Teacher's resource
150 Literacy Hours

YEAR R

Contents	Page
How to use this book	3
Summary of outcomes	5
Strand 1: Communication	10
Strand 2: Language for Thinking	18
Strand 3: Linking Sounds and Letters	28
Strand 4: Reading	46
Strand 5: Writing	58
Strand 6: Motor Skills & Handwriting	72
Copymasters	75
Glossary	145

Acknowledgements

Every effort has been made to trace and acknowledge ownership of copyright material but if any have been inadvertently overlooked, the publisher will be pleased to make the necessary alterations at the first opportunity.

First published 2001
exclusively for WHSmith by

Hodder & Stoughton Educational,
a division of Hodder Headline Ltd.
338 Euston Road
London NW1 3BH

Text and illustrations © Hodder & Stoughton Educational 2001

All rights reserved. This work is copyright. Permission is given for copies to be made of pages provided they are used exclusively within the institution for which this work has been purchased. For reproduction for any other purpose, permission must first be obtained in writing from the publishers.

A CIP record for this book is available from the British Library.

Author: Kris Winthorpe
Series editor: Gill Matthews

ISBN 0340 78995 6

Typeset by Fakenham Photosetting
Printed and bound in Spain by Graphycems

Foundation
How to use this book

Introduction

This book provides a range of generic strategies and materials to resource the Communication, Language and Literacy strand of the Foundation Stage curriculum.

The Curricular guidance for the Foundation Stage (QCA 2000) is the core reference document for practitioners to plan and match the opportunities to learn about language that children aged three to five should experience. This curriculum is organised into a set of progressive 'Stepping Stones' which illustrate and guide the sort of developmental opportunities, incidental and planned activities which can be used to take children forward in their ability to use, understand and apply spoken and written language well.

Children should move from a sensitisation and awareness that language is there in their play, from the age of three, to a gradual and explicit focus on the control and application of language as a tool in their speech, reading and writing as they near the end of the Foundation Stage at the age of five. By the end of the Reception Year, the last term of the Foundation Stage, children will be experiencing many of the activities outlined in this resource book in a sequence that prepares them for the Literacy Hour at the beginning of Year 1.

Organisation of the book into strands

- *The strands of Communication, Language and Literacy (CLL)*

This book is organised to resource the six strands that run through the Communication, Language and Literacy area of learning in the Foundation Curriculum. These strands are: Communication, Language for Thinking, Linking Sounds to Letters, Early Reading, Early Writing, and Motor skills for Handwriting.

- *Learning Objectives*

Each strand begins with a short introduction and this includes the coverage of the Steeping Stones, Early Learning Goals and the links to the Teaching Objectives for the Reception Year in the National Literacy Strategy Framework.

- *Differentiation*

Each strand is organised into three broad levels of differentiation linked to progression through the Stepping Stones in the Foundation Stage. Activities are roughly grouped into the appropriate level of challenge but teachers should note that activities can be modified to extend and be built upon once introduced. Observation will lead to assessment and this information should be used to modify activities to meet the needs of the groups of learners.

Early – corresponds to yellow and blue Stepping Stones, and activities more appropriate to Foundation Year 1 (3/4 year olds).
Developing – corresponds to blue to green Stepping Stones, and activities more appropriate to the beginning of the Reception/ Foundation Year 2.
Challenging – corresponds to leading to/ beyond the Early Learning Goals, and activities more appropriate to more able children and the end of the Reception year/ Foundation Stage.

- **Themes**

Each activity is self-contained but most are organised into collections of similar activities or themes. It is not intended that teachers work through these in order, but rather that they use them as a resource bank to supplement and enrich planned provision and opportunities to meet and extend children's needs.

- **Activities**

Each activity is organised with the following headings:
- **Activity title**
- **CLL** – indicates which Communication, Language and Literacy Early Learning Goal this activity contributes toward. The following indicates which Stepping Stone the activity contributes towards: (y)- yellow, (b)- blue, (g) -green, (CLL)- the Early Learning Goal itself.
- **Specific Learning Outcomes** – details the focus of the activity.
- **Group** – the size and type of group recommended for this activity;
Shared – large group with demonstration and leadership from an adult;
Guided – small group, e.g. key worker groups, adult led with an emphasis on independence;
Supported – small groups derived from play- child-led;
Collaborative – small groups with emphasis on co-operative working;
Independent – once set up this activity can run without further input or support from an adult. All such activities are much enriched by the presence of an adult, even if only in the role of parallel play.
- **Resources** – specifies the necessary items or photocopiable masters (copymasters) needed to run and resource the activity.
- **What to do** – tells the teacher how to set up and run the activity.
- **Variation, differentiation and extension** – provide possible variations and extensions to the activity. Where there is a significant variation then there will be a separate activity.
- **Assessment focus** – details criteria for assessment.

How to use this book

- **Photocopiable masters (copymasters)**

Many themes are accompanied by copymasters for use to support and resource the activity. These are not worksheets and have been designed to encourage and support practical and active learning by the children. Many of these copymasters provide and add to the range of generic resources available to support learning in settings providing for Foundation age children.

- **Homework**

There is no specific resourcing of activities for homework in this collection. However, many of the activities and resources are suitable for parents/carers to use to support language activities at home. Where they are used in this way it will be necessary to provide some guidance to parents/carers to ensure that the most is made of the opportunities to learn through and about language. Indeed, many activities can be used in this way to provide a focus for talking and learning about reading and writing at home.

- **Links to the Literacy Hour**

The guidance from the Qualifications and Curriculum Authority and the National Literacy Strategy state that children should have experience of the Literacy Hour by the end of the Reception Year, that is, by the end of the Foundation Stage. The activities and resources in this publication provide a comprehensive set of materials to support the elements that eventually combine to form the sequence of teaching styles that make up the Literacy Hour. Young children use language all the time in their play and learning, but the activities in this publication are distinguished by their emphasis on helping children become aware of the existence and the power of language. The 'Linking Sounds to Letters' strand is based on the Seven Steps of Phonics teaching outlined by the National Literacy Strategy Progression in Phonics.

- **Equality of opportunity and inclusion**

All these activities have been designed with all children in mind, however, teachers should be sensitive to the fact that different activities will appeal to some children more than to others, and that equality of provision does not always equate to equality of uptake. Most of these activities will be provided for children on the basis of careful observation and matching activities to take children forward to their next step of learning. The activities are broad enough to be adapted and modified to meet the needs of specific individual children, and many of the activities provide useful ways of allowing some children to consolidate or deepen their understanding of specific aspects of language. Teachers should also be sensitive to the language that some children use at home, in that children for whom English is not their first language may have a very different expectation of how language works. This may include different expectations about the direction of the text and different constructions of grammar in spoken language. The activities and resources in this collection are particularly appropriate for these children because of their explicit focus on how English language works and is used. Where possible, children should be encouraged to undertake some of these activities in their first language as well as in English.

- **ICT**

Many of the activities in this collection use ICT such as tape recorders and computers. These are clearly marked and reference is made to ICT in many of the extension and variation possibilities.

There are a number of useful collections of resources on the Internet, particularly in the collection of Kindergarten and Nursery websites that can be found from America. These constantly change and are updated but the easiest way to find these resources is with a bit of patience and searching for key words and phrases in a powerful Internet search engine such as www.google.com. The best tip is to type exactly what you want to find in inverted commas, search and try finding a web site with a good set of links. Let someone else take some of the legwork out of your hunting!

Foundation Stage
Summary of outcomes

Autumn term

Number	Activity title	Specific Learning Outcome
Strand 1	**Communication**	
	Early	
1	The Greeting Song	To encourage children to listen for their names and to establish a pattern and routine for registration. To pattern a greeting and response.
2	Get ready to listen	To develop a routine to settle children and prepare them to listen.
3	Circle of Friends (1)	To develop children's confidence in saying their own name and the name of other children. To encourage children to learn to co-operate and develop some circle time routines.
4	Circle of Friends (2)	
5	What do you want to do today?	To raise children's confidence in group participation. To practise asking and answering questions. To follow simple rules of a game.
6	Runaways	To develop confidence and participation in speaking through a simple drama game.
7	Postie! Postie!	To develop confidence and participation in speaking through a simple drama game.
8	Watch for the Bear	To develop confidence and participation in speaking through a simple drama game.
9	Puppy patrol	To give and follow simple instructions using body language and simple phrases.
10	The Listening Centre ICT	To be able to use a tape recorder/listening centre with independence.
	Developing	
11	Talking Circles	To gain confidence in speaking aloud in a large group.
12	Tape the circle	To listen carefully to the talk of others by listening to a tape recorder. Children will become more confident in speaking to a large group and will listen to and discuss comments made by other children.
13	The Talk about Table (1)	To be able to talk confidently about objects of interest. To be able to listen to the talk of others offering relevant comments.
14	The Talk About Table (2)	
15	Mobile phone	To become familiar with the conventions of turn taking in telephone conversation.
	Challenging	
16	What's in the bag?	To develop and refine children's descriptive language and questioning skills.
17	Mystery box	To develop and refine descriptive and imaginative language and learn to refine questioning skills.
18	The Story Teller	To be able to retell or make up stories and rhymes based on familiar stories and rhymes.
19	Story Circles	To be able to retell and extend stories and rhymes based on familiar stories and rhymes.
20	Star Kid Box	To positively reward good communication and use of good manners.
Strand 2	**Language for Thinking**	
	Early	
1	Role-play/dramatic play and small world play	To provide children with the opportunity to explore actions and events through stimulating imaginary environments and props.
2	What are you doing and how are you doing it?	To develop thinking skills through encouraging children to verbalise their actions. To expand and develop correct vocabulary.
3	Mr and Mrs Sock	To develop awareness of the conventions of social behaviour.
4	Mini-me (1)	To role-play and explore different scenarios and situations and to use appropriate dialogue to the context of the small world play.
5	Mini-me (2)	
	Developing	
6	Planning time	To enable children to plan and state intentions and intended outcomes ahead of actions. To enable children to plan and to work with other children with increasing co-operation.
7	The Share and tell Circle (Review)	To develop confidence in describing activities and reviewing what has been done and what has been learned.
8	News Circle	To be able to structure and recount events and experiences to small and large groups.
9	Tell-me puppet	To listen to and talk to a puppet, asking questions and responding to prompts.
10	Teacher in role	To listen and respond appropriately to an adult in role.
11	How are you feeling today?	To be able to adopt a role and give an explanation for what is happening in role.
12	Read my mind	To develop questioning and interaction amongst group members.

Summary of outcomes

Number	Activity title	Specific Learning Outcome
	Challenging	
13	Neat Knees (Think-pair-share)	To begin to be able to work collaboratively to talk, think and negotiate responses to a question, challenge or task.
14	What comes next?	To be able to listen carefully and follow a set of instructions.
15	Funny faces	To be able to listen carefully and follow a set of instructions.
16	Crazy creatures	To be able to listen carefully and follow a set of instructions.
17	Where in the house?	To be able to listen carefully and follow a set of instructions.
18	Robo-kid	To encourage children to give clear instructions. To develop careful listening and response to instructions. To encourage children to ask questions when instructions are not clear.
Strand 3		
1	Developing Phonological Awareness	Introduction and alignment to the NLS Progression in Phonics.
	Early	
2	The Listeners	(Environmental sound discrimination). To explore the sounds in the environment and to practise focusing attention on environmental sounds
3	Sound spotter (1)	(Instrumental sound discrimination). To match objects with their sounds. To describe the sound made and to discuss how the sound was made.
4	Sound spotter (2)	(Instrumental sound discrimination). To listen for a discrete sound amongst a sequence of sounds.
5	What is the sound?	(Instrumental sound discrimination). To develop an ability to listen carefully to discrete sounds.
6	Segment your tune	(Instrumental sound discrimination). To listen to and repeat sequences of sound.
7	Sound sequencer (1)	(Instrumental sound discrimination). To use a symbol to represent a sound. To blend a sequence of sounds using symbols to represent each sound.
8	Sound sequencer (2)	(Instrumental sound discrimination). To blend sequences of instrumental sound.
9	Sound buttons	To develop an ability to listen carefully to discrete sounds. To create opportunities for children to explore the sounds that they can make with their voices. To begin to link phonemes to letters.
10	Where are you?	(Environmental sound discrimination). To be able to distinguish one specific sound from many similar sounds that are heard at once.
11	Finger-rhyme time	To link motor movements with rhymes to aid the learning of rhymes; to explore patterns in rhymes and to tune children into listening to the sounds of words; to be able to predict and continue rhyming patterns.
12	Nonsense Songsense	To develop an ability to listen carefully to and innovate on familiar rhymes. To be able to predict and continue rhyming patterns.
13	Humpty Dumpty	To use nursery rhymes as a frame to sensitise children to rhyme and to explore and make new rhymes.
	Developing	
14	Word Count (1)	To understand that sentences are made up of words and that words are units of print.
15	Word Count (2)	
16	Sound sequencer (3)	(Instrumental sound discrimination). To segment and blend sequences of instrumental sound.
17	Word beat (1)	To enable children to hear syllables in words.
18	Word beat (2)	
19	Syllable Sally (1)	To enable children to segment orally and blend syllables in words.
20	Syllable Sally (2)	
21	Mnemonics for Alliterative Phonemes (MAPs) 1	(Progression in Phonics – PiP- Step 2). To hear and say phonemes in the initial position.
22	Pop the phoneme	To practise the correct articulation of the phonemes a-z, ch, sh and th.
23	Phoneme snap (1)	To reinforce the link between graphemes and phonemes.
24	Sound shopping	To segment the initial phoneme from spoken words and to make a collection of pictures of objects that start with this phoneme.
25	It's behind you!	To describe the features of letter shapes.
26	Treasure letters	To match and link letters to initial phonemes of objects and words.
	Challenging	
27	The Naughty Microphone 1 (or Drop the phoneme)	To attend and identify initial, final and medial phonemes in words. To practise phoneme segmentation skills.
28	The Naughty Microphone 2 (adding and deleting phonemes)	To attend and identify initial, final and medial phonemes in words. To practise phoneme segmentation skills. To explore how the meaning of words changes if phonemes are taken away, added or changed.

Summary of outcomes

Number	Activity title	Specific Learning Outcome
29	The Naughty Microphone 3 (Phoneme substitution)	To attend and identify initial, final and medial phonemes in words. To manipulate phonemes.
30	Mnemonics for Alliterative Phonemes (MAPs) 2	(PiP Step 6). To know one representation of each of ten vowel digraph phonemes ai/ee/ie/oa/oo/or/ar/ir/oi/ou. To equip children with the tools for phonic spelling.
31	Phoneme snap (2) (Long vowel phonemes)	(PiP Step 7). To segment and blend words containing vowel digraphs and tri-graphs. To learn the different spellings of long vowel phonemes.
32	Scaffolded spellings 1 (dictation)	To increase speed in application of phonics and known words to independent writing.
33	Scaffolded spellings 2 (dictation)	
Strand 4	Early Reading	
	Early	
1	Souvenirs and Story Treasures	To involve parents in supporting retellings of stories.
	Developing	
2	Environmental Print and reading – Word Walls	To understand the rationale to Word Walls
3	Build the wall	To recognise common key words on sight. To build knowledge of alphabetic letter names and alphabetical order.
4	Word Wall chants	To recognise common key words on sight. To link graphemes to phonemes.
5	Searchlights for reading (1)	To read on sight high frequency words recognising critical features such as shape and letter combination.
6	Searchlights for reading (2)	To use knowledge of rhyme to identify high frequency words with similar spelling patterns. To use knowledge of 'onset' and 'rime' to help spell words using clue words.
7	Jammy words	To develop knowledge of the critical features of words.
8	Mystery word	To develop strategies for cross checking across reading and spelling.
9	Read around the room	To notice and contribute to environmental print.
10	Cross the river (1)	To describe the features of letter shapes.
11	From reading into writing (using Big Books as text models for reading and writing)	To understand the rationale for shared reading using big books.
12	The new book (first read through of a big book)	To introduce and discuss a new text with the class. To read the text through and focus on response to the text.
13	Returning to the text (second read through of a big book)	To read the text through and to explore an aspect of the text in more depth. To increase child participation.
14	Reading to Teddy (book handling and directionality)	To understand how to handle books and follow text.
	Challenging	
15	'Wordo!'	To recognise rapidly high frequency words on sight.
16	Cross the river 2 (Beat the Troll)	To describe the features of letter shapes.
17	Independent Reading Area and resources	To provide opportunities for children to apply strategies that they have been taught elsewhere with independence and confidence. To consolidate reading skills and strategies and provide an opportunity to challenge and extend individual pupils.
Strand 5	Early Writing	
1	Independent activities and Literacy centres	To understand the rationale to opportunities for writing and mark making across a setting.
	Early	
2	The Writing Area	To provide a permanent area for children to explore different ways of 'mark-making' and 'writing'.
3	A shop	To provide a permanent area for children to explore different ways of 'mark-making' and 'writing'.
4	Hospital (human or animal hospital)	
5	A house	
6	Travel agents	
7	Restaurant/café	

Summary of outcomes

Number	Activity title	Specific Learning Outcome
	Developing	
8	My Name is	To help children develop their understanding of what a word is. To recognise and begin to be able to write their own name.
9	Shared Writing 1 (Innovating in a text)	To understand that text in books is written by a person. To have a clear model to imitate when writing independently.
10	Shared Writing 2 (Innovating on a text)	
11	Shared Writing 3 (Innovating from a text)	
12	Scrambled words	To write and spell their own name correctly. To write and spell high frequency words correctly.
	Challenging	
13	Scrambled sentences	To be able to sequence words to form a simple sentence.
14	Caption it!	To speak in and begin to write simple sentences.
15	Colourful sentences (1)	To write simple sentences with a given structure.
16	Colourful sentences (2)	To write simple sentences with a given structure.
17	Ketchup on your cornflakes	To write and explore simple sentences with a given structure.
18	Drama Day (using drama as a starting point for writing)	To begin to write simple narratives and recounts and dictate and invent their own compositions. To think about what to write ahead of writing it.
19	Story faces ('I am feeling … because')	To dictate and invent their own compositions. To think about what to write ahead of writing it. To use experience and drawing as a basis for writing and to understand the difference between drawing and writing.
20	Consequences (verb pictures) Day 1 and 2	To use experience and drawing as a basis for writing. To think about what to write ahead of writing it. To dictate and invent their own compositions.
21	Consequences (verb pictures) Day 3 and 4	
22	Information and communication technology	To be able to use a keyboard and a mouse to enter and manipulate text and writing.
Strand 6	**Motor skills and Handwriting**	
	Early	
1	Motor Skill Moments	To develop motor skills and co-ordination of the whole-body Gross Motor skills and hand/finger Fine Motor skills.
2	Brain Workout	To build gross motor skills and hand-eye co-ordination through multi-sensory co-ordinated movements.
3	The Three Letter Roots	To learn to form the three basic movements for letter formation.
	Developing	
4	Snake letters/Snake letter snacks	To learn the correct formation of lower case letters.
5	Feely letters	To learn the correct formation of lower case letters.

Early learning goals

Early Learning Goals for communication	NLS Teaching Objectives
Teachers should plan for: *opportunities for children to communicate thoughts, feelings and ideas to an adult and to each other; speaking and listening activities which include children speaking and listening to an adult and each other.*	
CLL A Interact with others, negotiating plans and activities and taking turns in conversation. **CLL B** Enjoy listening to and using spoken and written language and readily turn to it in their play and learning. **CLL C** Sustain attentive listening, responding to what the have heard with relevant comments, questions or actions. **CLL D** Listen with enjoyment and response to stories, songs and other music, poems and rhymes and make up their own songs, music, poems and rhymes. **CLL E** Extend their vocabulary, exploring the meanings and sounds of new words **CLL F** Speak clearly and audibly with confidence and control and show awareness of the listener – for example by their use of conventions such as greetings, 'please; and ;thank you'.	There are no NLS Teaching Objectives for speaking and listening
Early Learning Goals for language and thinking	
CLL G Use language to imagine and recreate roles and experience. **CLL H** Use talk to organise, sequence and clarify thinking, ideas, feelings and events.	

Theme 1) Early communication

Teachers should plan for:
Opportunities for children to communicate thoughts, feelings and ideas to an adult and to each other;
Speaking and listening activities which include children speaking and listening to an adult and each other;

Objectives

- **CLL A** Interact with others, negotiating plans and activities and taking turns in conversation;
- **CLL B** Enjoy listening to and using spoken and written language, and readily turn to it in their play and learning;
- **CLL C** Sustain attentive listening, responding to what they have heard by relevant comments, questions or actions;
- **CLL D** Listen with enjoyment and response to stories, songs and other music, rhymes and other poems and make up their own stories, songs, rhymes and poems;
- **CLL E** Extend their vocabulary, exploring the meanings and sounds of new words;
- **CLL F** Speak clearly and audibly with confidence and control and show awareness of the listener, for example by their use of conventions such as greetings, 'please' and 'thank you'.

---

1. The Greeting Song

CLL F Use isolated words and phrases and/or gestures to communicate with those known to them (yellow). Begin to use more complex sentences; use a widening range of words to express or elaborate ideas (blue).
Specific Learning Outcomes – to encourage children to listen for their names and to establish a pattern and routine for registration. To pattern a greeting and response.
Group – shared.
Resources – none.
What to do – start the session off with a tuneful registration. Sing to the children as you register them.
Teacher: Good morning, Sarah. How are you?
Child: Good morning, Mrs Seena. I'm fine, thank you.
Teacher: Good morning, Thomas. How are you?
Child: Good morning, Mrs Seena. I'm fine thank you.

Good Morning To You
Good morning to you, good morning to you.
We're all in our places,
With bright shining faces.
Good morning to you.
Children could clap along to the pattern of the rhythm.
Variation, differentiation and extension – ask a child to be in the middle of the circle. This child rolls the ball to children around the circle and they return it to him/her.
Spider webs: One child is in the middle (the spider) and rolls a ball of string or wool instead of a ball. After about ten rolls the spider winds up the web and greets each child, in turn, as they collect the web in.
Assessment focus – I can greet other children appropriately.

---

2. Get ready to listen

CLL C Respond to simple instructions (yellow).
Specific Learning Outcomes – to develop a routine to settle children and prepare them to listen.
Group – shared.
Resources – none.
What to do – there are many signals that can be used to stop children in the flow of activity and prepare them to listen. Some of the subtlest techniques are the most powerful *e.g.* **hand raising** – raise your hand and wait for all children to notice, stop and raise their hand. Lower your hand and talk to the children;
By the numbers – children are instructed that if you say 'Number 1' it means 'Sit down on the carpet and listen to me'. 'Number 2' means 'Stop, freeze, look and listen'. 'Number 3' means 'Line up quietly'. These three instructions are sufficient to control most Reception classes.
Routine rhymes *e.g.*
Have a seat, everybody have a seat
Have a seat, have a seat
Everybody have a seat on the floor
Not on the ceiling, not on the door.
Everybody have a seat on the floor.

Open, shut them, open, shut them, open, shut them.
Give a little clap.
Open, shut them, open, shut them.
Lay them in your lap.

Wiggle them, wiggle them, wiggle them so.
Wiggle them high. Wiggle them low.
Wiggle them to the left, and wiggle them to the right.
Wiggle them out of sight

Creeping, creeping, creeping, creeping,
To my head.
Down again, down again
Put them all in bed.

These are Grandma's spectacles,
This is Grandma's hat.
This is the way she folds her hands,
And puts them in her lap.

Variation, differentiation and extension – n/a
Assessment focus – I know when to stop what I am doing and listen to an adult.

Strand 1

3. Circle of Friends (1)

CLL F Join in with repeated refrains, anticipating key events and important phrases; listen to others in small groups when conversation interests them (yellow).
Specific Learning Outcomes – children develop confidence in saying their own name and the name of other children. Children learn to co-operate and develop some circle time routines.
Group – shared.
Resources – a soft ball.
What to do – children sit in a circle with an adult as a participant in the circle. Warm up to this activity by passing the ball round and saying their name. 'Hello I'm...' Select a child and roll the ball to them whilst saying 'Hello (child's name), please will you look after my ball?'
The child receiving the ball responds with 'Thank you (sender's name), I don't mind at all'. He/she then rolls the ball across the circle to someone else and says 'Hello _____, please will you look after my ball?'.
Play continues faster and faster until all the children have had several turns.
Variation, differentiation and extension – circle games are all about developing a sense of community and sharing. A nice way to end this activity is with a circle game called *Balloon*. One child is in the middle of the circle. All the other children hold hands and come together as close as they can. The child in the middle of the circle pretends to blow. With each breath the circle gets a little larger as the 'balloon' 'fills with air'. The circle expands until it is so big that it bursts and the children fall to the floor with a 'Bang!' Someone else is selected to blow up another balloon.
Assessment focus – I can say my name confidently. I say 'please' and 'thank you'. I can speak aloud in a large group.

4. Circle of Friends (2)

CLL F Join in with repeated refrains, anticipating key events and important phrases; listen to others in small groups when conversation interests them (yellow).
Specific Learning Outcomes – children develop confidence in saying their own name and the name of other children. Children learn to co-operate and develop some circle time routines.
Group – shared.
Resources – a soft ball.
What to do –
• Play some music and pass the ball. When the music stops, whoever is holding the ball has to roll it across the circle to someone else as outlined above.
• Choose an attribute such as hair colour or gender.
Roll the ball across the circle to someone with the same or different attribute whilst describing yourself and the person chosen.
'I am a boy. You are a girl.'
'I am a girl. You are a girl.'
'I am a girl. You are a boy.' etc.
Variation, differentiation and extension – introduce new phrases for children to ask across the circle e.g.
'Hello, Tom. Do you like sausages?'
'Thank you, Treena. No I don't.'
'Excuse me, Suami. Do you like pizza?'
'Thank you, Tom. Yes I love pizza!...'
Assessment focus – I can say my name confidently. I say 'please' and 'thank you'. I can speak aloud in a large group.

5. What do you want to do today?

CLL F Use isolated words and phrases and/or gestures to communicate with those well known to them (yellow). Use a widening range of words to express or elaborate ideas (blue).
Specific Learning Outcomes – raised confidence in group participation. Practice in asking and answering questions. Ability to follow simple rules of a game.
Group – shared.
Resources – none.
What to do – sit the children in a circle. Teach the children the chant 'Who stole the cookie from the cookie jar?'
Teacher: 'Did Tamsin steal the cookie from the cookie jar?'
Tamsin: 'Who, me?'
All: 'Yes, you!'
Tamsin: 'That's not true!'
All: 'Then who?'
Tamsin: 'Mmm, Kyle'
All: 'Did Kyle steal the cookie from the cookie jar?'
Kyle: 'Who, me?' etc.
Once the pattern and routine of the chant has been established it can be used to innovate upon to explore question and answers e.g.
Teacher: 'What do we want to find out about today?'
Sam: 'I want to find out who likes having a bath.'
Teacher: 'Does Julie like having a bath?'
Julie: 'Who, me?'
All: 'Yes, you!'
Julie: 'Yes I do!' or 'No I don't'
All: 'Good for you'
Teacher: 'Now who?'
Julie: 'Does Pina like having a bath?'
Variation, differentiation and extension – let a child decide on the next question, or alternate questions with each child.
Assessment focus – I can ask a question.

Theme 1) Early communication

6. Runaways

CLL B Join in with repeated refrains, anticipating key events and important phrases; respond to simple instructions, listen to others in small groups (yellow). Question why things happen and give explanations (blue).
Specific Learning Outcomes – to develop confidence and participation in speaking through a simple drama game.
Group – shared/guided.
Resources – a PE mat. A towel.
What to do – sit with the children and pretend you are all near some water (the PE mat). An adult starts the game with the following chant:
*'Please listen to (name), (name) is the boss;
Please don't go in the water, Or I'll be CROSS!'*
The adult turns and faces away and another child is chosen to sneak from the group and pretend to play in the water. Suddenly, the first adult turns round and says *'Come out and get dry at once!'*
The runaway child slowly comes off the PE mat and pretends to dry him/herself with the towel and this child then becomes the 'boss'.
Talk about water dangers with the children.
Variation, differentiation and extension – *'Don't play with the….', 'Don't go off with strangers'* etc. The game can be used as fun way into exploring important safety issues with young children.
Assessment focus – I can explain why I should do as an adult tells me.

---

7. Postie! Postie!

CLL B/C Join in with repeated refrains, anticipating key events and important phrases. Respond to simple instructions. Listen to others in small groups (yellow).
Specific Learning Outcomes – to develop confidence and participation in speaking through a simple drama game.
Group – shared/guided.
Resources – a space made from chairs or blocks etc. Some string or elastic. A collection of noisy objects such as musical instruments to drape over and through the string. A bag with some envelopes in. A mask for a dog [Copymaster 1].
What to do – mark off a large enclosed area for the group to sit inside using the chairs. At one or two points make an entrance to the enclosed area and drape the string across the entrance. Hang some of the noisy instruments and objects on the string, so that if they are touched they will make sound.
The children should spread themselves around in the enclosed area. The child selected to be the 'dog' should put the mask on and 'patrol' around inside the area. The child selected to be the 'Postie' should have the sack of letters and stand outside the circle.
Say with the group of children:
*'Postie! Postie! Postie!
Don't go past the door,
If you've got a letter,
Tell us who it is for?'*
The Postie chooses one of the children sitting inside the enclosed area and takes a letter out of the sack. He/she enters the area as quietly as possible trying to avoid the dog. The seated children can say: 'Shh! Mind the dog!'. The 'dog' has to try and catch the Postie by listening to where he/she is before the Postie can give the chosen child their letter. The Postie's sack could contain some bells to aid the dog in tracking her/him down!
Swap and let other children take the roles.
Variation, differentiation and extension – older children could identify the children using names on the envelopes or symbols to match symbols or colours with children inside the enclosed area.
Assessment focus – I can sit quietly and listen carefully.

---

8. Watch for the Bear

CLL B/C Join in with repeated refrains, anticipating key events and important phrases. Respond to simple instructions. Listen to others in small groups (yellow).
Specific Learning Outcomes – to develop confidence and participation in speaking through a simple drama game.
Group – shared/guided.
Resources – a drum and some percussion instruments. A bear mask (Copymaster 1). A trolley or vehicle to transport a child around the room. A large space (outdoors).
What to do – one child is selected to pretend to be the bear. This child has the bear mask with eyeholes so they can see where they are going. This child pretends to be asleep. The instruments are shared out amongst the children. The vehicle is put in the middle of the area near the bear. Set up a slow and menacing drumbeat. Say quietly: *'Watch out for the Bear! The Bear is fast asleep. The Bear is in the woods. Can you creep to your jeep?'* Select a child to sneak up to the trolley as quietly as possible. While this is happening the drumming should continue and the bear should begin to roar as it slowly wakes up. Use a signal such as symbol to indicate that the child should get to the trolley and escape. The bear chases the child around, roaring but never quite catching it, and finally gives up.
Select new children to take on the roles.
Variation, differentiation and extension – have the vehicle move backwards away from the bear, so that the child can see the bear chasing it.
Assessment focus – I can tell you how I feel.

Strand 1

9. Puppy Patrol

CLL A Use words and/or gestures, including body language such as eye contact and facial expression, to communicate (yellow). **CLL B** Respond to simple instructions (yellow). **CLL F** Use isolated words and phrases and/or gestures to communicate with those well known to them (yellow).
Specific Learning Outcomes – to give and follow simple instructions using body language and simple phrases.
Group – guided/supported.
Resources – small PE apparatus.
What to do – tell the children that they are going to pretend to be puppies at Puppy School. Today you are going to train the puppies to do some tricks. Let the children pretend to be puppies. Tell them to 'sit' and make up a gesture that means 'sit'. Let the children, in role, obey the command and then continue teaching them new instructions, e.g. 'roll-over', 'shake paw', 'sit-up and beg', 'fetch' etc. With each instruction make up a gesture or sign. Let other children be the Puppy Patrol teacher. Let the children carry this game into free play, encouraging them to make use of the gesture as well as the spoken instruction.
Variation, differentiation and extension – develop a set of instructions and gestures to co-ordinate and control the children in the group.
Assessment focus – I can give and follow instructions using gesture.

10. The Listening Centre ICT.

CLL B/C/D Listen to favourite nursery rhymes, stories and songs. Join in with repeated refrains, anticipating key events and important phrases. Listen to others in small groups when conversation interests them (yellow). Listen to stories with increasing attention and recall and describe main story settings, events and principal characters (blue).
Specific Learning Outcomes – to be able to use a tape recorder/listening centre with independence.
Group – independent.
Resources – a tape recorder, headphones, microphone, finger puppets, sound discrimination games and tapes, musical instruments, barriers for barrier games, story and nursery rhyme tapes, a telephone, paper, crayons and pencils, blank tapes.
What to do – set up and resource an activity area with a focus on listening and sound discrimination activities. Teach the children how to control the tape recorder and to play, rewind and turn over tapes. Introduce new sound discrimination activities through small group time and let children have further opportunity to explore and develop them with time in the listening centre.
Variation, differentiation and extension – teach children how to record their own tapes. The listening centre is a good place to locate many of the early Linking Sound to Letter activities from Strand Three.
Assessment focus – I can set up, play and listen to a story or music tape by myself.

Theme 2 — Developing communication

11. Talking Circles

CLL F Begin to use more complex sentences; use a widening range of words to express or elaborate ideas (blue). Use statements and stick to the main theme or intention (green). **CLL C** Question why things happen and give explanations (blue).
Specific Learning Outcomes – to gain confidence in speaking aloud in a large group
Group – shared/guided.
Resources – a toy animal.
What to do – sit the children in a circle, with you. You have the soft toy Select a focus for the talking circle e.g. 'I like to....'/ 'I am happy when …'/'I don't like …'/ 'My favourite colour is …' etc., based on whatever is topical and will engage the group.

Model the phrase 'I like to work' and pass the toy to the child next to her. Each child says and completes the phrase when they are holding the toy. Children do not have to say anything and can pass the toy straight to the next child if they do not wish to contribute or have nothing to say. You should note children who regularly pass in this way.
Variation, differentiation and extension – the routines of contributing to a circle in this way underpin much of the work in the early years. Initially children will tend to contribute little, with much repetition. However, when the routines are internalised children will gradually widen their contributions to talking circles.
Assessment focus – I can take my turn. I can contribute to a whole class discussion.

12. Tape the circle

CLL F Begin to use more complex sentences; use a widening range of words to express or elaborate ideas (blue). Use statements and stick to the main theme or intention (green). **CLL C** Question why things happen and give explanations (blue).
Specific Learning Outcomes – to listen carefully to the talk of others by listening to a tape recorder. Children will become more confident in speaking to a large group and will listen to and discuss comments made by other children.
Group – shared/guided.
Resources – a tape recorder and a microphone.
What to do – this activity builds upon the talking circle in Activity 7. Young children tend to focus so much on what they are going to say in a talking circle that they do not listen to other children's contributions. The use of a tape recorder enables speech to be captured and replayed to enable children to listen to comments and contributions from other children. These can then be used as the basis for further discussion and development. Sit the children in a talking circle. Place the tape recorder in the centre of the circle. Plug the microphone in and set the tape to record. Model for the children the correct way to hold the microphone whilst speaking. Hold the microphone in your hand, raise your thumb and place your thumb onto your chin. This keeps the microphone just the right distance from the mouth and ensures that children keep the microphone close enough to record their speech.

Practise passing the microphone round with the correct handhold and thumb to chin guide. Remind the children that they should only speak when they have the microphone. Agree a signal that means that it is time to pass the microphone on e.g. make a 'T' shape with your hand. Explain how the controls on the tape recorder work. Have a test run and record the children as they say: 'Hello, my name is…..'. Rewind the tape and let the children listen to their own voices. For many children, this may the first time that they have heard their own voices, so there will be plenty to discuss.
When you are ready, select the theme for the talking circle e.g. 'At the weekend I..'. Press record and pass the microphone around to record the children's contributions.
When all the contributions have been recorded, rewind the tape. Now you can play the tape and pause it after each child's contribution. This enables children to focus on listening to the contribution rather than worrying about what they are going to say. Pausing the tape enables you to lead a discussion on contributions that children have offered.
Variation, differentiation and extension – modelling the use of tape recorders in this way enables children to use tape recorders with growing independence to record spoken language in collaborative and independent activities.
Assessment focus – I can use a tape recorder. I know what my voice sounds like.

13. The Talk about Table (1)

CLL F Begin to use more complex sentences. Use a widening range of words to express or elaborate ideas (blue). Link statements and stick to a main theme (green). **CLL E** Use vocabulary and forms of speech that are increasingly influenced by experience of books (green).
Specific Learning Outcomes – to be able to talk confidently about objects of interest. To be able to listen to the talk of others offering relevant comments.
Group – guided.
Resources – a display table with a sign 'The talk about table' in a speech bubble, a drape, objects brought in by children to put onto the table. Copymaster 2.

What to do – set up the *talk about table* in a prominent position in the room. Bring in an object to start the *talk about table* off and model how to talk about an object. During a *sharing circle*, either at the beginning or end of the session, you should talk about the object that they have brought in. Ask whether anyone wants to ask any questions about the object. An adult helper should be primed to model asking some questions to prompt the children e.g. 'Where did you get it?', 'Why do you like it so much?', etc.
The questioning should expand the initial description of the object.
Establish a rota for children to bring in items of personal

Strand 1

interest in to put on the *talk about table*. Let children have the option of looking at the objects during the session. During the *sharing circle* the chosen child should talk about their object. Children should be prompted to ask questions about the object. You can lead in this questioning in the early stages to build up an expanded description. Over time the children will question more and you will need to talk and prompt less.

Variation, differentiation and extension – see the *talk about table (2)*.
Assessment focus – I can talk about an object for a sustained time. I can answer questions. I can ask relevant and interesting questions.
Copymaster 2 Whole class observation sheet.

14. The Talk About Table (2)

CLL F Begin to use more complex sentences; use a widening range of words to express or elaborate ideas (blue). Link statements and stick to a main theme (green).
CLL E Use vocabulary and forms of speech that are increasingly influenced by experience of books (green).
Specific Learning Outcomes – to be able to talk confidently about objects of interest. To be able to listen to the talk of others offering relevant comments.
Group – supported, collaborative and independent.
Resources – a display table with a sign 'The Talk About Table' in a speech bubble, a drape, objects brought in by the children to put onto the table. A magnifying glass, photographs and suitable reference books (as available). A tape recorder.
What to do – show the children how to work at the *talk about table* by modelling its use. Sit the children so that they can see you doing the following:
- Look at the objects on the table, talking and thinking aloud as you describe the objects on the table and what interests you about them;
- Model looking at some of the objects on the table and talk to the children about what is really interesting. Pick one object in particular and describe it in detail.
- Use the magnifying glass and see if you can find a picture of it in one of the books;
- Summarise all the things you have noticed and discovered about the object and orally share this with the children. Tell them what you would like to find out more about this object and say what your question would be;
- Now record this summary onto the tape recorder including the question.

Explain to children that when they come to the table they should listen to what is on the tape, look at the objects on the table and record their own findings. Some of the children may even be able to answer some of the questions asked by other children on the tape.
In the early stages some adult support may be needed to keep the amount of talk on the tape to a minimum and to establish the routines.
Over time the tape should build up into an interesting record of what children were interested in on the *talk about table*. This activity can lead to some interesting work away from the table, as children attempt to find the answers to some of their friends' questions.
Variation, differentiation and extension – n/a.
Assessment focus – I can listen to a recorded message and I can record my own.

15. Mobile phone

CLL A Use intonation, rhythm and phrasing to make their meaning clear to others (blue). Have emerging self-confidence to speak to others about wants and interests. Use simple grammatical structures. Ask simple questions, often in the form of 'where' or 'what'.
CLL F Use language for an increasing range of purposes (green).
Specific Learning Outcomes – to become familiar with the conventions of turn-taking in telephone conversation.
Group – shared/guided to model for independent use.
Resources – two cuboid wooden bricks, or two toy mobile phones.
What to do – sit the children in a circle. Make a telephone ringing noise and pick up the wooden brick and pretend it is a mobile phone. They should role-play a telephone conversation.
Ask the children who they think telephoned and what sorts of things were talked about.
Explain that you are going to phone some children. You should put one brick in front of you and the other brick should be passed around the circle to some music. When the music stops, whoever has the brick holds onto it and you make a ringing noise.
The target child pretends to answer the phone whereupon you have a conversation similar to one that was modelled. You should model greetings and formalities, and this should be followed by questions to elicit responses and discussion.
After a short exchange, start the music and continue with short telephone conversations during the musical pauses.
Variation, differentiation and extension – once children are familiar with the basic game, both phones can be passed in opposite directions to encourage children to phone each other within the circle. Two red bricks and two yellow bricks would enable children with the same coloured bricks to talk to each other.
When children are quite familiar with this activity, give them each a brick and let them partner up and have a 'telephone' conversation. After a minute encourage children to swap and partner up with other people to share the news of the first person etc. Provide opportunities to access realistic and pretend telephones in various activity areas.
Set up a system whereby children take it in turns to be on the end of a telephone hotline. When other individuals are stuck, they are able to 'phone a friend' who will help then resolve their problem.
Assessment focus – I can talk with a partner. I can listen to what my partner says and share this with someone else.

Theme 3 — Challenging communication

16. What's in the bag?

CLL C Sustain attentive listening, responding to what they have heard by relevant comments, questions or actions.
Specific Learning Outcomes – children develop and refine their descriptive language and learn to refine their questioning skills.
Group – shared and guided.
Resources – a large bag. Some unusually shaped objects. Copymaster 2.
What to do – collect together several unusually shaped everyday objects e.g. an iron, a brass kettle, a furry toy animal, a rubber glove, a key, a candlestick, a slipper. Put one of the objects into the bag without the children seeing what it is.
Explain that they have to guess 'What is in the bag?' and that you can only respond 'yes' or 'no'.
Invite a child up to be the 'feeler'. Their job is to put their hand into the bag and touch the object and to say a word to describe what the object feels like e.g. cold, smooth, round.
The other children in the group can ask the 'feeler' what the object feels like and can ask you questions e.g. Is it a pot? Is it used in the house?. Remember that you can only answer 'yes' or 'no'. This game works very well if children are encouraged to close their eyes and imagine a picture of what they think the object is.
You can give clues if necessary.
Variation, differentiation and extension – n/a.
Assessment focus – an additional adult can use an observation sheet to check that over time all children have contributed either descriptions or questions over a period of sessions. See observation sheet (Copymaster 2).

17. Mystery box

CLL C Sustain attentive listening, responding to what they have heard by relevant comments, questions or actions.
Specific Learning Outcomes – children develop and refine their descriptive and imaginative language and learn to refine their questioning skills.
Group – shared and guided.
Resources – a box with the back cut off and a hole for a hand to go through the front (to let the rest of the class see what is happening when the 'feeler' can see nothing). Some interesting objects.
What to do – a child is invited to come and be the 'feeler'. The 'feeler' chooses four children who come and sit on chairs next to the 'feeler'.
The 'feeler' is handed one of the unusually shaped objects, and they handle it in the box, without seeing what the object is. As they feel the object they are encouraged to describe the object. You should prompt the 'feeler' to describe and talk about the picture they are seeing in their mind.
Encourage the feeler to use language that describes parts of the object as if they were parts of something else e.g. 'it feels all furry like a soft cat'. 'Oooh! this bit feels like a snake skin, all bumpy and cold, and here there is a sort of hole like a mouth' (a slipper!).
Ask an adult helper to scribe the description that the 'feeler' gives.
After a few minutes of this, the 'feeler' may have an idea of what the object is but they should not say what it is just yet. The 'feeler' says: 'Can I phone a friend?' and they choose a number – either 1, 2, 3, or 4. This corresponds to the seating order of children in the chairs. The 'feeler' pretends to telephone their friend and they can ask them one question, but the friend can only answer 'yes' or 'no' They are able to ask three questions but the fourth friend can be a bit more helpful.
The fourth friend is allowed to give a clue (without saying what the object is). The clue might be a description of what the object is used for.
The 'feeler' then has to describe what they think the object is in as much detail as possible. The adult helper should scribe this again.
If the child is not correct then, before they look at the object, they can select another child from the 'audience' to offer a description of the object so that the 'feeler' gets a mental picture.
However, if they are correct in their guess and description of the object then the other children should give them a clap.
Variation, differentiation and extension –
Extension 1 The better the description offered, the 'richer' they are, so see if they are able to describe the object, its use, its colour, etc.
Extension 2 – as children move toward an understanding that a sentence is a complete idea, then they can be encouraged to describe objects in sentences, without the use of the 'and' connective.
Extension 3 – at the end of the Reception year and into Year 1 objects could be placed in boxes with a hole for a hand to go in and feel. The task being to write a description of what they think is in the box. This can be a good starting point for creative writing, especially if the objects are very unusual e.g. a rubber glove filled with water (and frozen!), a small tub of jelly with salt sprinkled on the top!
Assessment focus – I can describe an object in simple phrases/sentences. I can ask simple questions.

18. The Story Teller

CLL D Listen with response and enjoyment to stories, songs and other music, rhymes and other poems and make up their own stories, songs, rhymes and poems.
CLL E. Extend their vocabulary, exploring the meanings and sounds of new words. Use vocabulary and forms of speech that are increasingly influenced by experience of books (green).
Specific Learning Outcomes – to be able to retell or make up stories and rhymes based on familiar stories and rhymes.

Strand 1

Group – shared/guided.
Resources – a mask on a stick (Copymaster 3).
What to do – read a big book or tell the children a story several times so that they are familiar with the characters, events and actions.
Model retelling the story while holding the mask up to your face. Pretend that you cannot remember what happens next and ask for a volunteer to continue telling the story. Pass them the story-telling mask and let them continue the story, prompting to elicit detail. Ask another child to continue and pass the mask on.
Let children explore characters, settings and events in the story through activity areas such as small world play, construction equipment (small and large), role-play or outdoor play. This experience can be structured by asking the children how they are resolving some of the issues from the story that prompted their play. For example, after a reading of *Three Billy Goats Gruff* some children might use large construction equipment to build a bridge and act out the story. You could talk to the children in role as characters both during and after the play. The children could retell their version of the story using the story-telling mask. Whoever has the mask provides the voice of the narrator.
Variation, differentiation and extension – over time children will move toward retelling stories using similar language to the original text. This should be encouraged by the wearing of a story-telling mask whilst retelling and sharing new stories.
Assessment focus – I can retell a story or a rhyme to a large group of listeners.

19. Story Circles

CLL D Listen with response and enjoyment to stories, songs and other music, rhymes and other poems and make up their own stories, songs, rhymes and poems.
CLL E Extend their vocabulary, exploring the meanings and sounds of new words. Use vocabulary and forms of speech that are increasingly influenced by experience of books (green).
Specific Learning Outcomes – to be able to retell and extend stories and rhymes based on familiar stories and rhymes.
Group – shared/guided.
Resources – an object to pass round the circle.
What to do – sit the children in a circle. Prompt them to recall a familiar story, nursery rhyme or song. Start to retell the story or rhyme. After one sentence, pass the object to the next child who carries on with the next part of the story. The object continues to be passed round until the story is complete. If children are unsure what to say then they can pass.
Variation, differentiation and extension – the story or rhyme could be written up on a large sheet of paper. The paper could be cut up. Bits of the writing could be distributed round the group to be retold and re-ordered correctly.
Assessment focus – I can listen to and continue a story with an understanding of what a sentence is.

20. Star Child Box

CLL F Speak clearly and audibly with confidence and control and show awareness of the listener, for example by their use of conventions such as greetings, 'please' and 'thank you'.
Specific Learning Outcomes – to reward positively good communication and use of good manners.
Group – shared.
Resources – reward vouchers (Copymaster 4), a decorated box with a hole cut in the top, some rewards.
What to do – explain to the children that every time any of the teachers or classroom assistants catch them being a good talker or listener they will get one of the reward vouchers. Their name will be put on the voucher and they can put it into the *star child box*.
Discuss what you mean by good talking and listening, including for example the use of the conventions 'please' and 'thank you'. At the end of each week, hold a special ceremony to draw one voucher out of the box.
Whoever this child is should win the weekly award and become the Star of the Week. N.B. it can be helpful to note on the vouchers why the child's name went into the box.
Variation, differentiation and extension – create a display to show who the Star of the Week is and why their name went into the box.
Assessment focus – I speak clearly with an awareness of the needs of my listeners. I have good manners.

Theme 4 — Early language for thinking

Objectives
- **CLL G** use language to imagine and recreate roles and experiences;
- **CLL H** Use talk to organise, sequence and clarify thinking, ideas, feelings and events.

1. Role-play/ dramatic play and small world play

CLL G Use action, sometimes with limited talk, that is largely concerned with the 'here and now' (yellow). Use talk to give new meanings to objects and actions, treating them as symbols for other things (blue).
Specific Learning Outcome – to provide children with the opportunity to explore actions and events through stimulating imaginary environments and props.
Group – collaborative/independent.
Resources – see suggested lists in the Early Writing Strand 4.
What to do – small world play, role-play and dramatic play are the early foundations of narrative story-telling and writing. They provide an opportunity for children to explore events that are personally meaningful, to rehearse alternative possibilities and to explore fantasy situations well beyond their experience. Children will naturally tend to play and converse when presented with small world figures and props – the challenge is to structure and extend the quality of language being used in these situations. One of the key aims of extending the language aspect of this play is to sensitise children to ways of presenting their experiences to others. This oral retelling shares many of the features of storytelling and children are developing the skills of storytelling by retelling their imagined and role-played experiences. To this end children should be provided with opportunities to:
- set the scene, so it is meaningful to them;
- explore the 'world' created in the drama or small world play;
- transform objects in the world, using everyday objects to stand for other objects and things;
- present their world to others, by sharing their play or by involving them in their play and use of objects; and by telling others how they have played and what happened;
- reflect upon the events explored through the play and consider how they relate to other situations.

Variation, differentiation and extension – N.B. for further ideas on resourcing the role-play area see the areas outlined in the Early Writing Strand.
Assessment focus – I can pretend to be someone else, somewhere else, doing something else.

2. What are you doing and how are you doing it?

CLL H Use action, sometimes with limited talk, that is largely concerned with the 'here and now' (yellow). Talk activities through, reflecting and modifying what they are doing. Use talk to connect ideas, explain what is happening and anticipate what might happen next (blue).
CLL A Use words and/or gesture, including body language such as eye contact and facial expression to communicate (yellow). Use intonation, rhythm and phrasing to make their meaning clear to others (blue).
Specific Learning Outcomes – to develop thinking skills through encouraging children to verbalise their actions. To expand and develop correct vocabulary.
Group – supported and independent.
Resources – planned activities in structured play.
What to do – adults observe and play alongside the Reception children and prompt them to offer a commentary of their play. You may need to model this as they play in parallel with the child, or it may happen spontaneously.
The commentary can be prompted by the question 'What are you doing?' and (to explore problem-solving strategies) 'How are you doing it?' and 'What was hard?', 'How did you do that?', 'Why are you doing that?'.
Be careful not to ask questions that are too general or infer criticism, but rather be specific and relate the question to the context, material and strategies that you wish the child to comment upon.
Try to lead the child to discuss how they overcame problems and use questioning to keep the dialogue going, but let the child talk more than you. Introduce appropriate vocabulary to the context and materials being used to expand the child's vocabulary set.
Echo and expand: echo back to the child comments and responses that they offer to you, modelling correct phrasing, and use of vocabulary and expanding the phrase e.g
(context: child is making a model)
Teacher: 'What are you doing?'
Child: 'I'm making this go on here.'
Teacher: 'You are joining that tube onto the box. How are you doing that?'
Child: 'Stickin' it.'
Teacher: 'You are sticking it with Sellotape; that's a good idea. Why are you using Sellotape?'
Child: 'Glue don't work.'
Teacher: 'You tried the glue and it didn't work, so now you are using the Sellotape and it is working.'
Variation, differentiation and extension – children in small groups can be taken forward in their thinking when an adult works and plays in parallel to the group and models their thinking aloud. This demonstrates to children that it is appropriate to talk about what they are thinking and how they are doing it. If this pattern is established, children playing in groups will share their thinking aloud and this is a way to move children from solitary/parallel play into social and collaborative play.
Assessment focus – I can describe what I am doing. I can tell you how I solve problems that I encounter.

Strand 2

3. Mr and Mrs Sock

CLL G Use action, sometimes with limited talk, that is largely concerned with the 'here and now' (yellow). Use talk to give new meanings to objects and actions, treating them as symbols for other things (blue).
Specific Learning Outcomes – awareness of the conventions of social behaviour.
Group – shared.
Resources – Two sock puppets (Copymaster 5).
What to do – sit children down while you model a role-play and discussion with Mr Sock the sock puppet. Encourage the children to join in with the discussion about appropriate behaviour to try to teach Mr Sock how to behave. Possible scenarios include:
- You say 'hello' to Mr. Sock and he ignores and fails to respond. Mrs. Sock models appropriate behaviour.
- You are telling some news and are rudely interrupted by Mr Sock who demands attention.
- Mrs Sock is making a model and Mr Sock comes and takes some bits and/or knocks the model over;
- Mrs Sock is doing some writing with the children and Mr Sock demands the pen, argues and snatches it.
- Mr Sock is doing some writing and gets stuck. The children help but the puppet does not say 'thank you'.
- Mr Sock has an argument or is teasing another soft toy. The children have to help sort out this scenario.

Variation, differentiation and extension – children could be invited to play the part of Mrs Sock and help resolve the problem. The Mrs Sock puppet could be passed around for different children to advise.
The solutions that the children devise could be written up as shared writing to form part of the 'rules for the classroom'. Pupils could do some independent drawing and writing on Copymaster 5.
Assessment focus – I can tell you the 'rules' for our class. I am helpful and considerate of the needs of others.

4. Mini-me (1)

CLL G As above.
Specific Learning Outcomes – to role-play and explore different scenarios and situations and to use appropriate dialogue to the context of the small world play.
Group – guided, supported, collaborative and independent.
Resources – small play figures (play-people, dolls etc.). Small world play props and resources. A setting or activity area for the action to take place.
What to do –
1. Enabling This is the phase of setting up environments and opportunities for small world play. It involves providing small figures for the children to project their characters on and to engage with the play equipment. The small figures should be placed into the setting or activity area to be used. Typical settings might include:
- the sand tray along with plastic dinosaurs;
- the construction area;
- the cars, trains and road mats resources;
- the play-dough or plasticine area;
- the garden or outdoor area along with some vehicles and animals;
- the dolls house.

Children could explore and create scenarios just by engaging with the resources provided.
2. Supporting roles You join in with a scenario that has been developed by the children and support the play in-role. Encourage the children to sustain the context of the imagined play and let the children lead and direct the play.
Variation, differentiation and extension – see below.
Assessment focus – I can play with small world figures.

5. Mini-me (2)

CLL G As above.
Specific Learning Outcomes – As above.
Group – guided, supported, collaborative and independent.
Resources – small play figures (play-people, dolls etc.). Small world play props and resources. A setting or activity area for the action to take place.
What to do –
3. Modelling – demonstrate a possible context and scenario for the group of children by modelling and role-playing the small world characters. Pretend to be one of the small world characters and engage in the fantasy scenario. You should model some of the dialogue of the figures in role.
Model transforming everyday objects into objects relevant to sustaining the imagined world. Model presenting the 'story' of what happened to small-world characters. A modelled session could commence by telling the children what had happened previously and by providing the problem facing the characters today. It should end by leaving the children with a problem to resolve.
4. Sharing roles – assume the character of one of the small figures and engage children in dialogue through the play figure. Help to create and sustain the developing 'story' through this dialogue. You can step out of the role of the small character and talk directly to the other children, asking them what is happening to the small characters, what they think will happen next and how they will solve problems they are having.
Variation, differentiation and extension – n/a.
Assessment focus – I can play with small world figures. I can tell you what the small-world people have been doing.

Theme 5 — Developing language for thinking

6. Planning time

CLL H Begin to use talk instead of action to rehearse. Reorder and reflect on past experience, linking significant events from own experience and from stories, paying attention to sequence and how events lead into one another (green).
CLL A Have emerging self-confidence to speak to others about wants and interests (green).
Specific Learning Outcomes – to enable children to plan and state intentions and intended outcomes ahead of actions. To enable children to plan and to work with other children with increasing co-operation.
Group – shared and guided.
Resources – None.
What to do – when children are familiar with the range of activities available to them, encourage them to verbalise what they intend to do ahead of actually doing it.

Over time children should be held to their planned actions, at least as their first activity
Sessions can then be organised around a structure where children verbally plan what they intend to do, are encouraged to talk about how they are doing it as they engage with activity and review how their activities went in a sharing circle. This structure for sessions not only places language and communication into the centre of all activity and reflection on activity, but also begins to prepare children for the structure of the Literacy Hour, which is essentially the same as this in structure.
Variation, differentiation and extension – the type of talk in planning time will grow in sophistication as children mature and become more aware of the options available to them.
Assessment focus – I can talk about what I am going to do before I do it. I can plan my activity.

7. The Share and tell Circle (review)

CLL F Link statements and stick to a main theme or intention. Use language for an increasing range of purposes (green). **CLL G** Talk activities through, reflecting on and modifying what they are doing. Use talk to connect ideas, explain what is happening and anticipate what might happen next. Use talk, actions and objects to recall and relive past experiences (blue). Begin to use talk to reflect on past experience, linking significant events. Begin to make patterns in their experience through linking cause and effect, sequencing, ordering and grouping (green).
Specific Learning Outcomes – to develop confidence in describing activities and reviewing what has been done and what has been learned.
Group – supported, guided and shared.
Resources – Usually something that the child has done or made as a prop to support the sharing. A hoop. Share and tell prompts (Copymaster 6).
What to do – children are frequently encouraged to share their thoughts and descriptions of activities informally as they are doing them. Most children naturally begin to share and describe both what and how they went about making a model or a picture they have been working on in structured play. Typically, children move through labelling parts of their work, to describing the parts in more detail. Gradually they are able to explain how they went about making or doing, and with support can be encouraged to reflect, analyse and consider improvements or different ways forward. The 'Share and Tell Circle' presents a structured way of building upon this from small groups up to the whole class.
Tell the children that at the end of the activity period there will be a 'share and tell circle'. Let the children engage in their usual range of structured play activities. Remind children that at the end of the session they will be talking about what they have done. Encourage children to rehearse orally some of the things that they might say about what they have been doing and how they overcame any problems they were having.

At the end of the activity time, encourage the children to bring an object or a prop to help them talk about what they have been doing. Make as many 'share and tell circles' as your number of supporting adults will allow. Place a hoop in the middle of each circle.
An adult should model how to share. It can be helpful to have a set of question prompts to support e.g.
- What did you do/make?
- What does it look like?
- What does it do?
- What is the best thing about it?
- How did you make it and what did you use?
- What did you do first … next …a nd last?
- What was difficult? How did you solve that problem?
- Tell me something else …

These can then be used as prompts to extend the contributions from the children. Over time children should begin to be able to talk more confidently around these points.
Variation, differentiation and extension – the 'share and tell circle' is a useful routine to put into place to close all sessions. It enables children to reflect upon their learning and to think through and talk about how they met their intentions and resolved problems. It will eventually grow into the plenary sessions of the Literacy and Numeracy lessons.
Over time, and with constant routine children will become more confident with the conventions of talking about their learning. With support, other pupils should be encouraged to ask questions to the child sharing. This can be developed through adult modelling and prompting with questioning and gradually handing over some of this to the children.
It is important to establish the ground rules to ensure positive contributions (Share and Tell Guidelines).
Assessment focus – I can share and describe what I have done/made confidently and with only a little prompting.
I can describe how I overcame problems and answer questions from an adult or another child.

Strand 2

8. News Circle

CLL H Use talk, actions and objects to recall and relive past experiences (blue).
Specific Learning Outcomes – to be able to structure and recount events and experiences to small and large groups.
Group – collaborative, guided and shared.
Resources – Copymaster 7, a puppet.
What to do – You could use a puppet to model sharing news. You could reinforce with the puppet important points of presentation, such as speaking clearly and remembering to talk about who, where and what. You could then prompt the puppet using the chart from Copymaster 7. This copymaster can be enlarged and cut apart to make prompt cards. It would help if the different prompts were different colours.
Use the 'when' prompt to ask when the event happened. The 'who' prompt to discuss who was there. Use the 'where' and 'what' cards to elicit what happened where and the 'why' card can be used to explore some finer detail. These can be used to support children as they retell their news.
Variation, differentiation and extension – children can be encouraged to share their news. Initially they will probably just retell their news but it would be useful to revisit the news using the prompts to help them restructure their retelling. This works best if children are introduced to this activity in smaller groups building up to the larger group.
Children can be introduced to Copymaster 7 as a way of recording their news with pictures. As children move through the Reception year they will begin to be able to add written detail under these headings too (bottom of Copymaster 7). Copymaster 7 can be folded to make 2 zigzag books (these may need to be enlarged to A3). The zigzag books can form part of the class library. They could be used to make news bulletins for a role-play TV news area. A T.V. could be made out of a large cardboard box, turned upside down with a hole cut in the front for a screen. When the box is rested on two chairs a child can pop up inside the box to 'read' the news from News bulletins that children have produced. This can lead into fictional news items, linked to stories such as *Goldilocks and the Three Bears*, for example. Children could record their news onto a tape recorder for other children to listen to, both of these could be independent activities once they were set up
Assessment focus – I can share my news using a basic frame to structure my retelling. I can draw and write my news, using a simple frame to help me.

9. Tell-me puppet

CLL C/ D Listen to stories with increasing attention and recall. Describe main story settings, events and principal characters. Question why things happen, and give explanations (blue). Initiate a conversation, negotiate positions and pay attention to and take account of others' views (green). **CLL G** Use talk to give new meanings to objects and actions, treating them as symbols for other things (blue). Begin to use talk to pretend in imaginary situations (green).
Specific Learning Outcomes – to listen to and talk with a puppet, asking questions and responding to prompts.
Group – shared/guided.
Resources – a puppet, a story for the puppet to tell.
What to do – let the puppet tell the children a familiar story or relate a set of events that happened to the puppet, e.g. *a wolf puppet, could tell the story of the three little pigs, but from his point of view!* Encourage the children to listen to the puppet and then to ask the puppet questions about the story that it has told.
Encourage children to take the lead in using the puppet to relate stories or events. Model asking questions to the children when they are operating the puppet e.g. *How did you feel when? Why did you do that? Did you know that doing that was wrong? etc.*
Variation, differentiation and extension – let children use the puppet to tell stories or to act out stories to other small groups of children. The puppet can be used to model both correct and incorrect forms of spoken Standard English.
Assessment focus – I can tell a story using a puppet to speak for me.

10. Teacher in role.

CLL C/ D Listen to stories with increasing attention and recall and describe main story settings, events and principal characters. Question why things happen, and give explanations (blue). Initiate a conversation, negotiate positions and pay attention to and take account of others' views (green). **CLL G** Use talk to give new meanings to objects and actions, treating them as symbols for other things (blue). Begin to use talk to pretend in imaginary situations (green).
Specific Learning Outcomes – to listen and respond appropriately to an adult in role.
Group – shared/guided/collaborative.
Resources – props to support the adoption of the character in role.
What to do – gather the children together as for the normal routines of stories or sharing circles. Explain that someone else is going to tell the story on this occasion. At this point adopt the appropriate props e.g. *a hat, scarf and shawl* and change your voice appropriately.
This role should be kept up until the tale is finished and children should be given the opportunity to talk to the character in role. This is often best supported with another adult leading the questioning to show the children how to do this. In character, explain that you have to go and say 'Goodbye'. Take the props off and return to 'normal'. Ask the children what happened and what they found out.
Variation, differentiation and extension – put a similar set of props into the role-play costumes to let the children explore and act out the role you modelled.
Assessment focus – I can listen and talk to an adult pretending to be someone else.

Theme 5 — Developing language for thinking

11. How are you feeling today?

CLL F Begin to use more complex sentences. Use a widening range of words to express or elaborate ideas (blue). Link statements and stick to a main theme or intention. Consistently develop a simple story, explanation or line of questioning. **CLL G** Use talk to give new meanings to objects and actions, treating them as symbols for other things (blue). Begin to use talk to pretend in imaginary situations (green).

Specific Learning Outcomes – to be able to adopt a role and give an explanation for what is happening in role.

Group – shared, guided.

Resources – a tambourine, prop for a microphone (real microphone and tape).

What to do –

1 use a large comfortable space and let the children sit in their own space. Tell the children that when you tap the tambourine they should freeze and that you are going to ask some of them what they are doing. Use the pretend microphone as you ask the question and let them reply into the microphone.

Ask the children to stand up and walk round. Give the instruction *'Be yourself at home'*. Let the children pretend to do something at home. Tap the tambourine so they freeze and ask some of them to tell you what they are pretending to do.

2 As before, but this time ask the children to be someone else known to them (for example, someone from the setting) and again to act out something that they are doing. Try and encourage them to do this without talking. Freeze the children and ask some of them what they are doing and why they are doing it. Ask them how they are feeling today and why.

Variation, differentiation and extension –

3 As before, but let the children explore characters from nursery rhymes and familiar stories that they have experienced. Again ask them the questions about what they are doing, how they feel and why?

Record their comments to listen to in the Listening Area.

Assessment focus – I can pretend to be someone else and tell you how I am feeling.

Strand 2

12. Read my mind

CLL H Begin to make patterns in their experience through linking cause and effect, sequencing, ordering and grouping (green).
Specific Learning Outcomes – to develop questioning and interaction amongst group members.
Group – guided and shared.
Resources – a tray with a selection of objects on.
What to do – make a collection of various objects and put them onto a tray or into a hoop in the middle of a circle. Ask a child to choose one of the objects on the tray and to whisper the name of that object to the teaching adult.
The children in the circle ask questions to try and find out which object was chosen. The child who has chosen can only answer 'yes' or 'no'.
Whoever guesses the right object becomes the next child to choose.
Variation, differentiation and extension – variations on this game could include a collection of pictures, objects around the classroom, a large and detailed picture or poster (in a big book for example), children in the circle, Compare Bears, mathematical shapes etc. This game can develop into the traditional game of 'I Spy' when children begin to be able to segment initial letter sounds from words (step 2 of Progression in Phonics).
Variation, differentiation and extension – as children become used to the conventions of this game they can begin to move into eliminating sets of objects by reference to collective attributes such as size, shape, colour and position. Children should be encouraged to develop thinking along these lines. This could be linked to games such as *'Who stole the cookie?'*. One child leaves the room and the cookie is given to a child in the classroom. The 'Cookie Catcher' returns and has to find out who has the cookie in the least number of questions *e.g. 'Is it someone with blond hair?'*
Assessment focus – I can ask questions by thinking about the attributes of objects.

Theme 6 — Challenging language for thinking

13. Neat Knees (think-pair-share)

CLL H Use talk to organise, sequence and clarify thinking, ideas, feelings and events. **CLL A** Interact with others, negotiating plans and activities and taking turns in conversation.
Specific Learning Outcomes – children will begin to be able to work collaboratively and to talk, think and negotiate responses to a question, challenge or task.
Group – shared, guided and collaborative.
Resources – none.
What to do – both the Literacy and Numeracy strategies recommend the use of interactive teaching and learning. It is important to engage and involve all pupils particularly during small and large group work. When children are asked a question they may need some thinking time before responding to the question. 'Neat knees' or 'time out' enables children to talk through a question or challenge they have been set, and is a way of ensuring more children contribute to discussion.
First of all you will need to establish the 'neat knees' routine.
Sit the children cross-legged on the carpet. Ask them to turn to face a partner. They should sit so that their knees are touching each other.

When this has been sorted out, tell the children that they can talk to each other. Give them about a minute. Ask some children to share what their partner said with them. Establish this routine in spare moments by practising 'neat knees' and letting the children have an opportunity to free-talk.
Variation, differentiation and extension – when you think the children are ready, you should begin to structure the topic of talk. Plan a suitably engaging context, for example shared reading of a new story, and ask the children what they think will happen next. Instruct the children to 'Neat Knees' and to talk about what they think will happen. Take contributions from children and if possible make some notes of what they contribute as shared text.
You should be able to utilise this strategy whenever you feel the children would benefit from the opportunity to talk to each before responding. Over time it will be possible to step up the challenge of the questioning to the pupils. You should be able to use this strategy with slightly larger groups of three to four children as the children become trained to collaborate.
Assessment focus – I can talk with a partner. I can listen to what my partner says and share this with someone else.

14. What comes next?

CLL C Sustain attentive listening, responding to what they have heard by relevant comments, questions or actions.
CLL H Use talk to organise, sequence and clarify ideas, feelings and events.
Specific Learning Outcomes – to be able to listen carefully and follow a set of instructions.
Group – guided groups/collaborative pairs.
Resources – a barrier screen for the leader (barrier screens can be made using some thick card to provide each child with a screened off area to keep their beads away from the eyes of the other children until the end of the game).
Coloured threading beads and a threading string. Each participating child will need to be able to select from their own set of threading beads. Each child's set should include a similar number of similar coloured and shaped beads. (Note: any similar set of objects that can be threaded onto a threading string or stick can be used for variation.) Copymaster 8.
What to do – this game is probably best developed in small groups before expanding to larger groups. Provide a set of threading beads and threading string for each child and one for the adult leader (a similar set for each participant). The adult leader should set up the barrier screen so that the children are unable to see which beads are being selected and threaded onto the threading string. The adult begins the game by giving the first instruction: *'Please take a round blue bead and thread it onto the string'*. The other players follow the instruction and thread the bead that they think corresponds to this instruction onto their string. When they have all done this, together, they should say:
'Thank you, thank you,
We have done our best,
Now please can you tell us
WHAT COMES NEXT?!'
The instructor selects another bead and gives the next instruction e.g. *'Please take a square shaped yellow bead and thread it onto your string'*. Again the players follow the instruction and recite the rhyme.
Play continues like this for as many times as seems appropriate until the instructor decides to stop. The instructor tells the other players:
'That's it, I've finished,
No more to go!'
To which they reply:
'O.K., Boss,
Now it's time to show!'
The instructor lowers the barrier screen and the other players all line their threading string up next to the instructor's string to see if they have followed the instructions correctly. The beads are returned to the pots and play starts again, this time with a different instructor.
Variation, differentiation and extension – once an adult has led this game a few times it can become an independent game that pairs or small groups of children can play without adult support. The game becomes a bit more challenging when all the children have their own screen so that they cannot see what the other children are doing each time.
Extension – instructions could be recorded onto tape and children could check the answer with a colour-coded sequence using Copymaster 8. This copymaster could be used to help children plan and record sequences of beads, or it could be used to play the game with coloured counters or other objects *e.g. Compare Bears*.
Assessment focus – I can listen to and follow a sequence of instructions.

Strand 2

15. Funny faces

CLL C Sustain attentive listening, responding to what they have heard by relevant comments, questions or actions.
CLL H Use talk to organise, sequence and clarify ideas, feelings and events.
Specific Learning Outcomes – to be able to listen carefully and follow a set of instructions.
Group – guided groups/collaborative pairs.
Resources – a barrier screen for the leader.
A copy of Copymasters 9 and 10 suitably prepared for each child – the game will be much more interesting if the parts of the face are coloured in and will last longer if the parts are laminated. Laminating the face enables the children to draw on hair and wipe it off with dry wipe markers.
What to do – each player has a copy of the funny face from Copymaster 9 along with the various bits and pieces to add to the face (Copymaster 10).
The adult leader of the game puts up their screen and selects one of the parts of a face. They instruct the other players by describing the part of the face that they will need to select to add to their picture.
Play continues in this fashion until a completed face has been made. The screen is removed and the other players compare the face they have made with the leader.
Variation, differentiation and extension – once an adult has led this game a few times it can become an independent game that pairs or small groups of children can play without adult support. The game becomes a bit more challenging when all the children have their own screen so that they cannot see what the other children are doing each time.
Extension – 'Detective Identifit'. Blu-tack the parts of the face onto the face template, photocopy and reduce the photocopy. Make a set of faces like this to produce a set of cards. A child turns over a card and instructs the other children to try to make a face like the one on the card, but without showing them the card. Again instructions could be recorded onto tape and children could check the answer by reference to the photocopy.
Assessment focus – I can listen and follow a simple sequence of instructions. I can give simple instructions.

16. Crazy creatures

CLL C Sustain attentive listening, responding to what they have heard by relevant comments, questions or actions.
CLL H Use talk to organise, sequence and clarify ideas, feelings and events.
Specific Learning Outcomes – to be able to listen carefully and follow a set of instructions.
Group – guided groups/collaborative pairs.
Resources – a barrier screen for the leader. A copy of Copymasters 11 and 12 suitably prepared for each child (the game will be much more interesting if the parts of the face are coloured in and will last longer if the parts are laminated).
What to do – each player has a set of creature pieces cut up and prepared from Copymaster 12. The adult leader of the game puts up their screen and selects a creature head and places it onto the background. They instruct the other players by describing the next creature part that they are adding. Play continues in this fashion until a completed creature has been made. The screen is removed and the other players compare the crazy creatures to the creature made by the leader.
Variation, differentiation and extension – once an adult has led this game a few times it can become an independent game that pairs or small groups of children can play without adult support. The game becomes a bit more challenging when all the children have their own screen so that they cannot see what the other children are doing each time.
Extension – 'Detective Identifit'. Blu-tack the creature parts onto the background, photocopy and reduce the photocopy. Make a set of crazy creatures like this to produce a set of cards. A child turns over a card and instructs the other children to try to make a crazy creature like the one on the card, but without showing them the card. Again, instructions could be recorded onto tape and children could check the answer by reference to the photocopy.
Assessment focus – I can listen and follow a sequence of instructions. I can give simple instructions.

17. Where in the house?

CLL C Sustain attentive listening, responding to what they have heard by relevant comments, questions or actions.
CLL H Use talk to organise, sequence and clarify ideas, feelings and events.
Specific Learning Outcomes – to be able to listen carefully and follow a set of instructions.
Group – guided groups/collaborative pairs.
Resources – a barrier screen for the leader. A copy of Copymaster 13 suitably prepared for each child (photocopy Copymaster 14 onto coloured card or use colour to make sets of furniture for each child). Small play figures such as Play People or Compare Bears.
What to do – each player has a copy of the house (Copymaster 13). The adult leader has a screen to obscure their house from the view of the other players. The leader instructs the other players by telling them where to put different objects and items of furniture into the different rooms. Play continues until the leader is satisfied with the arrangement of furniture. The adult leader lowers the screen and the other players compare furniture arrangements with the leader.
Variation, differentiation and extension – once an adult has led this game a few times it can become an independent game that pairs or small groups of children can play without adult support. The game becomes a bit more challenging when all the children have their own

Theme 6 — Challenging language for thinking

screen so that they cannot see what the other children are doing each time. Each player could take it turn to give the instruction for the next item of furniture.
Extension – once the furniture has been arranged, other objects could be added to different rooms, such as different sized and coloured Compare Bears.
Assessment focus – I can listen to and follow a sequence of instructions. I can give simple instructions.

18. Robo-kid

CLL C Sustain attentive listening, responding to what they have heard by relevant comments, questions or actions.
CLL H Use talk to organise, sequence and clarify ideas, feelings and events.
Specific Learning Outcomes – to encourage children to give clear instructions. To develop careful listening and responses to instructions. To encourage children to ask questions when instructions are not clear.
Group – guided groups/collaborative pairs.
Resources – the robot mask on Copymaster 15 (note – with younger children cut out the eyes so that they can see, with older children leave the eyes in the mask so that they are effectively blindfolded and have to listen and follow the instructions literally).

What to do – this is a variation on the traditional game 'Simon Says'. Children can be introduced to this game informally by playing 'Simon Says' *e.g. only following instructions when preceded by the phrase 'Simon says…'.*
The game should be introduced by adult modelling. One adult leaves the room and a child is selected to hide an object such as a key. The adult returns to the class in role as a robotic person that will only follow instructions if preceded by the phrase: 'Controller says … ', and then the 'adult-in-role' will follow instructions literally. The remaining adult in the room should select children to give instructions to the robot to locate the hidden object, but the 'robot' should follow the instructions literally *e.g.*
Child: *'Controller says take four steps towards the door.*

Strand 2

Robot: 'What do you mean "step"?, what do you mean "door"?'.

This will encourage children to define the words they use to give instructions and to choose words carefully. This will become particularly apparent when it gets to finer instructions, such as *'Controller says lift up your arm and take the box from the shelf'* to which the response could be *'What do you mean arm, box and shelf?'* (It should be assumed that the robot understands some words such as up, forward and numbers.)

When the object is located a child can be chosen to be the Robo-kid and leaves the room whilst the object is hidden. The Robo-kid returns to the room and the procedure above is repeated with adults intervening to check that the rules of the game are being followed.

Variation, differentiation and extension –

Extension – once the game has been played a few times it can become an independent game for collaborative or independent work and the robot mask can be used in activity areas such as construction or painting. One child assumes the role of Robo-kid and the other of controller to instruct the robot in completing a task *e.g. building a tower, painting a picture*. It will be much more challenging if the robot mask has the eyes left in to blindfold the robot whilst the task is being given.

Early version of the game – before playing 'Simon Says' there is an earlier version of this game called 'Do this! – Do that!'. An adult, or a child, gives instructions to the group by demonstrating the action. If the demonstration is preceded by the phrase 'Do this!' then all the children should copy the leader. However, if the instruction is preceded by the phrase 'Do that!' the children should ignore the action. This can work quite well in small guided or collaborative groups with construction materials, when the game becomes a bit like follow the leader. Children should only copy, or 'follow', the lead, when the action is preceded by the phrase 'Do this!'.

Assessment focus – I can give clear instructions. I can listen to and follow instructions. When instructions are not clear I can ask for more detail.

Theme 7 — Linking sounds to letters

Early Learning Goals for linking sounds and letters	NLS Word level work: Phonics spelling and vocabulary
Teachers should plan for: • Opportunities to participate in musical activities; • Opportunities to link sounds to letters; • Opportunities for children to hear, use, see and read familiar words.	Pupils should be taught: • Phonological awareness, phonics and spelling.
• **CLL L** Explore and experiment with sounds, words and texts; • **CLL I** Hear and say initial and final sounds in words, and short vowel sounds within words.	**W1** to understand and be able to rhyme through: • Recognising, exploring and working with rhyming patterns, e.g. *learning nursery rhymes*; extending these patterns by analogy, generating new and invented words in speech and spelling.
	W2 knowledge of grapheme/phoneme correspondence through: • Hearing and identifying initial sounds in words.
	W4 to link sound and spelling patterns by: • Identifying alliteration in known and new and invented words.
• **CLL J** Link sounds to letters, naming and sounding the letters of the alphabet.	**W2** knowledge of grapheme/phoneme correspondence through: • Reading letter(s) that represent(s) the sounds(s): a-z, ch, sh, th; • Writing each letter in response to each sound: a-z, ch, sh, th.
	W3 alphabetic and phonic knowledge through: • Sounding and naming each letter of the alphabet in lower and upper case; • Writing letters in response to names; • Understanding alphabetical order through alphabet books, rhymes and songs.
• **CLL K** Use phonic knowledge to write simple regular words and make phonetically plausible attempts at more complex words.	**W2** knowledge of grapheme/phoneme correspondence through: • Identifying and writing initial and dominant phonemes in spoken words; • Identifying and writing initial and final phonemes in consonant-vowel-consonant (CVC) words, e.g. *fit, mat, pan*.
	W4 to link sound and spelling patterns by: • Using knowledge of rhyme to identify families of rhyming CVC words, e.g. *hop, top, mop, fat, mat, pat*, etc; • Discriminating 'onsets' from 'rimes' in speech and spelling, e.g. *'tip', 'sip', 'skip', 'flip', 'chip'*.

1. Developing Phonological Awareness

This strand focuses on helping children become aware of the relationship between the sounds of speech (phonemes) and the symbols that we use to represent these sounds (the letters of the alphabet/graphemes). Young children are not aware that language exists and the activities in this strand help sensitise them to the mechanics and structure of the language that they already can use.

The National Literacy Strategy has provided a Seven Step Progression in Phonics (PiP) to organise the sequence by which children are introduced to the code of sounds and letters in English. The games and activities included in this strand complement the games outlined in the NLS publication.

Strand 3

NLS Progression in Phonics mapped to the Early Years curriculum.

NLS Progression in phonics Step:	Timing and link to Stepping Stones

Step 1
• General sound discrimination
  • Environmental
  • Instrumental
  • Body percussion
  • Rhythm
• Speech sound discrimination
• Rhythm and rhyme
• Alliteration
	Birth and through the Foundation Stage
	
	Explicit focus of activities at yellow and blue Stepping Stones and Foundation Year 1

Step 2 • To be able to continue a rhyming string • To hear and say phonemes in initial position	Green Stepping Stone
Step 3 • To hear and say phonemes in the final position	Early Learning Goal
Step 4 • To hear and say phonemes in medial position • To segment to spell CVC words • To blend to read CVC words	Early Learning Goal
Step 5 • To hear phonemes within consonant clusters • To segment to spell words containing consonant clusters in the initial and final positions • To blend to read consonant clusters in the initial and final positions	Reasonable expectation for some children by the end of the Foundation Stage
Step 6 • To know one representation of each of ten vowel phonemes (digraphs) • To segment to spell words containing vowel phonemes represented by more than one letter • To blend to read words containing vowel phonemes represented by more than one letter	Reasonable expectation for some children by the end of the Foundation Stage
Step 7 • To know the different spellings of the long vowel phonemes	

The activities in this section are organised against the Progression in Phonics for convenience. Each activity is mapped to the Early Learning Goal at the appropriate level also.

Theme 7 — Sound discrimination and awareness

2. The Listeners

CLL I Distinguish one sound from another.
Specific Learning Outcomes – (environmental sound discrimination) to explore the sounds in the environment and to practise focusing attention on environmental sounds.
Group – shared, guided.
Resources – a tape recorder, Copymaster 16 (the ear), and a piece of doweling or wood to mount the copymaster on.
What to do – settle the children and speak to them in a quiet voice. Explain that they are going to become 'the listeners', and they are going to listen very carefully to the sounds that they can hear. Explain that they will be able to listen even more carefully if they close their eyes. Let the children listen to the sounds that they can hear in the environment and then ask them to share the sounds that they heard. Some of the sounds the children will be able to label, such as cars, breathing, wind, voices; but others will be sounds that they may have to imitate to convey.
In a group give each child a copy of Copymaster 16. Visit different locations within the setting and let children settle quietly, close their eyes and listen. When they open their eyes, instead of raising their hands they should raise the ear to contribute.
Take the children on a 'Listening Walk' outside and let them listen to the various sounds in the environment
Variation, differentiation and extension –
Extension – when a group visits different locations, they should use a tape recorder to record the environment sound picture at each different location. The tape can be played to the group who, with their eyes closed, try and picture the location. Children should describe what they can hear and add detail into their description of the setting e.g. *what kind of weather do they think it was, sunny or windy? How and why can they tell?*
Assessment focus – I can listen carefully and discriminate between environmental sounds.

3. Sound spotter (1)

CLL I Distinguish one sound from another.
Specific Learning Outcomes – (instrumental sound discrimination) to match objects with their sounds. To describe the sound made and to discuss how the sound was made.
Group – shared, guided collaborative.
Resources – several pairs of objects that make different sounds. A screen.
Copymaster 16 (the ear), and a piece of doweling or wood to mount the copymaster on
What to do – collect together a range of objects that make different sounds, including everyday objects from which a sound could be made e.g. *water in a bottle (to be shaken), paper (to be torn or scrunched), some musical instruments, some different materials that could be tapped together (two stones, two sticks, two wooden bricks).*
Put the objects behind the screen and put a similar set of objects in front of the screen.
Choose a child to go behind the screen and make a sound using one of the objects on display. The other children listen carefully to the sound.
Hold up each of the objects in front of the screen in turn. When the object that the children think made the sound is held up the children should raise their 'ear' (from Copymaster 16) to vote for it.
Choose a child to describe in words the sound that the object made and how it was made. This child should instruct another child to select the object with the most votes and instruct them to make the sound to compare it to the sound behind the screen.
Listen and compare the sound to the sound behind the screen once more to check whether the children are correct and then remove the screen.
Repeat with an alternative object.
Variation, differentiation and extension – once children are familiar with this game they should be able to select their own sets of objects to compare sounds. Objects can be made that make sounds. A set of sounds could be recorded onto a tape instead of using the screen. Children have to listen to the tape, select the correct object and repeat the sound.
Assessment focus – I can listen carefully to the sounds made by objects. I can describe the sounds made by objects and I can make these sounds using the objects.

4. Sound spotter (2)

CLL I Distinguish one sound from another.
Specific Learning Outcomes – (instrumental sound discrimination) to listen for a discrete sound amongst a sequence of sounds.
Group – shared, guided collaborative.
Resources – several pairs of objects that make different sounds. A screen.
Copymaster 16 (the ear), and a piece of doweling or wood to mount the copymaster on.
What to do – collect together a range of objects that make different sounds, including everyday objects from which a sound could be made. All the other children sit in front of the screen; each child has a copy of Copymaster 16 (the ear) on a handle.
Select a child to go behind the screen. This child selects one object to make the target sound and uses the object to make the sound e.g. *tapping two stones together*. The other children listen very carefully to this sound.
The game commences with the child behind the screen putting together sequences of sounds using the objects. Every time the children who are listening hear the target sound they hold up their ear signals (Copymaster 16) to indicate that they have spotted the sound.
At an appropriate moment change the child behind the screen and the target sound and continue with the game.

Strand 3

Variation, differentiation and extension – use a tape recorder to record sequences of sound in a similar way. Play the tape. When children hear the target sound they hold up the ear signals to indicate that they have spotted the sound.
Some interesting sound sequences can be made if you have access to a keyboard that has a range of sound effects and sound samples. Some of these sound effects can be played at a different key thereby increasing the challenge as children decide when one sound ends and another begins, and whether the sound they heard belongs to the original target sound or a different sound altogether.
Children could record sound sequences like this for other children to sound spot. Background 'noise' could be added through instruments, body percussion and the use of vocal effects. A group of children could produce quite a challenging 'soundscape' from which to spot the target sound.
Assessment focus – I can listen carefully for a discrete sound. I can describe the sounds made by an object.

5. What is the sound?

CLL 1 Distinguish one sound from another.
Specific Learning Outcomes – (instrumental sound discrimination) to develop an ability to listen carefully to discrete sounds.
Group – shared, guided collaborative.
Resources – a set of objects that make different sounds. A tape recorder.
What to do – collect together objects with which you can make interesting and distinctive sounds *e.g. water being poured/splashed/shaken in a bottle, paper being torn/screwed up/flapped*. Sounds can be made with the body such as claps, knee pats, foot stamps and clicks of the tongue, and you can make other sounds such as paper being cut, things being dropped, a box being opened and a pencil being sharpened.
Record the sounds onto the tape recorder. Leave a space between each sound to pause the tape.
Play the tape to children. Ask them to close their eyes and try to picture the object that is making the sound. Encourage them to try to visualise the object that is making the sound. Ask the children to tell a partner what they think is making the sound. Make a list of their suggestions for each sound before showing the children how the sound was made.
Variation, differentiation and extension – encourage the children to imagine what the sound could be rather than what it actually is. Slapping knees could be a duck walking over a concrete path.
Let children record their own unusual sounds and sound effects.
Assessment focus – I can listen to and identify sounds.

6. Segment your tune

CLL 1 Distinguish one sound from another (yellow).
Specific Learning Outcomes – (instrumental sound discrimination) to listen to and repeat sequences of sound.
Group – shared, guided collaborative.
Resources – a tape recorder.
What to do – sit the children in a circle. Tell them that you are going to make a sound and that you want them to copy what you do. Clap once and let the children clap once back to you. Clap twice and let them clap back.
Explain that there are two types of pattern that you will use. One is called 'tap' and it is the same as a single clap or knee slap or tap on the floor. Show them what you mean by saying 'tap-tap-tap' and clapping three times slowly as you say each 'tap'. Let them echo this back to you.
Tell them that the other pattern is called 'tapper' and this is the same as a double-time clap, slap, click or tap. Show them the pattern 'tap-tapper-tap-tapper' and let them echo this back to you. Try some other patterns *e.g. 'tapper-tap-tapper-tap'/'tap-tapper-tapper-tap'/'tap-tap-tap-tapper'* and let the children echo these back to you.
You can introduce children to the 'rest' symbol and card, which simply means to mark the beat with a silence or a rest.
Variation, differentiation and extension – record some simple sequences onto a tape. Play the tape and let the children echo the sequence.
Give the children different percussion instruments and let them echo the 'tap-tapper' sequences to you.
Tell the children the sequence by saying, for example, 'tapper-tapper-tapper-tap' and letting the children play it back to you using the instruments
Assessment focus – I can listen to a sequence of sound and repeat it.

7. Sound sequencer (1)

CLL 1 Distinguish one sound from another (yellow).
Specific Learning Outcomes – (instrumental sound discrimination) to use a symbol to represent a sound. To blend a sequence of sounds using symbols to represent each sound.
Group – shared, guided collaborative.
Resources – a whiteboard and pen. Copymaster 17 (one enlarged set of symbols and a set for each pair of children). A tape recorder.
What to do – recap the 'tap' and 'tapper' way of describing single and double time beats of percussion. Show the children the symbols used to represent the 'tap' and 'tapper' beats: '\' and '/\'.
Tell the children a pattern, *e.g. tap-tapper-tap-tapper* and show the children the pattern using the symbols used to represent this sequence: '\ /\ \ /\'. Let the children echo

Theme 7 — Sound discrimination and awareness

this back to you in claps or in beats on the percussion instruments that they have. Model reading the sequence from left to write with a pointer.

Model several patterns in this way and let children echo the patterns back to you.

Ask children to make up a simple pattern. Let them perform the pattern and write the pattern onto the board using the 'tap/tapper' key. Read the pattern back to the class and let the class perform the pattern from the symbols on the board.

Now just write the pattern onto the board and see if the children can follow the symbols to repeat the pattern.

Finally, using the set of enlarged symbols (Copymaster 17), let some children come and put a sequence of symbols onto the board (attached with Blu-tack). Let the children perform the sequence that has been created.

Let children make up their own sequences from the Copymaster 17 symbols. They can perform these to the class.

Variation, differentiation and extension – children can use these symbols and the sound frames to compose sequences of music as an independent activity in a music area. Children can use the sequences of symbols to recall the composition and perform their pattern to the class in a plenary session.

Assessment focus – I can compose a sequence of sounds by using symbols.

8. Sound sequencer (2)

CLL I Distinguish one sound from another (yellow).
Specific Learning Outcomes – (instrumental sound discrimination) to blend sequences of instrumental sound.
Group – shared, guided collaborative.
Resources – a set of simple percussion instruments (including a drum, a shaker, two wooden sticks and a chime bell). Copymasters 17, 18, 19 and 20 (enlarged to demonstrate to a group). A tape recorder.
What to do – children should be familiar with the idea of representing single beats with the '\tap' symbol and double beats with the '/\tapper' symbol. Enlarge the composing grid on Copymaster 19 and a set of percussion instrument symbols from Copymaster 18 along with a set of 'tap' and 'tapper' symbols. Give out percussion instruments to the children.

Select one of the percussion instrument symbols and place it into the first top space on the grid and select one of the 'tap' or 'tapper' cards to go beneath it. Select another percussion instrument for the second space and build up a sequence of instruments and a sequence of 'beat' cards to make a pattern, e.g. '/ /\ /'.

Let the children with the appropriate instruments perform the sequence. Change the sequence by substituting instruments and/or changing the pattern. Let children compose their own simple musical patterns using this way of working.

Important note: There are four beats to a bar in most musical sequences and it is useful to introduce and encourage children to think in sequences of four when composing music.. The sequencing grid on Copymaster 19 can be used to support this. The sequencing grid on Copymaster 20 presents 3 marked spaces for instruments. This is to draw a parallel with simple three letter 'consonant vowel consonant' words in English, and to support children's developing understanding of sounds being in the initial, final or medial position within a sequence.

Variation, differentiation and extension – sequences of sounds can be recorded onto tape and children can match the correct symbols to the sequence of sound on the tape.

Assessment focus – I can sequence and perform a series of sounds using written notation.

9. Sound buttons

CLL I Distinguish one sound from another (yellow).
Reception Literacy Objective (PiP Step1 and Step 2) Speech sound discrimination.
Specific Learning Outcomes – to develop an ability to listen carefully to discrete sounds. To create opportunities for children to explore the sounds that they can make with their voices. To begin to link phonemes to letters.
Group – shared, supported, and independent.
Resources – Copymaster 21.
What to do – introduce the sound buttons from Copymaster 21 to the children. Explain that although these things have a name they all make a distinctive sound. Rehearse the sounds that go with each picture with the children.

Explain that these pictures are special 'sound buttons'. When they are pressed, whoever presses them should make the sound that goes with the picture. Demonstrate that when you press the sound button with a picture of a sheep on it, you make a 'Baa-a-a-a!' sound, etc.

Let the children stick the sound buttons around the room with Blu-tack. Provide opportunities for them to add additional pictures onto the sound buttons. Model pressing sound buttons from time to time, adding the appropriate sound effects.

When children are used to the idea of sound buttons they can be used in lots of ways – for example, to make a display more interactive by providing sound buttons that relate to sounds of objects in the picture. The buttons could be placed next to the objects or at the bottom of the display (like a key) for children to interact with and add sound effects.

Variation, differentiation and extension – work with sound buttons can lead into supporting children as they learn letter sound correspondence. The letter combinations that represent phonemes can be written

Strand 3

onto sound buttons and placed around the room (use the blank sound buttons on Copymaster 21) The same rules apply: as before, a letter has both a name and a sound and when the sound button is pressed the person pressing it should say the sound, i.e. the phoneme. Sound buttons can be used to support sound sequencing activities, such as those outlined in the sound sequencer activities, and also used to tell sound stories.
Assessment focus – I can make the correct sound for an object using my voice.
I can link the speech sound (phoneme) to the correct letter combination.

---

10. Where are you?

CLL I Distinguish one sound from another (yellow).
CLL C Listen to others in small groups (yellow).
Reception Literacy Objective (PiP Step1) *Speech sound discrimination.*
Specific Learning Outcomes – (environmental sound discrimination) to be able to distinguish one specific sound from many similar sounds that are heard at once.
Group – shared.
Resources – a blindfold.
What to do – one child is selected and blindfolded. A target word, such as a child's name, is selected and that child whispers their name loudly three times. The children jumble themselves up randomly around the room. On a given signal all the children begin to whisper their own names over and over. Guide the blindfolded child around the children until the target child is located. The children swap and another child is selected as the target child.
Variation, differentiation and extension – another word or sound could be selected as the target sound Alternatively an object that makes a distinguishable sound such as a ticking clock could be hidden someone in the room. The children enter the room and have to locate the object by listening for the sound.
Assessment focus – I can listen carefully and locate a specific sound.

---

11. Finger rhyme time

CLL I Enjoy rhyming and rhythmic activities (yellow). Show awareness of rhyme and alliteration. Recognise rhythm in spoken words (blue). **CLL D** Listen to favourite nursery rhymes, stories and songs. Join in with repeated refrains, anticipating key events and important phrases (yellow).
Reception Literacy Objective (PiP Step1) *Rhythm and rhyme.* **Pip Step 2** *Be able to continue a rhyming string.*
W1 Understand and be able to rhyme through:
- recognising, exploring and working with rhyming patterns, e.g. learning nursery rhymes;
- Extending these patterns by analogy, generating new and invented words in speech and spelling.

Specific Learning Outcome – to link motor movements with rhymes to aid the learning of rhymes. To explore patterns in rhymes and to tune children into listen to the sounds of words. To be able to predict and continue rhyming patterns.
Group – shared/guided.
Resources – prompts for finger rhymes and plays. Copymasters 22, 23 and 24.
Books of nursery rhymes, jingles and finger plays.
What to do – introduce the rhyme and finger play, showing the children the actions. Emphasise the rhythm and exaggerate the rhymes. Repeat it slowly, letting the children echo each line of the rhyme. Speed it up, letting the children take the lead.
Use some of the rhymes in this section that have been chosen for their onomatopoeia and actions.
Variation, differentiation and extension – vary the voice used to recite the rhyme *e.g. say the rhyme in a whisper voice but with rhyming words said aloud, loud voices but whispered rhymes, voices getting louder or quieter and softer.* Say the rhyme around the circle with each child or group saying a line or a word at a time. Use the following rhyme to choose the style of recital:
*'It's finger-rhyme time, it's finger-rhyme time,
But......we've......got.....to make a choice,
Whose turn is it to choose the voice?'
Sarah!
'Whisper voice'
All recite the rhyme and actions.*
Assessment focus – I can continue a nursery rhyme or action song.

---

12. Nonsense Songsense

CLL I Enjoy rhyming and rhythmic activities (yellow). Show awareness of rhyme and alliteration and recognise rhythm in spoken words (blue). **CLL D** Listen to favourite nursery rhymes, stories and songs. Join in with repeated refrains, anticipating key events and important phrases (yellow).
Reception Literacy Objective (PiP Step1) *Rhythm and rhyme.* **Pip Step 2** *Be able to continue a rhyming string.*
W1 Understand and be able to rhyme through:
- Recognising, exploring and working with rhyming patterns, e.g. learning nursery rhymes;
- Extending these patterns by analogy, generating new and invented words in speech and spelling.

Specific Learning Outcome – to develop an ability to listen carefully to and innovate on familiar rhymes. To be able to predict and continue rhyming patterns.
Group – shared/guided.
Resources – prompts for finger rhymes and plays. Copymasters 22, 23 and 24.
Books of nursery rhymes, jingles and finger plays.

Theme 7 — Sound discrimination and awareness

What to do – *warm-up:* select a nursery rhyme or poem that children are familiar with. Say the rhyme but leave a silence for children to contribute the rhyming words. Use some of warm up ideas from 'Finger-rhyme time'.

Ask the children to close their eyes so that they can concentrate on the listening. Tell them that they have to put up their hands if they spot any changes that you make to the rhyme (they could hold up the ear from Copymaster 16). The changes could be made at any level from phonemes in words, to reordering the words, to substituting words, to inserting nonsense words e.g. 'Daa, Daa, Dack sheep, have you any dull?', 'Twinkle twinkle little car' etc.

Let children make up their own versions of rhymes with hidden changes.

Variation, differentiation and extension – this activity can be revisited later in the Reception year, when the children can read some of the rhymes. Type up a nursery rhyme and print two copies. Laminate (if possible). Cut the nursery rhyme up and let children resequence one copy of the rhyme. The child reads their version of the rhyme to another child who has to sequence the cut pieces into the same order. Match and compare the two versions. Prepare the text of a nursery rhyme for children to cut up and re-order into a new version.

Assessment focus – I can continue a nursery rhyme or action song.

Strand 3

13. Humpty Dumpty

CLL I Enjoy rhyming and rhythmic activities (yellow). Show awareness of rhyme and alliteration; recognise rhythm in spoken words (blue). **CLL D** Listen to favourite nursery rhymes, stories and songs. Join in with repeated refrains, anticipating key events and important phrases (yellow).
Reception Literacy Objective (PiP Step1) Rhythm and rhyme. **(Pip Step 2)** Be able to continue a rhyming string
W1 Understand and be able to rhyme through:
- Recognising, exploring and working with rhyming patterns, e.g. learning nursery rhymes;
- Extending these patterns by analogy, generating new and invented words in speech and spelling.

Group – shared/guided.
Resources – a hard-boiled egg (or egg shaped piece of dry clay/plasticine) decorated to look like Humpty Dumpty. Copymaster 25.
Outcome – to create rhyming strings
What to do – use nursery rhymes as a frame to sensitise children to rhyme and to explore and make new rhymes.
Sit children in a circle and warm up by rehearsing the traditional version of Humpty Dumpty.
Game 1: Say to the children: *'Humpty Dumpty sat on a cat'*. Pass the egg to the child next to you in the circle. They continue by saying: *'Humpty Dumpty sat on a bat'*, i.e. they have to think of a word (real or nonsense) that rhymes with the lead word –'cat'. The egg goes round the circle with each child adding a rhyming word. Children could clap in time to keep the rhythm and pace going.
Game 2: Exactly the same as Game 1, but if you put up your hand, all the children say-*'All the King's horses and all the king's men told Humpty never to sit down again!'*. Whichever child has the egg at this point makes up a new rhyming phrase, e.g. *'Humpty Dumpty sat on an egg'* and play continues round the circle again.
Variation, differentiation and extension – *Game 3* – Same as Games 1 and 2, but this time teach the children this rhyme:
'Humpty Dumpty went to Lumpty
To get his cheese and meat.
But when he got there,
The shops were all bare,
So he had nothing to eat.'
Use this rhyme for children to innovate a rhyme to nonsense words e.g.
'Hampty Dampty went to Lampty, to get his cheese and meat etc…..' and *'Hippty Dippty went to …… (Lippty)'*. Once the children have got the hang of this oral frame you can venture quite far from the original rhyme e.g. *'Heeping Deeping went to ……(sleeping)'*, *'Bixing Fixing went to ….(tixing/mixing/sixing etc..)'*, *'Speaking Leaking went to Peeking...'*, etc.
You could use the format from Game 2 to enable children to contribute rhymes until a given signal and then all join in with the body of the verse, before changing the rhyme, e.g. *'Higgledy Piggledy went to Jiggledy, Higgledy Piggledy went to figgledy, Higgledy Piggledy went to Miggledy'* (signal) – all children: *'To get his cheese and meat, But when he got there …',*.
Many nursery rhymes provide the oral framework for this kind of rhyme awareness activity e.g. *'Little Miss Mofat sat on a ……',* *'Little Bo Cat has lost her …',* *'Little Bo Peeping has lost her….',* *'Little Bo chopper has lost her …'.*
Assessment focus – I can create a rhyming string.

Theme 8 — Progression in Phonics Steps 2-3

14. Word Count 1

CLLO Understand the concept of a word (blue).
Reception Literacy Objective
T1 through shared reading:
- to understand and use correctly terms about books and print:....page, line, word, letter....
- to track the text in the right order, ...left to right, top to bottom, pointing while reading ... making written correspondence between written and spoken words.

Specific Learning Outcomes – to understand that sentences are made up of words and that words are units in a sentence.
Group – shared.
Resources – a pointer, shared writing resources, Copymasters 26 and 27.
What to do – young children who have listened to spoken language will not be aware that words are separate units in sentences. They will just extract the meaning. They will not understand the terms *word* or *sentence*. The development of this understanding takes some time to accomplish.
Technique 1: whilst reading a big book, point at each word as it is read. This models directionality and one to one correspondences between spoken words and written words. Talk to the children about how you are reading, telling them that you are saying the words that are written on the page. Show them the words, pointing to the spaces between the words. Pick a sentence on a page from the book. Count the words in this sentence.
Technique 2: tell the children that you are going to be counting words again. Say a simple sentence orally and then write it onto the board or strip of paper. Draw a loop around each word as you count the words. Ask a child to give you a sentence, write it up, and together count the words. Compare the number of words in the first sentence with the number of words in the second. Use some of the sentence models on Copymaster 26 to teach the children to think about the numbers of words rather than the size of words in the sentences. Encourage them to focus on the number of words in the sentence rather than the size of the letters or the size of the objects described.
Sit the children in a circle with a train strip from Copymaster 27 and some counters or blocks. Tell the children that you are going to say a sentence and they have to put a counter onto the train for every word they think you have said. Use an enlarged copy of the train to write the words of the sentence on when they have listened a couple of times. Compare the number of counters with the actual number of words.
Variation, differentiation and extension – see Word Count 2.
Assessment focus – I know what a word is.

15. Word Count 2

CLLO Understand the concept of a word (blue).
Reception Literacy Objective – T1 through shared reading:
- to understand and use correctly terms about books and print:....page, line, word, letter....
- to track the text in the right order, ...left to right, top to bottom, pointing while reading ... making written correspondence between written and spoken words.

Specific Learning Outcomes – to understand that sentences are made up of words and that words are units of print.
Group – shared.
Resources – a pointer, shared writing resources. Copymaster 27 and counters or small bricks.
What to do – follow on from *Word Count 1*.

Sit the children in a circle with a train strip from Copymaster 27 and some counters or blocks. Tell the children that you are going to say a sentence and they have to put a counter onto the train for every word they think you have said. Use an enlarged copy of the train to write the words of the sentence on when they have listened a couple of times. Compare the number of counters with the actual number of words.
Variation, differentiation and extension – in pairs let children say a sentence and put the number of counters onto the train to match.
Put the number of counters onto the train first, perhaps with a dice roll; say a sentence with that number of words in.
Assessment focus – I know what a word is and I can count words in simple sentences.

16. Sound sequencer (3)

CLL L Distinguish one sound from another (yellow).
Reception Literacy Objective – (PiP Step1 Preparation for steps 2–4) *Instrumental sound discrimination and initial, final and medial sound segmentation and blending*
Specific Learning Outcomes – (instrumental sound discrimination) to segment and blend sequences of instrumental sound.
Group – shared, guided collaborative.
Resources – a set of simple percussion instruments, including a drum, a shaker, two wooden sticks (Copymaster 20).

Each child will need a copy of Copymaster 18 appropriately cut up and prepared.
Some sequences of music made from Sound Sequence (1) Copymaster 17 – enlarged with a set of symbol cards. A tape recorder.
What to do – as for Sound sequence (1). However, the focus is on segmenting sounds from a sequence of percussion sounds, so use Copymaster 20.
Instruct the children to listen very carefully to the sequence of sounds that will follow. Behind a screen, an adult should perform a sequence of 3 sounds by selecting from the range of instruments on Copymaster 18. An alternative to this would be to record the sequences onto audiotape.

Strand 3

The adult can ask the children how many different sounds the children heard in the sequence – they could indicate this with their fingers. The adult could ask how many beats they heard in total in the sequence, again to be indicated by fingers.

The adult instructs the children to listen very carefully to the first sound in the sequence and the sequence is played again. Remember to not let the children actually see the sequence being played. The children are asked to point to the symbol on their keyboard (Copymaster 18) or to the instrument itself to indicate which instrumental sound they thought they heard first.

Variation, differentiation and extension – when the procedure is clear to children they can be trained to listen to the final sound in a sequence of three or four sounds and to indicate by pointing.

Ultimately, as attention develops they will be able to discriminate the medial instrumental sound in a sequence of three sounds. With practice they should develop an ear to distinguish sounds in initial, final or medial positions.

These activities are a useful grounding in teaching children to distinguish phonemes in these positions later on. The ability to distinguish instrumental sound is a more obvious way into training children to segment sounds and develop the skills of segmenting and blending that can be later applied to the less obvious phonemes of speech.

Assessment focus – I can sequence and perform a series of sounds using written notation.

---

17. Word beat 1

CLL I Show awareness of rhyme and alliteration, recognise rhythm in spoken words (blue).
Reception Literacy Objective *Step 1 Instrumental and body percussion linked to awareness of syllables*
Specific Learning Outcome – to enable children to hear syllables in words
Group – shared.
Resources – musical percussion instruments.
What to do – sit the children in a circle and tell them that you are going to count how many syllables they have in their names. Say your own first name and as you say it put your hand in a fist at the top of your chest with the thumb sticking up (a thumbs up signal), so that with each syllable your chin touches the top of your thumb. Go around the circle and ask each child to say their name and feel how many times their chin touches their thumb. Clap the syllables to the child after they have said their name.

Experiment with different ways of saying a name e.g. *slowly, fast, loudly etc.* Count the syllables: are they still the same? Go around the circle and let children clap the syllables in their names.

Pass round the percussion instruments and let children perform their names or beat out their names.

Variation, differentiation and extension – when children are sure of the number of syllables in their name, beat out a number of syllables e.g. 3 and ask children with that number of syllables in their name to stand. One of these children thinks of a child's name and beats out the number of syllables and the appropriate children stand.

Assessment focus – I can tap and count the syllables in my name.

---

18. Word beat 2

CLL I Show awareness of rhyme and alliteration, recognise rhythm in spoken words (blue).
Reception Literacy Objective *Step 1 Instrumental and body percussion linked to awareness of syllables.*
Specific Learning Outcome – to enable children to hear syllables in words.
Group – shared.
Resources – musical percussion instruments. A selection of objects.
What to do – sit the children in a circle and tell them that you are going to count how many syllables there are in the words for some objects.

Take the first object out of a box or bag and put it into the circle. Say the word e.g. 'elephant', showing the children how you are feeling for the syllables by letting your thumb touch your chin. Now clap the syllables for elephant as you say it, and finally play the syllables using a percussion instrument.

Pass one or two percussion instruments into the circle. Take the next object out of the bag and let the children holding the instruments play the syllables for the object using the instruments. Ask the other children whether they think they are correct. Move onto the next object.

Variation, differentiation and extension – use two sets of objects, or picture cards with different numbers of syllables. Put three objects/cards into the centre of the circle, ensuring that each object has a different number of syllables. Choose one of the objects but keep it behind a screen or out of sight. Clap the syllables for the object and let the children work out which object you have chosen by counting the syllables.

Assessment focus – I can count the syllables in a word.

Theme 8 — Progression in Phonics Steps 2–3

19. Syllable Sally 1

CLL I Show awareness of rhyme and alliteration; recognise rhythm in spoken words (blue).
Reception Literacy Objective – Step 1 Speech sound discrimination linked to an awareness of syllables.
Get up and Go/ Show me
Specific Learning Outcome – to enable children to orally segment and blend syllables in words.
Group – shared.
Resources – a puppet or Copymaster 28.
What to do – introduce a new puppet as Syllable Sally. Explain that she likes to play games with words and her favourite game is to play 'Speaking in syllables'. Put a selection of objects into the middle of the circle. The objects should be selected to give a range of polysyllabic words. Tell the children that Sally will say the word of one of the objects in the circle and the children have to decide which object she has said.
Sally says –   'Ummmmm..................
                 brelllllllll...............aahhhhhhh'.
She speaks slowly with a large pause between each syllable. Let children echo back to Sally what she has said and wait for the 'Ah Ha!' moment when one child works out that she said umbrella. Continue with a couple more examples.

Give objects to children. When Syllable Sally says their object they stand up and show it to her, saying the word correctly and saying it as Sally would say it.
Pass the puppet, or Copymaster 28 on a stick, round the circle and let children name objects using 'syllable speak'. Whichever child has the object should stand up and name their object correctly.
Variation, differentiation and extension – Sally could beat out a syllable pattern on a percussion instrument. Children with objects that have the same number of syllables should stand up and come into the middle of the circle and tell Sally in syllable speak what they have got. She will check with the instrument. Children swap places and sit somewhere else in the circle.
Play I-Spy with syllables. Pick an object in the room and say it in syllable speak. Children have to blend the syllables together and name the object.
Say words at normal speed and let children tell you how many syllables are in the word.
Assessment focus – I can orally segment a word into syllables. I can orally blend syllables to pronounce words.

20. Syllable Sally 2

CLL I Show awareness of rhyme and alliteration, recognise rhythm in spoken words (blue).
Reception Literacy Objective – Step 1 Speech sound discrimination linked to an awareness of syllables.
Get up and Go/ Show me
Specific Learning Outcome – to enable children to orally segment and blend syllables in words.
Group – shared.
Resources – a puppet or Copymaster 28. A percussion instrument. Some objects or pictures of objects.
What to do – when children are familiar with the activities in Syllable Sally 1 you can omit a syllable in a word and let children tell you what has been dropped out.
Pick an object, such as an umbrella. Say the word 'umbrella', then let Syllable Sally say the word in syllable Speak: 'Ummm......brell....aahhh'. Let children say the word and count the syllables using thumbs under chins to count the jaw opening movements. Agree with the children that there are three syllables (three beats). Now ask them to close their eyes and listen very carefully. Use the percussion instrument to put a beat for the first syllable without saying it, then say the other two syllables. It will sound like: '#......brell......ah'. Ask the children what was missing from the word. Try omitting the final syllable: 'Ummm....brell....#' and the middle one: 'Ummm....#.....aahh'. Play this game with several objects that have two or three syllables.
Variation, differentiation and extension –
Extension – put several objects into the middle of the circle and tell the children that Sally is going to choose one of the objects. Objects could include, an umbrella, a toy elephant, a camera. Sally uses the percussion instrument to omit syllables. She might start off '#...#....#'. Next she might offer: '#....#...aaahh', next: '#...merrr....ahhh' and so on. Play continues until the majority of the class have selected the correct object. Children could select objects by pointing or by getting up and standing next to the objects, providing they are well spaced out. Children could play this game as an independent activity in a small group, once they have mastered it as a class.
Assessment focus – I can orally segment a word into syllables. I can orally blend syllables to pronounce words.

21. M.A.P.s (Mnemonics for Alliterative Phonemes) 1

CLL I/CLL J Hear and say the initial sound in words and know which letters represent some of the sounds (green).
Reception Literacy Objective –
W2 knowledge of grapheme/phoneme correspondences through:

- hearing and identifying initial sounds in words;
- identifying and writing initial and dominant phonemes in spoken words;
- reading letter(s) that represent(s) the sound(s).

Specific Learning Outcome – Pip Step 2 to hear and say phonemes in the initial position
Group – shared/guided.
Resources – Copymasters 29, 30, 31, 32, 33 and 34. Cut out the cue cards and write the lower case letter

Strand 3

that represents the phoneme with a thick marker pen, in the style of letter formation appropriate to your school. Laminate for longevity.
A collection of objects and/or pictures that begin with the chosen phoneme.
What to do – use the cue cards on the copymasters and the short alliterative stories that go with the illustrated pictures. Tell the children a short alliterative story based on the cue card e.g. *One bright day, Billy and Brenda bought the paper. Billy saw that a b-b-b-band was playing in the beautiful park. Billy and Brenda packed a bag and bounced down to the park. They sat on a blanket to wait for the b-b-b-band. Billy dropped a bottle but it didn't break on the grass. Suddenly Brenda took a deep breath. She could hear a b-b-b-b-b!! It was the band. The b-b-b-band was brilliant. Billy and Brenda were bowled over.*
Show the children the cue card for the /b/ phoneme – the picture of the band. Say to the children b-b-b-band.

With each /b/ pretend to hit a big drum swinging your arms from side to side.
Once the cue card is introduced it can be used to remind children of the action that prompts the phoneme. Try and encourage children to pronounce just the phoneme without adding an /uh/ e.g. /t/ and not /tuh/. Once children have got the actions under their belt, use a set of letters as the prompts to remind the children of the actions and use the cue cards just for reference.
Variation, differentiation and extension – once the children have begun to be able to respond with the phoneme from a cue from a letter card, you can begin to introduce blending simple 3 letter words together e.g. ccc-aaa-ttt, cat, building on the syllable blending from the work with Syllable Sally.
Assessment focus – I can say the correct phoneme when shown an initial letter. I can hold up the correct letter in response to hearing a phoneme.

22. Pop the phoneme

CLL I/CLL J Hear and say the initial sound in words and know which letters represent some of the sounds (green).
Reception Literacy Objective:
W2 knowledge of grapheme/ phoneme correspondences through:
hearing and identifying initial sounds in words ;
Reading letter(s) that represent(s) the sounds(a-z, ch, sh, th).
Specific Learning Outcome – to practise the correct articulation of the phonemes a-z, ch, sh and th.
Group – shared/guided.
Resources – Copymaster 36, some mirrors.
What to do – select the phoneme to be practised and revisit the cue card and action. Look at the letter and model writing and forming the letter on a large board with the children skywriting the letter in the air.
Show the children how you shape your lips and talk about how you are making the sound, where it is coming from and what your tongue is doing. Let the children use small mirrors to look at the shape of their mouths and compare with their friends and your face. Explore different ways of saying the phoneme, letting children choose e.g. *loud, soft, getting louder, in a sad way, in a happy way* etc. Revisit the balloon game from the Circle of Friends Activity 3 extension. Form a circle with

all the children close in and one child in the middle. This child pretends to blow up the balloon by saying the phoneme. The class join in and with each time the circle gets wider and wider until 'pop!' – all the children fall down as the 'balloon' bursts. A new child is selected and a different phoneme is used to 'blow' up the balloon.
Use Copymaster 36 to provide some follow up to these activities. Show the children how to use the copymaster. Prepare it by cutting out the balloon shapes and selecting the phonemes to be practised. Show the children how the phoneme is positioned on the balloon and then how the 'balloon' is rolled up round a pencil. With each unrolling of the pencil the child should pronounce the phoneme until the balloon gets fully unrolled and springs back with a 'pop!'. The child can then select another phoneme to pop.
On the balloon part of the copymaster the child can have a try at writing the chosen phoneme and practising its formation.
Variation, differentiation and extension – if you have a digital camera take a photograph of a child forming a phoneme to illustrate the correct mouth positioning. This could be linked to the cue card display and with a tape recorder could form an independent workstation in the class.
Assessment focus – I can write and say the phonemes that correspond to the letters of the alphabet.

23. Phoneme snap (1)

CLL I/CLL J Hear and say the initial sound in words and know which letters represent some of the sounds (green).
Reception Literacy Objective:
W2 knowledge of grapheme/ phoneme correspondences through:
• hearing and identifying initial sounds in words;
• reading letter(s) that represent(s) the sounds(a-z, ch, sh, th).
Specific Learning Outcome – to reinforce the link between graphemes and phonemes.

Group – collaborative group.
Resources – Copymasters 29, 30, 31, 32 and 33, 32 identical sets of cards shuffled into one deck.
What to do – there are several variations of familiar card games that can be played with the sets of phoneme cards from the copymasters:
Snap 1 Shuffle the cards up with the picture cards. Reduce the number of pairs of phoneme cards to a manageable quantity. Deal out the cards between the players so that each player has the same amount. Each player takes it in turn to put down a card. If two cards match then the first child wins all the cards that have

39

Theme 8 — Progression in Phonics Steps 2–3

been played. Play continues until either one player is out or one player has won all the cards.
Pairs Put cards from the set face down and spread out on a flat surface. Each player takes it in turns to turn over a card and to try and find a matching card with the same initial phoneme. Play continues until all are matched. The player with the most pairs is the winner.
Assessment focus – I can link sounds (phonemes) to letters (graphemes).

24. Sound shopping

CLLI/ CLL J Hear and say the initial sound in words and know which letters represent some of the sounds (green).
Reception Literacy Objective:
W2 knowledge of grapheme/ phoneme correspondence through:
• reading letters that represent the sounds a-z, ch, sh, th;
• identifying and writing initial and dominant phonemes in spoken words.
Specific Learning Outcome – to segment the initial phoneme from spoken words and to make a collection of pictures of objects that start with this phoneme.
Progression in Phonics Step 2 – to hear and say phonemes in the initial position.
Group – guided/collaborative.
Resources – catalogues/magazines, scissors and glue.
What to do – select a group of children that need some further consolidation with hearing, segmenting, identifying and matching initial phonemes with graphemes.
Fold a large piece of paper for each child and write 4 graphemes, one in each corner, so that the group has a spread of letters between them. (You could draw a large shopping basket for each phoneme.) Discuss the phonemes and rehearse the mnemonics to remember the letters.
Instruct the children that they are going 'shopping' for phonemes. They have to look through the catalogue for objects starting with one of their four phonemes and when they have found them they cut them out and stick them onto to their paper in the appropriate place. Encourage the children to work collaboratively and share objects they find so that they are all hunting for more objects than the just the four on their piece of paper.
Variation, differentiation and extension –
Extension – with a more advanced group the task would be to select objects where the phoneme occurs at any point in the word. Before the children go 'shopping', rehearse segmenting words into phonemes and blending the phonemes back together again. As children find objects they can try and label the objects using phonemic spelling; alternatively objects could be labelled with correct spellings and the part of the word making the phoneme can be used as a way of collecting different spellings of that phoneme. This latter alternative makes a useful interactive display that can be added to over the course of a couple of weeks, especially if children are encouraged to cut out pictures from home and bring them in.
Assessment focus – I can segment initial phonemes and match sounds to letters.

25. It's behind you!

CLL J Hear and say the initial sound in words and know which letters represent some sounds (green).
Specific Learning Outcome – to describe the features of letter shapes.
Group – shared.
Early Learning Goal:
LL12 link sounds to letters, naming and sounding letters of the alphabet
Reception Literacy Objective
W3 alphabetic and phonic knowledge through
• sounding and naming each letter of the alphabet in lower and upper case;
• understanding alphabetical order through alphabet rhymes and songs.
Resources – a set of alphabet cards (e.g. Copymasters 34 and 35).
What to do – the children sit in a circle with you. A child is selected and they take an alphabet (or phoneme cue card) from you. They must make sure that the other children do not see which card is selected. This child walks around the circle whilst the other children chant an alphabet song e.g.
'a,b,c,d,e,f,g,
I wonder who it's going to be?
h,i,j,k,l,m,n,
Round and round you go again.
o,p,q,r,s,t,u,
Soon it will be behind you,
v,w,x,y,z-
Which letter is behind your..........
HEAD?'
At the word 'head', the child walking round the circle should stop and show the letter to all the children but the child that they are standing behind. This child has to guess the letter by asking questions about the letter. The other children can only answer 'yes' or 'no' until the letter is guessed.
Variation, differentiation and extension – this game could be played with words from the word wall.
Assessment focus – I can describe the letters of the alphabet and chant the alphabet in order.

Strand 3

26. Treasure letters

CLL J Hear and say the initial sound in words and know which letters represent some sounds (green).
Reception Literacy Objective
W3 alphabetic and phonic knowledge through:
• sounding and naming each letter of the alphabet in lower and upper case;
• understanding alphabetical order through alphabet songs.
W3 knowledge of grapheme/ phoneme correspondence through:
• reading letters that represent the sounds a-z.
Specific Learning Outcome – to match and link letters to initial phonemes of objects and words.
Group – guided/independent.

Resources – the sand tray, small plastic or foam letters, objects beginning with the same initial letter as the letters of the alphabet.
What to do – bury the plastic or foam letters in the sand along with some of the objects and words with initial letters highlighted. Show the children that they need to dig the letters out and match letters to the initial letters of the objects.
Variation, differentiation and extension – objects could be hidden round the room for children to collect to match the letter and its sound. This could form an ongoing and interactive display.
Assessment focus – I can sort objects and match initial sounds of objects to written letters.

Theme 9 — Challenging Progression in Phonics Steps 4 +

27. The Naughty Microphone 1 (or Drop the phoneme)

CLL I Hear and say initial and final sounds in words, and short vowel sounds within words.
Reception Literacy Objective:
W2 knowledge of grapheme/ phoneme correspondences through:
- identifying and writing initial and final phonemes in consonant-vowel-consonant (CVC) words, e.g. *fit, mat, pan*.

Pips Steps 2 – 5 Demonstration Activity
Specific Learning Outcome – to attend and identify initial, final and medial phonemes in words. To practise phoneme segmentation skills.
Group – shared/guided.
Resources – a microphone or Copymaster 37, some objects or pictures in a bag, letter cards, whiteboards.
What to do – explain to the children that you are going to play a game where they have to listen and tell you which part of the word is missing. Explain that when the phonemes (sounds) in words are changes new or different words are made.
Explain that the microphone you are using to talk with the children is broken and sometimes sounds get left out of words. Explain that sometimes the microphone changes the phonemes or sounds of bits of words.
Pick an object from the bag and show the children the object *e.g. a toy fish*. Holding the microphone up to your mouth say to the children '…ish'. The children repeat the correct pronunciation of the word, but ask the children what phoneme the naughty microphone has left off. Prompt the children to supply the /f/ phoneme. Alternatively for 'fish' the microphone might change the initial phoneme to /d/ and the word to '/d/ish'. The children should supply the correct phoneme, *e.g. '/f/-/f/-/f/-fish'*. This time the microphone might pronounce the word '/w/ish'. The children prompt again until the microphone offers the correct pronunciation- *e.g. '/f/ish'* The same method can be used at Step 4 in Progression in Phonics for final phonemes, and at Step 5 for initial and final consonant clusters, *e.g. target word- 'spider', mispronounced as '/s/t/ider'….'/s/m/ider' etc.*
When phonemes are changed in the medial position the meaning of the word will be changed. This might form an interesting discussion point that leads into, or arises from The Naughty Microphone 2.

Variation, differentiation and extension – an extension to this activity is for children to show the microphone the missing or 'dropped' phoneme, or for them to show the correct phoneme when the microphone mispronounces the phoneme. They could do this using letter cards or a strip of card with target phonemes on. Alternatively, towards the end of the Reception year they should be able to write the target letter onto a whiteboard or margarine tub lid with a dry wipe pen.
Let a child use the Naughty Microphone to lead the activity.

Assessment focus – I can segment and identify phonemes in the initial/ final/ medial position of words, I can write the phoneme that is 'dropped' from a word in the initial/ medial/ final position.

28. The Naughty Microphone 2

CLL I Hear and say initial and final phonemes in words, and short vowel sounds in words. **CLL K** Use their phonic knowledge to write simple regular words and make phonetically plausible attempts at more complex words.
Reception Literacy Objective:
W2 knowledge of grapheme/ phoneme correspondences through:
- identifying and writing initial and final phonemes in consonant-vowel-consonant (CVC) words, e.g. *fit, mat, pan*.

W4 to link sound and spelling patterns through:
- discriminating 'onsets' from 'rimes' in speech and spelling, *e.g. tip, sip, ship, flip, chip*.

Pips Steps 2 – 7 Demonstration Activity.
This activity is particularly suitable as a challenge and extension activity.
Specific Learning Outcome – to identify initial, final and medial phonemes in words. To practise phoneme segmentation skills. To explore how the meaning of words changes if phonemes are taken away, added or changed.
Group – shared/guided.
Resources – a microphone or Copymaster 37. Whiteboards.
What to do – select initial, final or medial phonemes and decide if the session will focus on removing, adding or changing phonemes. Stick with just one focus in a session. Ask the children to listen carefully because the Naughty Microphone is up to its tricks again. Explain that when phonemes are left off a word (or added to a word or changed) the meaning of the word often changes. Instruct the children to listen. They will have two tasks. The first task will be to decide if the second word you say, after something has changed, is a real word or a nonsense word. They can indicate this with a thumbs up or a thumbs down signal.
The second task is to decide what has been taken away, added or changed.
Examples:

Strand 3

Dropping a phoneme in the initial position.
farm- arm /f/
near- ear /n/
mat- at /m/
dog- og /d/
Adding a phoneme in the initial position
arm- /f/arm
ear- /n/ear
at- /c/at /m/at /h/at /s/at etc.
Adding a phoneme in a medial position
bid- bi/r/d
pet- pe/s/t
goat- /gh/o/s/t/
tie- ti/m/e
hat- ha/f/t
Dropping a phoneme in the final position
ots- pot /s/
house- hou(how) /se/
farm- far /m/
fox- fo /x/
Adding a phoneme in the final position
boo- boo/t/ boo/k/
pot- pot/s/
t/ie/- t/igh/t/
Removing a phoneme in a medial position
bi/r/d- bid
pe/s/t- pet
gh/o/s/t-goat
ti/m/e- tie
h/a/nd- hnd

N.B. Some of these examples reflect the level of challenge it is possible to reach in this activity. The activity can be kept to an easier level if it is done orally and the spellings of the phonemes do not change between the words.
Removing vowels from single syllable words is a way of reinforcing for children that every syllable needs a vowel.
Variation, differentiation and extension – the activity can be extended well into Step 7 of Progression in Phonics by encouraging children to segment and spell the words as they are changed. This activity can be used to explore some of the alternative spellings of medial vowel phonemes, silent letters, consonant clusters and inflexional endings.
The example of *'tie- ti/m/e ti/m/e- tie'* reflects the usefulness of this activity in teaching children about the split digraph.
Let a child use the Naughty Microphone to lead the activity.
Assessment focus – I can hear changes in words when phonemes are added, deleted or substituted. I can use my understanding of adding and changing phonemes to help me spell words.

---

29. The Naughty Microphone 3 (Phoneme substitution)

CLL I Hear and say initial and final phonemes in words, and short vowel sounds in words. **CLL K** Use their phonic knowledge to write simple regular words and make phonetically plausible attempts at more complex words.
Reception Literacy Objective
W2 knowledge of grapheme/ phoneme correspondences through:
• identifying and writing initial and final phonemes in consonant-vowel-consonant (CVC) words, *e.g. fit, mat, pan.*
W4 to link sound and spelling patterns through:
• discriminating 'onsets' from 'rimes' in speech and spelling, *e.g. tip, sip, ship, flip, chip.*
Pips Steps 4–7 Demonstration Activity.
Specific Learning Outcome – to attend and identify initial, final and medial phonemes in words. To manipulate phonemes.
Group – shared/guided.
Resources – a microphone or Copymaster 37. The fan on Copymaster 38 – one per two children. Paper or a whiteboard divided into three or four sections by two or three vertical lines, to make a 'phoneme frame'.
What to do – draw three vertical lines onto the board and write a consonant-vowel-consonant word at the top so that there is one phoneme in each section of the vertical lines *e.g. /p/e/t/.*
Give out the fans (Copymaster 38) to the pairs of children. Explain that the microphone will say the word but will

change one of the phonemes and the children have to listen and identify which phoneme has changed. They will have a chance to talk to their partner, select the right petal on the fan and, at the given signal, show you which phoneme changed. Show a start word *e.g. /p/e/t/* and a target word *e.g. /t/a/r/.*
Begin with a word like /p/e/t/ on the board and change one phoneme to get to /m/e/t/. The children should show you #— on their fans. The game continues:
Met -> mat -#-
Mat-> map —#
Map -> tap #—
Tap-> tar —# etc.
N.B. It is useful to have plotted out the phoneme changes before starting the activity. The level of challenge can reflect the level in the Progression in Phonics that the children are working at, e.g. Step4 CVC words; Step 5 initial and final consonant clusters, Step 6 vowel digraphs, Step 7 different spellings of digraphs including 'split digraphs'.
Variation, differentiation and extension – rather than using the fan, the children could write the changed spelling of the new word onto their own phoneme frame. The target word could be the original word. When it is reached the children could call out 'HOME!' or 'FULL CIRCLE!'.
Let children develop their own transitions using magnetic letters and then use the Naughty Microphone to lead others through the activity.
Assessment focus – I can manipulate phonemes. I can spell using my phonic knowledge.

Theme 9 — Challenging Progression in Phonics Steps 4 +

30. M.A.P.s (Mnemonics for Alliterative Phonemes) 2

CLL K Use their phonic knowledge to write simple regular words and make phonetically plausible attempts at more complex words.
Reception Literacy Objective
W2 knowledge of grapheme/ phoneme correspondences through:
- identifying and writing dominant phonemes in spoken words.

Specific Learning Outcome – PiP Step 6 to know one representation of each of ten vowel digraph phonemes /ai/ee/ie/oa/oo/or/ar/ir/oi/ou/. To equip children with the tools for phonic spelling.
Group – shared/guided.
Resources – Copymasters 39 and 40.
What to do – use the cue cards on Copymasters 39 and 40 to introduce the long vowel phonemes. Emphasise these phonemes by stretching and elongating them in simple monosyllabic words. At this stage just rehearse the pronunciation and association of the letters with the sound and action.
Variation, differentiation and extension – as children become more confident with the letter sound recognition you can begin to demonstrate how these phonemes are used when writing and spelling. This will be through shared writing and demonstration in which words are segmented into phonemes, written and blended back together into words.
Assessment focus – I can say the correct phoneme when shown its written representation. I can hold up the correct vowel digraph in response to hearing a long vowel phoneme. I can attempt to write and spell any word using phonic strategies.

31. Phoneme snap (2)

CLL J Link sounds to letters, naming and sounding the letters of the alphabet.
Reception Literacy Objective:
W2 knowledge of grapheme/ phoneme correspondences through:
- hearing and identifying initial sounds in words;
- reading letter(s) that represent(s) the sounds (s) a-z, ch, sh, th.

W3 alphabetic and phonic knowledge through:
- sounding and naming each letter of the alphabet in lower and upper case.

Specific Learning Outcome – Progression in Phonics Step 7 – to segment and blend words containing vowel digraphs and tri-graphs. To learn the different spellings of long vowel phonemes.
Group – guided group/collaborative group.
Resources – Copymasters 41 and 42; a set of cards with words containing different spellings of long vowel phonemes.
What to do – make a set of word cards with the vowel phonemes in different positions in the words. Choose words that have different spellings of the long vowel phonemes. Use a different colour card to the cards with the different spellings of the vowel phonemes on Copymasters 41 and 42. Choose a player to be the game leader (initially this will be you).
The game leader deals out the word cards between the players but keeps the vowel phoneme cue cards. The game leader picks up the first vowel phoneme cue card and reads the phoneme to the other players without them seeing the spellings of the phoneme.
The first player plays a word card, turning it over to put it down into the centre of play. The next player plays their word card and so on. If a word card contains the phoneme then the first player to say the phoneme wins all cards played. The winning player should identify the part of the word that makes the phoneme and the game leader should check this.
The game leader selects the next phoneme card and play continues as before. The winner is the player with the most cards. At this point the winner could be the game leader.
Variation, differentiation and extension – an alternative version of this game is to produce a set of cards with the different spellings of the vowel phonemes, one phoneme per card. Use the set of word cards made for the game above. The phoneme cards are dealt out to the players and the word cards are held by the game leader.
The game leader reads a word from a word card. The players segment the word to themselves. They take it in turns to turn over a vowel phoneme card. If they think the phoneme card matches a phoneme in the word read out they should say the phoneme to snap. If they are able to spell the word (with magnetic letters, a whiteboard or orally) they win the word card. The player with the most word cards is the winner.
Assessment focus – I can link vowel phonemes to graphemes.

32. Scaffolded spellings 1

CLL K Use their phonic knowledge to write simple regular words and make phonetically plausible attempts at more complex words.
Reception Literacy Objective
W2 knowledge of grapheme/phoneme correspondence through:
- identifying and writing initial and final phonemes in consonant-vowel-consonant (CVC) words e.g. *fit, mat, pan.*

W4 to link sound and spelling patterns by:
- using knowledge of rhyme to identify families of rhyming CVC words, e.g. *hop, top, mop, fat, pat,* etc. Discriminating 'onsets' from 'rimes' in speech and spelling, e.g. *tip, sip, skip, flip, chip,* etc.

W9 to recognise the critical features of words, e.g. shape, length, and common spelling patterns.

Strand 3

Specific Learning Outcome – to increase speed in application of phonics and known words to independent writing.
Group – guided, collaborative.
Resources – a story for dictation, e.g. texts that focus on onset and rime e.g. Rhymeworld, ORT Rhyme and Analogy. A set of plastic letters and a segmentation sheet e.g. Copymaster 20.
What to do –
Version 1 – read the story to the children and ask them to listen to the sounds of the words, particularly the repeated rime refrain. Talk about the story, the characters and the events. Spread the magnetic letters in the middle of the table and give each child a segmenting sheet. Start to read the story slowly and when you get to the focal rime word let the children collect the right letters to spell the word. Discuss the shape of the word and how the different letters make the sounds to build the word. Carry on with the story until you get to the next rime word. The children will probably just have to change the initial letter. (A more advanced version of this might require them to change the spelling of a focal phoneme.) Carry on like this but get faster and faster.
Version 2 – as above, but children are required to write the spellings of the focal words onto a whiteboard or piece of paper.
Variation, differentiation and extension – see below.
Assessment focus – I can listen to dictation and write and spell words using phonic strategies and knowledge of high frequency words.

---

33. Scaffolded spellings 2 (dictation)

CLL K Use their phonic knowledge to write simple regular words and make phonetically plausible attempts at more complex words.
Reception Literacy Objective – as above
Specific Learning Outcome – to increase speed in application of phonics and known words to independent writing.
Group – guided, collaborative.
Resources – a story for dictation, e.g. texts that focus on onset and rime e.g. Rhymeworld, ORT Rhyme and Analogy. A set of plastic letters and a segmentation sheet e.g. Copymaster 20.
Version 3 – towards the end of the Reception year, as children acquire the motor skills to be able to handle a writing tool with some degree of control, including keyboard, pencil and pen, this version of the dictation exercise helps them to build up their writing speed. On paper children should write the story as you dictate it to them. Initially the speed of dictation will be quite slow, with you prompting the children, perhaps with each phoneme of some words. Prompting can be offered using the mnemonics and reference to high frequency word charts round the room. As children become more accurate they will increase their speed, and with support can acquire quite a pace.
Encourage the children to draw upon these strategies in their independent writing. When the children realise that they can write half a page or a page of dense text, with support, then it gives them a goal to aim for in their unsupported writing.
Variation, differentiation and extension – once children are used to the routines of dictation, this activity can become an independent collaborative activity that two or three children can use to consolidate their skills. One child becomes the 'teacher' and dictates, from a book, to the other children. The real value in this activity comes when children begin to realise that you can innovate on familiar texts, using the structure and spellings of many of the words, but inserting your own characters, setting, events and actions. This makes a nice bridging activity between supported and independent writing.
Assessment focus – I can listen to dictation and write and spell words using phonic strategies and knowledge of high frequency words.

Theme 10: Early reading

Early Learning Goals for linking sounds and letters	NLS Word level work: Phonics spelling and vocabulary
CLL N Read a range of familiar and common words and simple sentences independently	Word recognition, graphic knowledge and spelling **W5** to read on sight a range of familiar words, e.g. children's names, captions, labels, and words from favourite books; **W6** to read on sight the 45 high frequency words to be taught by the end of YR from Appendix list 1 of the NLS Framework; **W7** to read on sight the words from texts of appropriate difficulty; **W8** to read and write own name and to explore other words related to the spelling of own name; **W9** to recognise the critical features of words, *e.g. shape, length, and common spelling patterns;*
	Vocabulary extension **W10** new words from their reading and shared experiences **W11** to make collections of personal interest or significant words and words linked to particular topics;
	Grammatical awareness **S1** to expect written text to make sense and to check for sense if it does not; **S2** to use awareness of the grammar of a sentence to predict words during shared reading and when re-reading familiar stories.
CLL L Explore and experiment with sounds, words and texts	**W10** to re-read and recite stories and rhymes with predictable and repeated patterns and experiment with similar rhyming patterns.
CLL O know that print carries meaning, and in English, is read left to right, top to bottom;	Understanding of print **T1** through shared reading: • To recognise printed and hand-written words in a variety of settings, *e.g. stories, notes, registers, labels, signs, notices, letters, forms, lists, directions, advertisements, newspapers;* • To recognise that words can be written down to be read again for a variety of purposes; • To understand and use correctly terms about books and print: book, cover, beginning, end, page, line, word, letter, title; • To track the text in the right order, page by page, left to right, top to bottom, pointing while reading/telling the story, and making one to one correspondences between written and spoken words.
	Reading comprehension **T2** to use a variety of cues when reading: knowledge of the story and its context, and awareness of how it should make sense grammatically. **S3** grammatical awareness that words are ordered left to right and need to be read that way to make sense. **T3** to re-read a text to provide context cues to help read unfamiliar words
CLL M Retell narratives in the correct sequence, drawing on the language patterns of stories;	**T4** to notice the difference between spoken and written forms through re-telling known stories; to compare 'told' versions with what the book says; **T5** to understand how story book language works and to use some formal elements when re-telling stories, e.g. 'Once there was…', 'She lived in a little…', 'he replied…'.
CLL P Show an understanding of the elements of stories, such as main character, sequence of events, and openings, and how information can be found in non-fiction texts to answer questions about where, who, why and how;	**T6** to re-read frequently a variety of familiar texts, *e.g. big books, story books, taped stories with texts, poems, information books, wall stories, captions, own and other children's writing;* **T7** to use knowledge of familiar texts to re-enact or re-tell to others, recounting the main points in the correct sequence; **T8** to locate and read significant parts of the text, *e.g. picture captions, names of key characters, rhymes and chants, e.g. 'I'm a troll …', 'you can't catch me I'm the Gingerbread Man …', speech bubbles, italicised, enlarged words;* **T9** to be aware of story structures, *e.g. actions/reactions, consequences,* and the ways that stories are built up and concluded;

Strand 4

1. Souvenirs and Story Treasures

CLL M Listen to and join in with stories and poems, one to one and also in small groups, Show interest in illustrations and print in books and print in the environment. Begin to be aware of the way in which stories are structured (yellow).

CLL P Have favourite books, handle books carefully, know information can be relayed in the form of print (blue).

Reception Literacy Objective
T4 to notice the difference between spoken and written forms through
- re-telling known stories; to compare 'told' versions with what the book 'says';

T5 to understand how story book language works and to use some formal elements when re-telling stories, e.g. 'Once there was ... ', 'She lived in..', 'he replied' ...;

T6 to re-read frequently a variety of familiar texts, e.g. *big books, story books, taped stories with texts, poems, information books, wall stories, captions, own and other children's writing;*

T7 to use knowledge of familiar texts to re-enact or to re-tell to others, recounting the main points in the correct sequence.

Specific Learning Outcome – to involve parents in supporting retellings of stories.

Group – collaborative pair.

Resources – appropriate to book.

What to do – when preparing a big book for shared reading consider what object, either in or related to the story, could be used to prompt and support the retelling of the story. The object should be something simple that can be given and shared amongst all the children, something that they can take home and start to make a collection of precious objects. These scraps of story bits provide a tangible reminder of stories shared in the class, and they can be used as prompts to support retellings of the story with parents, family and friends. The resources need to be simple and cheap, *e.g. a scrap of cloth, a shape cut from coloured paper, a seed, a stone, a shell.*

In the example of the *The Very Hungry Caterpillar*, read the story to the children and when you get to the part of the story where the caterpillar is feeling very sick show the children a real green leaf. Explain that this will remind you that the caterpillar was born on a leaf, and that he had to eat a leaf after he felt sick from eating lots of different food. Explain also that he made his cocoon on a leaf.

Variation, differentiation and extension – set up a tape recorder in the class for children to record their oral retellings of stories for others to listen to.
Link story treasures to small copies of big books that children can borrow to take home.

Assessment focus – I am starting to use story language like 'Once upon a time ...'
I can retell stories that I have heard before.
I can make up and tell new stories by changing parts of familiar stories.

Theme 11 Developing early reading

2. Environmental Print and reading – Word Walls

Children are surrounded by print in the environment. It can cover almost any surface from computer screens, mobile phone displays, to T-shirts, shop signs and billboards. Children seem to attend to the logos and symbols that form part of this immersion in print, and can point out familiar shops, signs and food outlets well before they can recognise their own name. The activities in this section build upon these experiences of 'real world' literacy and turn the classroom into a print-rich interactive learning environment. In the same way that a big book is used to demonstrate the reading of stories and extraction of information from texts, the walls of a classroom can be used to teach children about other kinds of reading and writing.

Teaching walls can be used to generate interactive display that focuses on aspects of reading and writing at word, sentence and text level. They can become part of the daily routine, providing fun activities that help children learn about specific aspects of language. They are particularly useful for work at word and sentence level, *e.g. phonics, spelling and high frequency sight vocabulary work*. This section focuses particularly on strategies for helping children with recognising and spelling high frequency words, but many of the activities from the auditory, visual and tactile section on phonics and spelling should have a home on a word wall for at least some of the time. When the activities are not being interacted with during shared whole class time, they provide constant visual reinforcement to aid independent application of these strategies throughout the rest of the day.

Word Walls should be used to enable children to understand that a word:
- is a series of letters, in a special sequence, with space at either end;
- can be long or short and stands for a spoken word;
- is written left to right (in English) and are read left to right and in a top to bottom orientation.

Word walls are systematically organised collections of words and interactive activities designed to support the teaching and learning of how words work and are used. They provide constant visual consolidation by displaying, and mapping, the connections between words and parts of words, and they show children ways of organising and categorising words and language. They support children's independent writing by providing a reference tool that is linked to the writing demands placed on children at any one given period of focussed teaching. That is, Word Walls link to the text range and teaching objectives that a teacher is focussing on over (usually) a term.

Word walls provide spaces for interactive 'real world' literacy opportunities such as daily routines, *e.g. day of the week, today's weather, today's helper, learning targets,* etc.

Any wall or surface can be used to develop, support and extend literacy activities that are introduced on the main teaching wall. Focal Teaching Wall activities have a life span that sees displays move to functional places around a class as they move from shared, to guided, to collaborative and independent usage. Many Word Wall games used with the whole class can be miniaturised to become independent learning and consolidation games or Literacy Centres.

---

3. Build the wall

CLL N/CLL O Understand the concept of a word (blue). Begin to recognise some familiar words (green).
W2 knowledge of grapheme/phoneme correspondences through reading letters that represent the sounds, a-z, ch, sh, th;
W3 alphabetic and phonic knowledge through:
- sounding and naming each letter of the alphabet in lower and upper case;
- understanding alphabetical order through alphabet books, rhymes and songs.

W5 to read on sight a range of familiar words, *e.g. children's names, captions, labels and words from familiar books*;
W6 to read on sight the 45 high frequency words to be taught by the end of YR from Appendix List 1;
W9 to recognise the critical features of words, *e.g. shape, length, and common spelling patterns*;
W11 to make collections of personal interest or significant words linked to particular topics.
T1 through shared reading to recognise printed and hand-written words in a variety of settings, *e.g. notes, labels, signs, notices, forms, lists, directions*. To understand and use the correct terms about print: word, letter.
Specific Learning Outcome – to recognise common key words on sight. To build knowledge of alphabetic letter names and alphabetical order.
Group – whole class.
Resources – sets of cards onto which to write children's names, labels, and the 45 high frequency words from Appendix List 1 of the NLS framework. Copymasters 43 and 44. Word cards for days of the week and weather. Set of cue cards, *e.g. The M.A.P.s prompt cards*. Pocket charts to hold strips of card. Backed display boards at child height. Ideally, it should be possible for children to detach and attach word cards, labels and pictures from the Word Wall with a minimum of difficulty. If possible, laminate the cards to extend their life-span..
What to do – introduce the Word Wall to the children. At the beginning of the year the display walls will be relatively empty apart from a few key daily routine managers.

Children should be introduced to the daily tasks part of the Word Wall. Initially you will be responsible for carrying out the daily tasks to model the 'What to dos' to the children. These daily tasks will include updating the calendar and weather cards, for example.
Initial Words to go up on the wall might include children's names. The children could be given their name cards to decorate before they become laminated. Name cards could include a digital photograph of the child, if a

Strand 4

digital camera is available. The making of these cards, including the writing of the card, could form small group activities through the first few sessions at the beginning of the year.
Introduce five words a week by: providing a context for the word in an oral sentence; writing the sentence on the board; underlining the focal word; letting the children see you practise writing the word onto the board whilst talking about its features. Let children see you write the word onto the Word Wall card, displaying the word card on the Word Wall and presenting the same word in a number of different fonts over the coming weeks.

Use some of the chants from the next activity to explore, consolidate and over-learn the words. Provide small versions of the word wall cards and display them around the room. Use different fonts and text sizes on these small versions of the words.
Variation, differentiation and extension – introduce three to six phonemes a week in the same way and place the cue cards onto the word wall. (See the section on auditory, visual and tactile perception and the M.A.P.s activities.)
Assessment focus – I can recognise key words on sight.

---

4. Word Wall chants

CLL N/CLL O Understand the concept of a word (blue). Begin to recognise some familiar words (green).
Reception Literacy Objective
W5 to read on sight a range of familiar words, *e.g. children's names, captions, labels and words from familiar books;*
W6 to read on sight the 45 high frequency words to be taught by the end of YR from Appendix List 1;
W9 to recognise the critical features of words, *e.g. shape, length, and common spelling patterns;*
W2 knowledge of grapheme/phoneme correspondences through:
• reading letters that represent the sounds, a-z, ch, sh, th
T1 through shared reading:
• recognise printed and hand-written words in a variety of settings, *e.g. notes, labels, signs, notices, forms, lists, directions;*
• understand and use the correct terms about print: word, letter.

Specific Learning Outcome – to recognise common key words on sight To link graphemes to phonemes.
Group – whole class.
Resources – Copymasters 45 and 46.
What to do – when a new word has been modelled and introduced to the Word Wall there are a whole range of ways of helping children to become familiar with the shape and letters that make up the word. Many high frequency words can be read and spelled using phonic knowledge but many others are irregular.
Select a chant to take the word apart and put it back together again.
The chants provide fun ways in which to help children remember how a word is made up.
Variation, differentiation and extension –
interactive chants can be used in many ways. They can be used to break up a long whole class shared session on the carpet. The children can be got up and re-energised with some activities from the word wall.
Assessment focus – I can recognise key words on sight.

---

5. Searchlights for reading 1

CLL N Begin to recognise some familiar words (green).
CLL E Extend vocabulary, especially by grouping and naming (green).
Reception Literacy Objective
W5 to read on sight a range of familiar words and words linked to particular topics;
W6 to read on sight the 45 high frequency words to be taught by the end of YR from Appendix 1;
W9 to recognise the critical features of words, *e.g. shape, length, and common spelling patterns.*
T1 through shared reading:
• recognise printed and hand-written words in a variety of settings, *e.g. notes, labels, signs, notices, forms, lists, directions;*
• understand and use the correct terms about print: word, letter.
Specific Learning Outcome – to read on sight high frequency words, recognising critical features such as shape and letter combination.
Group – shared, guided.
Resources – words up on the Word Wall, some torches (blinds/curtains to darken the room).

What to do – children are seated facing the word wall. You have a torch. The lights are turned out
Variation 1 – show the children a word card that matches one on the wall, shining a torch onto the card they are holding. The searchlight scans the wall and when the beam touches the word card on the wall the children make a buzzing sound, until the beam settles on the card guided by the intensity of buzzing.
Variation 2 – show the children a word card that matches one on the wall, shining a torch onto the card they are holding. The searchlight scans the wall and settles on the ceiling. The children have to guide the searchlight to the word using 'up', 'down' 'left/right' or 'over this way/that way' (indicating), until they get to the word.
Variation 3 – the torch is shone around the wall, scanning from word to word in circular arcs. Finally the 'searchlight' settles on a word. The children say the word together and you echo the word.
Variation 4 – the torch is shone around the wall scanning from word to word in circular arcs. Finally the 'searchlight' settles on a word. The children use one of the Word Wall chants to indicate the shape of the word
Variation, differentiation and extension – the

Theme 11 Developing early reading

children have some torches in pairs and the lights are turned out. Initially they shine their torches on you.
Variation 1 – say a word and the children search the word out using the torches. They should settle their torches on the word until they all agree.
Variation 2 – pretend to be a robot saying the word, segmenting the word into its phonemes. In pairs the children have to blend the words and find them on the wall.

Challenging variation 3 – use one of the chants that indicate either shapes of letters or the sequence of consonants and vowels e.g. 'snap and clap', clicking fingers for vowels and clapping for consonants. Children have to search for the word. Alternatively the word could be written onto a whiteboard and the children could show you the word at a given signal.
Assessment focus – I can recognise words on sight, using my knowledge of the features and shapes of words.

6. Searchlights for reading (2)

CLL N Begin to recognise some familiar words (green).
CLL E Extend vocabulary, especially by grouping and naming (green).
Reception Literacy Objective
W4 to link sound and spelling patterns using knowledge of rhyme to identify families of rhyming words;
W5 to read on sight a range of familiar words and words linked to particular topics;
W6 to read on sight the 45 high frequency words to be taught by the end of YR from Appendix 1;
W9 to recognise the critical features of words, e.g. shape, length, and common spelling patterns.
T1 through shared reading:
- recognise printed and hand-written words in a variety of settings, e.g. notes, labels, signs, notices, forms, lists, directions;
- understand and use the correct terms about print: word, letter.

Specific Learning Outcome – to use knowledge of rhyme to identify high frequency words with similar spelling patterns. To use knowledge of 'onset' and 'rime' to help spell words using clue words.

Group – shared/guided.
Resources – words up on the Word Wall, some torches, blinds or curtains to darken the room.
What to do – the children are seated facing the Word Wall. Choose a word on the wall, without telling the children what the word is, and think of a rhyming word that is spelt in the same way. Tell the children the rhyming word.
Turn out the lights and let the children shine their torches onto the word wall to search out the rhyming word. As they find it they should leave their torch beams on the word until all the beams are shining on it. At a given signal the class should say the word together. Sets of rhyming Consonant-Vowel-Consonant words could be used to search out rhyming families.
Variation, differentiation and extension –
Challenging – once the word has been spotted, children should write the rhyming words onto a piece of paper or whiteboard.
Assessment focus – I can use my knowledge of rhyme to read familiar words. I can use my knowledge of rime to spell new words.

7. Jammy words

CLL N Begin to recognise some familiar words (green).
CLL E Extend vocabulary, especially by grouping and naming (green).
Reception Literacy Objective
W4 to link sound and spelling patterns by discriminating 'onset' from 'rimes' in speech and spelling, e.g. *tip, sip skip, flip, chip.*
W8 to read and write own name and explore other words related to the spelling of own name;
W9 to recognise the critical features of words, e.g. shape, length, common, spelling patterns.
Specific Learning Outcome – to develop knowledge of the critical features of words.
Group – shared/guided.
Resources – a large jar or pot, name cards and/or Word Wall cards.
What to do – ensure the name cards and/or Word Wall cards are visible. Put the names of the children and/or the words from the Wall onto small pieces of card and put them into the jar or pot. 'Stir' them up and select a name or word from the pot. Prompt the children with clues using Word Wall chant ideas, and/or mnemonics to help children identify the initial letter; this letter is written up on the board.
The children have to try to guess the next letter in word in the correct sequence, left to right. Prompts can be offered using Word Wall chant strategies, *e.g, tapping your tummy and snapping fingers to indicate that it is a short letter and it is a vowel.*
Variation, differentiation and extension – children could write the letter that they think is coming up next by writing it on a whiteboard.
Assessment focus – I can build up words using a developing understanding of likely combinations of letters in English.

Strand 4

8. Mystery word

CLL E Extend vocabulary, especially by grouping and naming (green), **CLL N** Begin to recognise some common words (green), **CLL J** Hear and say initial sound in words and know which letters represent some of the sounds (green).
Reception Literacy Objective:
W4 to link sound and spelling patterns by discriminating 'onset' from 'rimes' in speech and spelling, e.g. *tip, sip skip, flip, chip.*
T1 through shared reading:
To recognise printed and hand-written words in a variety of settings, e.g. notes, labels, signs, notices, forms, lists, and directions.
To understand and use the correct terms about print: word, letter
Specific Learning Outcome – to develop strategies for cross checking across reading and spelling.
Group – shared/guided.
Resources – sticky notes, Word Wall cards
What to do – select a word from the Word Wall without the children seeing. Write a sentence that contains the word onto a strip of paper. Cover the word with two sticky notes, the first to cover the onset of the word, and the second to cover the rime. Read the sentence together and ask the children what the 'mystery word' could be. Let the children make several guesses. Write these guesses onto the board. Uncover the onset of the word and cross out the guesses that it couldn't be. Let the children make new guesses. Read the sentence and insert the guesses and decide which one fits best. Uncover the rime to reveal the whole word.
Variation, differentiation and extension – let children try to spell the mystery word on a whiteboard.
Assessment focus – I can cross check and work out words using context, and the parts of words.
I can use my knowledge of onset and rime to help me spell.

9. Read around the room

CLL N Begin to recognise some familiar words (green).
Reception Literacy Objective:
W11 to make collections of personal interest of significant words and words linked to particular topics
Specific Learning Outcome – to notice and contribute to environmental print.
Group – guided/independent.
Resources – clipboards, paper and pointers.
What to do – in a small group children use a clipboard and pencil to write down and collect environmental print from around the classroom. Objects not labelled should be drawn and an attempt at spelling could be made to add to the list. You could provide the correct spellings of words that need labelling so that over time the room becomes 'print-rich'. The children attach the labels to the objects to build up the vocabulary in the room.
Variation, differentiation and extension – environmental print could be collected at home. Children could be given copies of Copymaster 44. This could be sent home for children to label objects.
Assessment focus – I notice environmental print
I can label objects.

10. Cross the river 1

CLL J Hear and say the initial sound in words and know which letters represent some sounds (green).
Reception Literacy Objective:
W3 alphabetic and phonic knowledge through
• sounding and naming each letter of the alphabet in lower and upper case.
Specific Learning Outcome – to describe the features of letter shapes.
Resources – a set of large alphabet cards – laminated if possible. Two long skipping ropes.
Group – shared/guided.
What to do – lay the ropes out parallel to each other and tell the children that this is a river to be crossed. Divide the children into two groups and sit each on either side of the 'river' – one group are the 'steppers' and the others the 'callers'. Scatter the alphabet cards along the river and tell the children that these are stepping-stones. Select a child to cross the river from the 'steppers' group and a child to help them get across from the 'callers' group.
The 'caller' must tell the child which letter to step onto to cross the river. If the 'stepper' steps on the wrong one then they 'fall' into the river and have to return to the other side of the river again. When all the 'steppers' have crossed, they become the 'callers' and have to guide their friends back to the other side.
Variation, differentiation and extension – instead of letters, words could be used.
Assessment focus – I can recognise the letters of the alphabet.

Theme 12 From reading into writing

11. Introduction

Big books provide an opportunity to model the reading process and to show young readers how books work and how a reader reads. They provide an opportunity to engage the whole class in a powerful and shared experience that invites children to participate in the world of literature, story, poetry and information texts. The prime purpose of these shared reading and writing sessions is to motivate children to respond and become interested in getting the meaning out of text and in learning how to use the effects of story and book language in their own developing writing and story making.

Books have an inherent value, and the response and attitude engendered towards reading in the early years has a powerful and lasting effect upon the attitude of developing readers in terms of their own confidence and willingness to participate in the challenge of learning to read. Children will have experience of learning discrete skills through activities related to speaking and listening and phonological awareness, and it is through shared reading that the application of all these skills can be modelled by teachers who think aloud and show children how reading works.

Big books provide powerful vehicles for stimulating discussion. Often the quality of the illustrations immerses children in rich sub-plots and discussion opportunities that can be springboards to further creative opportunities across the areas of learning in the early years curriculum.

The language of story is special and distinctive. It is different from the way that we usually talk and big books provide stimulating models to frame and support children's early writing attempts. Stories can be reproduced through oral retellings, drama and puppet plays. Scenarios can be recreated and explored through small world play, art and construction materials. Texts can be used to provide a base upon which children can adapt and innovate, initially by changing one or two aspects of a story (for example, by changing the main character) until gradually children come to gain control of the structures that underlie both writing and reading.

The key to being a successful reader lies in understanding the writer and the key to successful writing lies in writing like a reader.

The National Literacy Strategy suggests, as a rule of thumb, the idea of reading and using at least one big book a week. This enables children to become increasingly familiar with a book and to gain insight into its pattern and structure. This puts children in a position to be able to use some of these structures in their own writing. The focus for shared reading and writing shifts through the course of a week as children become increasingly familiar with a book.

A typical model for this might be:
For reading
Monday – book introduction with teacher reading through the book and children listening and enjoying the story.
Tuesday – children begin to participate in the reading, joining in with repeating refrains. An aspect of the story becomes a focus for some further exploration, possibly through shared writing.
Wednesday onwards – more and more control is handed over to the children and different aspects of the story are explored in more detail.
For retelling and writing:
From Monday – encourage retellings and exploration through speaking and listening activities, drama and role-play, and independent learning centres.
From Tuesday – explore aspects of the story, characters or setting in more detail.
From Wednesday – retell and innovate through modelling and shared writing leading to picture sequencing, story frames and captioned pictures, for example.
From Thursday – encourage innovations on the basic story by adding, or changing significant details, characters and/or events.
Present a new version or interpretation of the text through drama, retelling, role-play and/or writing and storybook making.

12. The new book (first read through of a big book)

CLL O/P Hold books the correct way up and turn pages. Handle books carefully, Suggest how the story might end (blue).
Reception Literacy Objective
T1 through shared reading:
- recognise words in a variety of settings;
- understand and use correctly terms about books and print; book, cover, beginning, end, page, line, word, letter, title.

To track the text in the right order, page by page, left to right, top to bottom, pointing while reading/ telling a story, and making one to one correspondences between written and spoken words
T2 to use a variety of cues when reading

Specific Learning Outcome – to introduce and discuss a new text with the class. To read the text through and focus on response to the text.
Group – shared.
Resources – big book of the week. Copymaster 47.
What to do –
(For a fiction book)
Introducing the story
In order for children to get the most out of the story about to be read to them it is often helpful to precept and focus their minds ready for the context and characters in the story. Often the picture on the cover of the book and the title provide opportunities to ask open-ended questions that allow children to draw upon personally meaningful previous experience. Children should be encouraged to share anecdotes and observations to provide the backdrop to this new story.

Strand 4

E.g. What kind of book is it? What do you think it will be about? Where do you think it will happen? Have you ever been to a place like this? Who will be in the story? What do you think they are like?

Discuss the fact that the book was written by someone (an author) and illustrated by (usually) someone else. It is important to convey the fact that books are made by people for other people to read.

Walk through the pictures in the book, modelling predicting what you think will happen next. Stop before you get to the end of the book to leave this as added suspense.

Use open-ended questions where possible and ask the children a question that can only be answered by reading the story *e.g. What do you think will happen at the end of the story?* Return to this after the first reading.

Reading the story

Use a pointer to point to each word as you model one-to-one correspondence with spoken to written words, left to right directionality and top to bottom movement. Tell the children your thought processes as you do this. The children's eyes will follow the end of the pointer. Occasionally pause and model strategies for working out words such as predicting, missing out and reading on, then reading back and breaking the word up into syllables, and/or phonemes. The focus for these strategies will depend on what you have taught them discretely elsewhere. Do not over use these strategies as this point as the prime purpose of the reading today is to get through and let the children digest the text. Read the story, right through, deliberately over-emphasising expression, characterisation and suspense.

Model your engagement and response to the story at various points through the reading, *e.g. 'I can't wait to find out what happens next ... oh, no! I don't believe it!'*

Responding to the story

After the first reading, model the response that you have had to the story. Return to the question that you asked. Ask children to retell the story and explore why things happened at various points through the story. Ask open-ended questions that are as specific as you can make them. General questions get general answers. Who did what where, when and why? Descriptions of main characters and personality. What where the problems in the story? What would you have done? Why do you think s/he did that?

Variation, differentiation and extension – non-fiction books should be read differently. Try and present a purpose for needing to read the information text *e.g. to answer specific question or to find something out.* There is no need to read most information texts from cover to cover. Instead you should model strategies for extracting information from information texts, such as flicking and browsing, using contents and index, skimming and scanning. This can be done using the pointer whilst telling the children what it is your eyes do when you look at the layout of a page of information text *e.g. how you use titles, sub-titles and captions to steer you to the information you want.*

Assessment focus – if there is another adult present they could keep a record of who asks and answers questions, who offers contributions and who does not participate. Use the simple observation checklist on Copymaster 47.

---

13. Returning to the text (second read through of a big book)

CLL O/P/M/N Hold books the correct way up and turn pages. Handle books carefully. Suggest how the story might end (blue). Begin to recognise some familiar words; enjoy an increasing range of books (green).

Reception Literacy Objective:
T1 through shared reading:
• recognise words in a variety of settings;
• understand and use correctly terms about books and print *e.g. book, cover, beginning, end, page, line, word, letter, title.*
To track the text in the right order, page by page, left to right, top to bottom, pointing while reading/telling a story, and making one-to-one correspondences between written and spoken words
T2 to use a variety of cues when reading.

Specific Learning Outcome – to read the text through and to explore an aspect of the text in more depth. To increase child participation.

Group – shared.

Resources – big book of the week. Copymaster 47.

What to do –
(For a fiction book)
Reviewing the story
Ask the children to help build up a retelling of the story. You want to know who was in the story, where it was set, what happened, what the characters did, how they solved the problems they were having and how the story ended.

Recap on some of the organisational features of a book and the conventions of reading books in English. This is most effectively done by modelling the consequences of breaking the conventions *e.g. reading bottom to top.* Let the children correct this behaviour and offer guidance on correct reading technique and strategies.

Reading the story

As the children know the story a little bit you can focus more on the structure of the text and on involving children in the reading. Children will have probably involved themselves already if there is patterned language or a repeating refrain of text. This participation could be extended through choral reading with expression and intonation, exaggerated as in your initial reading, adding movements and sound effects. The second reading offers an opportunity to rehearse and model strategies for working out new and unfamiliar words, *e.g. a sticky note can be used to cover a word which children have to predict through context, initial letter and/or picture cues.*

Exploring the story

After the second reading you can focus on a specific aspect of the story relevant to the learning needs of the group. This could be developed through questioning and discussion, supporting retelling of the story or modelling

53

Theme 12 From reading into writing

the writing of a captioning sentence for one of the illustrations through shared writing, for example. This could be used for some focused word or sentence level work.

Variation, differentiation and extension – subsequent readings of the text allow children to gain more control and increase their participation through choral reading. This choral reading is a powerful way for them to begin to internalise the structures and patterns of story language. Subsequent re-readings enable all pupils to be included in the reading process, and provide children with books and stories that they know and are familiar with.

Assessment focus – if there is another adult present they could keep a record of who asks and answers questions, who offers contributions and who does not participate. Use the simple observation checklist on Copymaster 47.

I can participate in shared reading.

Strand 4

14. Reading to Teddy (book handling and directionality)

CLL O/P/M/N Hold books the correct way up and turn pages. Handle books carefully. Suggest how the story might end (blue). Begin to recognise some familiar words. Enjoy an increasing range of books (green).

Reception Literacy Objective:

T10 to re-read and recite stories and rhymes with predictable and repeated patterns and experiment with similar rhyming patterns;

T1 to understand print through shared reading:
To understand and use correctly terms about books and print *e.g. book, cover, beginning, end, page, line, word, letter, title;*
To track the text in the right order, page by page, left to right, top to bottom, pointing while reading/telling a story, and making one-to-one correspondences between written and spoken words.

Specific Learning Outcome – to understand how to handle books and follow text

Group – shared/independent.

Resources – a big book. A teddy bear or toy.

What to do – sit the teddy bear on a chair next to the big book stand. Explain that Teddy does not know how to read and that you are going to teach him. Select a big book to model correct and incorrect usage. Turn the book upside down and face the back of the book towards the children. Ask the children why you cannot start reading here. Ask them where you should start and turn the book to the front. Model reading the title from right to left – again ask the children what is wrong with this. As you do this modelling, use the terminology *cover, beginning, end, page, line, word, letter, title,* pretending that you are instructing the teddy bear.

Let the children help you read the story to the teddy.

Variation, differentiation and extension – put the bear in the reading area to let children read to the bear as an independent activity.

The bear can go home as part of a reading and writing pack each weekend. This can include a diary called *The Adventures of Ted*, into which parents can help write dictated sentences to tell the story of what the bear did at the weekend. The bear can form part of a pack, *e.g. a knapsack, which contains the bear, the diary, a book chosen by the child, a pretend camera, etc.*

Assessment focus – I know how to handle a book and what the different parts of a book are called.
I know that, in English, print is read left to right and from top to bottom.

Theme 13: Challenging early reading

15. 'Wordo!'

Early Learning goal:
CLL E Extend their vocabulary, exploring the meanings and sounds of new words.
CLL N Read a range of familiar and common words and simple sentences independently.
Reception Literacy Objective
W6 to read on sight the 45 high frequency words to be taught by the end of YR from Appendix list 1.
Specific Learning Outcome – to recognise rapidly high frequency words on sight.
Group – shared/guided.
Resources – Copymasters 43, 44 and 48. High frequency word cards. Counters or small cubes.
What to do – take a set of high frequency word cards and shuffle them up. Give pairs of children one of the Wordo grids from Copymaster 48. Ensure that it is matched to the attention span and capability of the children.
Turn over a high frequency word card. If a pair of children have that word on their Wordo boards they put a counter or cube to cover it.
If a pair of children get a row of words in any direction they should call out 'Wordo!'. Check the words. The children could read out their covered words and match them to the words that have been shown.
The children should swap cards and play can continue again.
Variation, differentiation and extension – *Wordo* could be played with phonemes, or parts of words such as 'rimes'. It could be used for alphabet matching activities.
Wordo games provide good opportunities to consolidate new words from reading and shared experiences along with other common and useful words, *e.g. pupils' names, common colour words, numbers to twenty, days of the week, key mathematical vocabulary such as shapes*. This strategy is also useful for consolidating word collections of personal interest, significant words and words linked to particular topics.
Assessment focus – I can recognise words high frequency words on sight.

16. Cross the river 2 (Beat the Troll)

CLL J Hear and say the initial sound in words and know which letters represent some sounds (green).
Reception Literacy Objective:
W3 alphabetic and phonic knowledge through:
• sounding and naming each letter of the alphabet in lower and upper case.
Specific Learning Outcome – to describe the features of letter shapes.
Resources – a set of large alphabet cards, laminated if possible.
Two long skipping ropes.
Copymaster 49 for reference.
Group – shared.
What to do – this game can be played indoors or outside.
Lay the ropes out parallel to each other and tell the children that this is a river that has to be crossed. Scatter alphabet cards to bridge the river in a pattern similar to Copymaster 49.
The object of this game is to get across the river without being caught by the troll. Four children start at the bottom by stepping onto one of the alphabet stepping-stones. A child is selected to be a troll. The four children choose which letter they want to step to and call it out as they step in turn. The troll tries to corner and catch the children by stepping onto the same stone as the child; again they move by naming the letter before they step on it. Only one child is allowed onto a stone at any time and only one step can be taken in any one turn.
Children who are caught are turned into frogs and have to stay on the stone while the troll tries to capture other children.
A game like this could be painted onto the playground to become a permanent play feature.
This sheet can be photocopied for children to play the game with counters.
Instead of letters, words could be used.
Variation, differentiation and extension –
Spell it – Rather than being chased by a troll, give each of the four children a word card (with the same number of letters in each word). Children take it in turns to step, again naming the letter before moving. They have to collect the letters that make up the word that they have. Variations on this might include collecting them in order or in any order. When they step on a letter in their word they can cross it off their word card. The first person to collect all their letters and cross the river is the winner.
Sentence stones – As above but with words on the stones. Children are given a simple sentence and they have to collect words from their sentence in order. Alternatively, they have to step across the river in the order of the words in their sentence.
Assessment focus – I can recognise and name the letters of the alphabet.

17. Independent Reading Area and resources

Specific Learning Outcome – to provide opportunities for children to apply strategies that they have been taught elsewhere with independence and confidence. To consolidate reading skills and strategies and provide an opportunity to challenge and extend individual pupils.
Group – guided, collaborative and independent groups.

Strand 4

Resources –
Independent reading from class library – organised by genre.
Word Wall activities – interacting with display to investigate, look for patterns, or to sort and classify words.
Text marking activities for high frequency words in newspapers etc.
Graded book baskets – colour coded to Reading Recovery book bands.
Word Wall games as independent and collaborative activities
Read around the room – looking for target letters or letter combinations, collecting and listing. Child has clipboard and pen; partner has pointer.
Big book re-reading – with pointer.
Reordering words/letters etc.
Story props and manipulatives *e.g. finger puppets, transparencies of characters on the OHP.*

What to do –
The above activities should first have been introduced through guided or small group work. Once the children understand how to undertake the tasks, a set of resources should be left set up to encourage children to work independently on consolidating and extending specific skills.
Variation, differentiation and extension – the activities above make good activities for children to do at home with the support of parents/carers.
Assessment focus – I select and complete reading tasks with independence and confidence.

Theme 14 Early writing

Early Learning Goals for linking sounds and letters	NLS Word level work: Phonics spelling and vocabulary
CLL Q Attempt writing for different purposes, using features of different forms such as lists, stories and instructions; **CLL R** Write their own names and other things such as labels and captions and begin to form simple sentences, sometimes using punctuation.	Understanding of print: **T11** through shared writing: • To understand that writing can be used for a range of purposes, e.g. to send messages, record, inform, tell stories; • To understand that writing remains constant, i.e. will always 'say' the same thing; • To distinguish between writing and drawing in books and own work; • To understand how writing is formed directionally, a word at a time; • To understand how letters are formed to spell words; • To apply knowledge of letter/ sound correspondences in helping the teacher to scribe, and re-reading what the class has written.
CLL K Use their phonic knowledge to write simple regular words and make phonetically plausible attempts at more complex words.	Composition **T12** through guided and independent writing; • To experiment with writing in a variety of play, exploratory and role-play situations; • To write their own names; • To write labels or captions for pictures and drawings; • To write sentences to match pictures or sequences of pictures; • To experiment with writing and recognise how their own version matches and differs from conventional version, e.g. through teacher response and transcription. **T13** to think about and discuss what they intend to write, ahead of writing it; **T14** to use experience of stories, poems and simple recounts as a basis for independent writing, e.g. re-telling, substitution, extension, and through shared composition with adults; **T15** to use writing to communicate in a variety of ways, incorporating it into play and everyday classroom life, e.g. recounting their own experiences, lists, signs, directions, menus, labels, greeting cards, letters

1. Independent activities and Literacy centres

The activities in this section consist of resource lists to equip some of the independent literacy centres that should be available to children in the Foundation Stage. Teachers should model the use of much of this equipment to demonstrate and provide guidance of appropriate and imagined usage. Adult demonstration models conventional usage of resources and provides templates for possible behaviours, but children should be encouraged to explore and innovate through their play. Many of these activities encourage children to develop and apply the skills of communication, language and literacy in real and/or imagined contexts, but with real independence. This independence and exploration of language and literacy skills is a crucial part of the Foundation Stage curriculum, but children should not just be left to reinvent social conventions or the conventions of literacy. Careful and considered adult observation and intervention can help children refine their understanding of how to communicate more effectively, use language more powerfully, extract meaning through reading and record and reflect through writing.

Independent activities and routines provide the backdrop of applied literacy and self-reliance that enables teachers to work with small groups in guided and collaborative play, scaffolded learning and, at times, structured teaching.

Many of the activities throughout this publication, after teacher modelling and guided support will become independent activities that children can engage with. Sometimes this engagement will be child initiated as the child pursues a line of thinking or investigation. At other times children will be steered towards specific activities as ways of consolidating, extending and/or enriching experiences appropriate to their learning and development.

Strand 5

2. The Writing Area

CLL Q Draw and paint, sometimes giving meaning to marks (yellow). Ascribe meanings to marks (blue). Use writing as a means of recording and communicating (green).
Specific Learning Outcomes – to provide a permanent area for children to explore different ways of 'mark-making' and 'writing'.
Group – collaborative, independent.
Resources –
Alphabet and number posters.
Alphabet and number sets, stencils etc.
Blank booklets *e.g. origami books, consequences booklets, blank scrap paper booklets, zig zag books,* cards, different format blanks, *e.g. forms, and environmental print templates etc.* Note books and blank books. Copymaster 50.
Chalkboards, chalk or whiteboards (magnetic) (large and small) and dry wipe pens (non-toxic).
Clipboards.
Computer.
Crayons and colouring tools.
Envelopes.
Glue.
Hole punch and tags.
Line guides and letter formation prompts.
Magnetic letters, magnetic boards.
Markers – large/small (non-toxic).
Name cards.
Newspapers.
Paper – different sizes.
Pencils and pens.
Pictures (from magazines e.g. backgrounds, pictures of people, faces).
Rulers and scissors.
Stamps and ink pads.
Stapler.
Tape.
Telephone and appointment book.
Typewriter.
Word books and simple dictionaries.
Activity sheets and copymasters linked to shared work.

What to do – set up a permanent writing resource area in your setting. Play collaboratively and in parallel to children using the writing area. Think aloud and model as you use the equipment and resources in the area.
Variation, differentiation and extension – rotate resources in the writing area and link to themes and other role-play areas.
Assessment focus – I have explored different tools and materials for writing and making marks. I tell you that I am writing something.

3. A shop

CLL Q Draw and paint, sometimes giving meaning to marks (yellow). Ascribe meanings to marks (blue). Use writing as a means of recording and communicating (green). **CLL G** Use talk to give new meanings to objects and actions, treating them as symbols for other things (blue).
Specific Learning Outcomes – to provide a permanent area for children to explore different ways of 'mark-making' and 'writing'.
Group – collaborative, independent.
Resources –
Computer.
Bags.
Bulletin/notice board <u>cards for notices.</u>
<u>Name tags designating roles.</u>
<u>Receipt book.</u>
Magazines.
<u>Money (notes)/credit cards.</u>
Cash register.
Baskets.
<u>Cheques.</u>
<u>Price stickers for sale/sale signs.</u>
Smocks.
Blank book.
Paper for shopping list.
Telephone and <u>telephone message pad.</u>
Boxes (empty e.g. cereal).
Markers.
<u>Coupons.</u>
Suggestion box.
Shelves.

59

Theme 14 Early writing

What to do – play collaboratively and in parallel to children using the writing area. Think aloud and model as you use the equipment and resources in the area. *Note that the <u>underlined</u> items above are provided as resources on Copymasters 51 and 52.*

Variation, differentiation and extension – rotate resources in the writing area and link to themes and other role-play areas.
Assessment focus – I can pretend to be someone else, somewhere else doing something else.

---

4. Hospital (human or animal hospital)

CLL Q Draw and paint, sometimes giving meaning to marks (yellow). Ascribe meanings to marks (blue). Use writing as a means of recording and communicating (green). **CLL G** Use talk to give new meanings to objects and actions, treating them as symbols for other things (blue).
Specific Learning Outcomes – to provide a permanent area for children to explore different ways of 'mark-making' and 'writing'.
Group – collaborative, independent.
Resources –
Bandages.
Booklet (blank for children to write and draw about experiences in hospital).
Walking stick.
Gloves.
Meal tray- plates, cutlery.
Markers and pens.
Telephone.
<u>First aid instructions – e.g. place doll on floor, check heart rate, listen for breathing.</u>
<u>Signs for parts of the hospital e.g. operating theatre, waiting room, X-ray department, etc.</u>
Blankets.
Clipboards – <u>medical records and charts.</u>
Dolls (both genders and multicultural) or animals.
White coats – head caps etc.
Medical kit.
Sterilised pots.
<u>Medical papers e.g. x-ray, picture of a person with labelling lines to head, arm, leg etc. (labels Blank).</u>
Medical posters.
Appointment diary.
Bed.
Cotton balls.
File folders.
Magazines.
Paper (graph paper and blank in different sizes).
Stethoscope.
Plasters.
<u>Medical name badges e.g. doctor, surgeon, nurse.</u>

What to do – play collaboratively and in parallel to children using the writing area. Think aloud and model as you use the equipment and resources in the area. *Note that the <u>underlined</u> items above are provided as resources on Copymasters 53 and 54.*
Variation, differentiation and extension – rotate resources in the writing area and link to themes and other role-play areas.
Assessment focus – I can pretend to be someone else, somewhere else, doing something else.

---

5. A house

CLL Q Draw and paint, sometimes giving meaning to marks (yellow). Ascribe meanings to marks (blue). Use writing as a means of recording and communicating (green). **CLL G** Use talk to give new meanings to objects and actions, treating them as symbols for other things (blue).
Specific Learning Outcomes – to provide a permanent area for children to explore different ways of 'mark-making' and 'writing'.
Group – collaborative, independent
Resources –
Blank book for writing about experiences in the house.
Clothes rack/ trunk.
Cupboard.
Hats.
Mirror.
Shoes.
Dustpan and broom.
Costumes.
Dolls and dolls clothes (both genders and multicultural).
Iron and ironing board.
<u>Paper, drawing and writing tools. Shopping lists, memo, message pads, calendar, stationery, envelopes, bills e.g. forms to fill in,</u>
Telephone.
Chopsticks.
Bed.
Dishes, dish cloth, cutlery sink.
Jewellery.
Notice board.
T.V./computer/books.

Strand 5

What to do –
Play collaboratively and in parallel to children using the writing area. Think aloud and model as you use the equipment and resources in the area. *Note that the underlined items above are provided as resources on Copymaster 55.*

Variation, differentiation and extension – rotate resources in the writing area and link to themes and other role-play areas.
Assessment focus – I can pretend to be someone else, somewhere else doing something else.

---

6. Travel agents

CLL Q Draw and paint, sometimes giving meaning to marks (yellow). Ascribe meanings to marks (blue). Use writing as a means of recording and communicating (green). **CLL G** Use talk to give new meanings to objects and actions, treating them as symbols for other things (blue).
Specific Learning Outcomes – to provide a permanent area for children to explore different ways of 'mark-making' and 'writing'.
Group – collaborative, independent.
Resources –
Booklets.
Brochures.
Business cards.
Cash register/money.
Cheque book and credit cards.
Computer – appropriate software, calculator.
Globe and maps.

Luggage and luggage tags.
Paper (receipts, hotel vouchers, booking forms, Passports, etc).
Telephone.
Tickets.
Travel posters.

What to do –
Play collaboratively and in parallel to children using the writing area. Think aloud and model as you use the equipment and resources in the area. *Note that the underlined items above are provided as resources on Copymasters 56 and 57.*
Variation, differentiation and extension – rotate resources in the writing area and link to themes and other role-play areas.
Assessment focus – I can pretend to be someone else, somewhere else doing something else.

---

7. Restaurant/café

CLL Q Draw and paint, sometimes giving meaning to marks (yellow). Ascribe meanings to marks (blue). Use writing as a means of recording and communicating (green). **CLL G** Use talk to give new meanings to objects and actions, treating them as symbols for other things (blue).
Specific Learning Outcomes – to provide a permanent area for children to explore different ways of 'mark-making' and 'writing'.
Group – collaborative, independent.
Resources –
Cash machine – calculator.
Table/chairs/cutlery/table cloth/candle/flowers.
Recipe books.
Blank books.
Day time name number of people.
Notice board.
Chef's hat and clothes, waiters waist coat and bow tie.
Money, cheque book, credit cards, receipt and bills.
Tray/ plates/ bowels.

Recipe cards (blank).
Booking diary.
Fridge/sink etc.
Empty boxes.
Place mat with children's puzzles etc.
Menu cards (just title) and bit of line art – children will fill in details.
Cooker/pans/pots/cooking utensils/.
Shopping list.
Blank posters to advertise restaurant.

What to do – play collaboratively and in parallel to children using the writing area. Think aloud and model as you use the equipment and resources in the area. *Note that the underlined items aboveare provided as resources on Copymasters 58 and 59.*

Variation, differentiation and extension – rotate resources in the writing area and link to themes and other role-play areas.
Assessment focus – I can pretend to be someone else, somewhere else doing something else.

Theme 15 Developing early writing

8. My Name is …

CLL R Ascribe meanings to marks (blue). Begin to break the flow of speech into words (green). **CLL N** Understand the concept of a word (blue). Begin to recognise some familiar words (green).
Reception Literacy Objectives:
T11 through shared writing:
- understand that writing remains constant, i.e. will always 'say' the same thing;
- understand how writing is formed directionally, a word at a time;
- understand how letters are formed to spell words.

T12 through guided and independent writing;
- write their own names.

Specific Learning Outcome – to help children develop their understanding of what a word is. To recognise and begin to be able to write own name.
Group – shared/guided.
Resources – a set of cards with children's names written on the cards. Each card should reflect the length of the child's name, with letters clearly printed and evenly spaced. A whiteboard and pen.

What to do – give the children their name cards and ask them to look at the word that says their name. Write the initial letter from one child's name up on the whiteboard, followed by a series of dashes to indicate the remaining letters. Try to get the letter size and spacing the same as on the child's name cards.
Ask children to stand up if they think you are writing their name. Get them to look at the initial letter. If more than one child's name begins with the initial letter bring them all out to match to the word you are writing on the board.

Variation, differentiation and extension – use some of the Word Wall chants and strategies to help them to spot the ascenders and descenders in their name.
Use the Letter Worms (Copymaster 69) to aid in the formation of the letters to make the name. Let the children trace their name using tracing paper and make the letters out of plasticine.

Assessment focus – I can recognise my name. I can write the initial letter of my name.
I can write my name.

---

9. Shared Writing 1 (innovating *in* a text)

CLL H Use talk to connect ideas, explain what is happening and anticipate what might happen next (blue). **CLL Q/R/K** Ascribe meanings to marks (blue). Begin to break the flow of speech into words. Use writing as a means of recording and communicating (green).
Reception Literacy Objective
T11 through shared writing:
- understand that writing can be used for a range of purposes, e.g. to send messages, record, inform, tell stories;
- understand that writing remains constant, i.e. will always 'say' the same thing;
- understand how writing is formed directionally, a word at a time;
- understand how letters are formed and used to spell words.

To apply knowledge of letter/sound correspondences in helping the teacher to scribe, and re-read what the class has written;
T14 to use experience of stories, poems and simple recounts and shared composition with adults.as a basis for independent writing, *e.g. retelling, substitution, extension.*
Specific Learning Outcome – to understand that text in books is written by a person.
To have a clear model to imitate when writing independently.
Group – shared.
Resources – a big book. Some paper to mask the text and some Blu-tack to stick the masks over the text in the big book.
What to do – read a big book or tell the children a story several times over several days so that they are familiar with the characters, events and actions in the story.

On the day of the shared writing, mask the text to be rewritten using the paper and Blu-tack. Stick the paper into the big book to cover the existing text. Model the decisions and how, as a writer, you would go about constructing the text *e.g. look at the picture and discuss the picture.* Consider the text that was in the book before it was masked and explain that you want to write something that is nearly the same, but that says it differently. Ask the children for suggestions and ideas. Explain why you make the choice that you do and rehearse the sentence aloud before you write it. Begin to write the sentence and model the strategies that you want the children to use when spelling known as well as new and unfamiliar words. Model writing at least two sentences like this. Leave out the punctuation and explain that you have forgotten to put it in. Ask the children to re-read what you have written and to put their hands up in the places where they think the full stops should go. Explain that a sentence is a complete idea and that a full stop should go at the end of every idea. Insert the full stops then check through for capital letters after the full stops.
Do one or two pages like this. Model substituting the main character for a different one, or changing the setting, but keep the structure of the text similar.
When you have finished writing, prompt the children to re-read chorally what has been written. Explain that the children are going to go and write some sentences to go with a picture. If they have not drawn the picture yet, let them talk to a friend about what they will draw and then rehearse what sentence they might write as a caption for this picture. If a picture, or picture sequence, is being provided, let them talk to a friend and rehearse what the sentences they will write about the picture(s) will say.
Let some children share their sentences with the group. Sometimes children will link several phrases together

Strand 5

with 'and….and', so echo back to the children what they have said but edit out the 'ands' and explain that you have turned their ideas into sentences. Remind the children what to do if they are stuck with spelling a word, i.e. try to spell it using phonic strategies, or to use some of the display that is on the Word Wall or around the class.
Let the children go and write.
Let some children share their text innovations with the class during a review/plenary session.
Variation, differentiation and extension – this strategy can be used with any genre of writing. The important thing is to give the children a clear model before they go and write independently. This is a particularly effective way of modelling non-fiction writing such as lists which when modelled with the class can be put into the writing or role-play areas. The demonstration of writing a list or filling in a form, using an enlarged version of the text, gives children the context and a framework to enable them to explore and work towards conventional writing based on adult modelling.
Assessment focus – I can draw a picture to help me with my writing. I can tell an adult what I want her/him to write for me.
I can make marks to caption my picture.
I can write a sentence to caption my picture.

---

10. Shared Writing 2 (innovating *on* a text)

LL H Use talk to connect ideas, explain what is happening and anticipate what might happen next (blue).
CLL Q/R/K Ascribe meanings to marks (blue). Begin to break the flow of speech into words. Use writing as a means of recording and communicating (green).
Reception Literacy Objectives:
T11 through shared writing:
* understand that writing can be used for a range of purposes, e.g. to send messages, record, inform, tell stories;
* understand that writing remains constant, i.e. will always 'say' the same thing;
* understand how writing is formed directionally, a word at a time;
* understand how letters are formed and used to spell words.

To apply knowledge of letter/sound correspondences in helping the teacher to scribe, and re-read what the class has written;
T14 to use experience of stories, poems and simple recounts as a basis for independent writing, *e.g. retelling, substitution, extension, and through shared composition with adults.*
Specific Learning Outcome – to understand that text in books is written by a person.
To have a clear model to imitate when writing independently.
Group – shared.
Resources – a familiar big book or rhyme. Several big book sized pieces of paper or a big book blank – these could be made up from large sheets of sugar paper folded to make a big book. Remember that you will be working in multiples of 4 (8, 12 or 16 pages).
What to do – read a big book or tell the children a story several times over several days so that they are familiar with the characters, events and actions in the story.
Explain that you are going to make a new big book/rhyme that will be based on the original. Look through the original again and decide what you will change *e.g. The Little Red Hen might become The Big Spotty Dog* (or any of the rhyme innovations *e.g. finger-rhyme time, nonsense songsense or Humpty Dumpty*).
Model making notes based on suggestions from the children. These will also function as a word bank both for you and the children if they are to write independently.
Look at the text in the original book and use your notes and the children's suggestions to write an alternative sentence onto a strip of paper. Do this for each page of the new big book. Use the strategies for modelling the writing of sentences from Shared Writing 1.
Share the sentence strips out amongst groups of children to illustrate on large sheets of paper, using paint or collage. Each group should work with the same medium for consistency. One group could work on the cover and a back page with blurb.
Cut and mount the pictures into the big book. Word process the written text ensuring that it is in a large legible font. If possible, laminate the sheets to provide longevity to the big books.
Place the big books into the class library.
Let children make small versions of big books in this way using the origami book template on Copymaster 50.
Variation, differentiation and extension – this strategy can be used with any genre of writing. The important thing is to give the children a clear model before they go and write independently. This is a particularly effective way of modelling non-fiction writing such as lists which when modelled with the class can be put into the writing or role-play areas. The demonstration of writing a list or filling in a form, using an enlarged version of the text, gives children the context and a framework to enable them to explore and work towards conventional writing based on adult modelling.
Assessment focus – I can draw a picture to help me with my writing.
I can tell an adult what I want her/ him to write for me.

Theme 15 Developing early writing

11. Shared Writing 3 (innovating *from a text*)

LL H Use talk to connect ideas, explain what is happening and anticipate what might happen next (blue).
CLL Q/R/K Ascribe meanings to marks (blue). Begin to break the flow of speech into words. Use writing as a means of recording and communicating (green).
Reception Literacy Objective:
T11 through shared writing:
- understand that writing can be used for a range of purposes, e.g. to send messages, record, inform, tell stories;
- understand that writing remains constant, i.e. will always 'say' the same thing;
- understand how writing is formed directionally, a word at a time;
- understand how letters are formed and used to spell words;
- apply knowledge of letter/sound correspondences in helping the teacher to scribe, and re-read what the class has written.

T14 to use experience of stories, poems and simple recounts as a basis for independent writing *e.g. retelling, substitution, extension, and through shared composition with adults.*
T15 to use writing to communicate in a variety of ways, incorporating it into play and everyday classroom life, *e.g. recounting their own experiences, lists, signs, directions, menus, labels, greetings cards, letters.*
Specific Learning Outcome – to understand that text in books is written by a person.

To have a clear model to imitate when writing independently.
Group – shared, guided to independent.
Resources – a familiar big book or rhyme.
What to do – read a big book or tell the children a story several times over several days so that they are familiar with the characters, events and actions in the story.
The purpose of this writing activity is to change the format or genre of the original text *e.g. a nursery rhyme could be retold in a big book story format, or a story could be retold as a list.*
This strategy is also useful for developing writing opportunities from texts, *e.g. if a character writes a list in the story then the shared writing could focus on modelling writing lists and lists could be provided through independent work areas – e.g. role-play lists: shopping, things to do: construction (instructions for making something), cars and trains (a list of instructions of how to get from one place on the road mat to another). Other opportunities for writing could be letters from and to characters, posters, forms and types of texts featured in stories, e.g. forms to be filled in, newspapers that characters are reading.*
Variation, differentiation and extension – possible opportunities for reading and writing could include: diaries, schedules *e.g. times of T.V. programmes, songs, wrappers and packaging for food and cereal packets, recipes, catalogues, menu's for role-play café's, get-well soon card to Humpty Dumpty.*
Assessment focus – I can draw a picture to help me with my writing.
I can tell an adult what I want her/him to write for me.

Strand 5

12. Scrambled words

CLL R Use writing as a means of recording and communicating.
Reception Literacy Objective:
S4 to use a capital letter for the start of own name;
W9 to recognise the critical features of words, e.g. shape, length, and common spelling patterns.
Specific Learning Outcome – to write and spell own name correctly. To write and spell high frequency words correctly.
Group – shared/collaborative.
Resources – name cards and word cards from high frequency list or words linked to particular topics
What to do – before the children enter, select a target word from the Word Wall, e.g. *a child's name*. Copy the name onto another word card. Cut the word card up into its individual letters. Mix the letters up and put them on the Word Wall.
Ask the children to look at the scrambled word. Tell them that it is someone's name. Remind the children that names begin with capital letters. Invite a child to identify the initial letter of the name by looking for the capital letter. Unscramble the word until it looks right – this can be by matching it to the unscrambled word.

Show the children another scrambled name. Let them unscramble it.
Repeat this with one of the high frequency words. This time there will be no capital letter. Select about six high frequency word cards and move them to the work area. Put the scrambled word in the middle of them and ask the children to tell you which letter to put first. Try different combinations of letters until one of the sight words is made.
Variation, differentiation and extension – this activity can be made into a collaborative game away from the Word Wall. Select four high frequency words and write them onto a strip of paper. Choose one of the words and copy it onto a piece of card. Cut the word up and put all the pieces into a sandwich bag. Children have to unscramble the word to make one of the words on the strip. Alternatively put one mixed up sight word per bag for children to unscramble and work out what the word is.
Assessment focus – I can put letters in the right order to make simple words.

Theme 16 Challenging early writing

13. Scrambled sentences

CLL R Write their own names and other things such as labels and captions and begin to form simple sentences, sometimes using punctuation (ELG).
Reception Literacy Objective
S1 to expect written text to make sense and to check for sense if it does not;
S3 that words are ordered left to right and need to be read that way to make sense
W11 through shared writing to understand how writing is formed directionally, a word at a time
Specific Learning Outcome – to be able to sequence words to form a simple sentence
Group – shared/collaborative.
Resources – strips of paper to write simple sentences on.
What to do – select a sentence either from a familiar big book or from something that needs to be written down. Orally rehearse the sentence aloud and think aloud as you model for the children the processes and decisions involved in writing the sentence. Write the sentence onto the strip of paper. Cut the sentence up and scramble the word order. Put the words on the floor and select some children to come and pick up the words. Let the children read the scrambled word order and ask the children to have a go at unscrambling themselves.
Put the words up on the Word Wall in the correct order. Read the sentence together. Ask the children to close their eyes or turn away and remove one of the words. Read the sentence again and ask them what word is missing. Ask them to tell you what letter it starts with, how many letters it has in it, etc. Use some of the Word Wall chants as ways of indicating the shape and composition of the missing word without actually telling you what the word was.
Variation, differentiation and extension – this activity can be made into a collaborative game away from the word wall. Make simple sentences, from nursery rhymes for example, and cut the words up. Children have to reassemble the rhyme, with the words in order. Include a copy of the rhyme or sentences for the children to compare and check. Simple games like this can be made up for children to play at home.
Assessment focus – I can put words in the correct order to make sense because I know that sentences are read from left to right and that a sentence has to make sense.

14. Caption it!

CLL E Extend their vocabulary, exploring the meanings and sounds of new words. **CLL F** Speak clearly and audibly with confidence and control and show awareness of the listener. **CLL R** Write their own names and other things such as labels and captions and begin to form simple sentences, sometimes using punctuation.
Reception Literacy Objectives
T11 through shared writing:
• understand that writing remains constant, i.e. will always 'say' the same thing;
• understand how writing is formed directionally, a word at a time;
• understand how letters are formed to spell words;
• apply knowledge of letter/ sound correspondences in helping the teacher to scribe, and re-read what the class has written.
T12 through guided and independent writing;
• write labels or captions for pictures and drawings;
• write sentences to match pictures or sequences of pictures.
T13 to think about and discuss what they intend to write, before writing it;

Specific Learning Outcomes – to speak in and begin to write simple sentences.
Group – shared/guided.
Resources – a bag with a collection of common objects from around the setting. A whiteboard and pen or strips of paper.
What to do – sit the children in a circle. Demonstrate a sentence that you would like the children to use by reaching into the bag and taking out an object. Carefully say to the children for example 'The puppy is brown'. Write on the board 'The puppy is brown'. Rub out 'puppy' and 'brown' to leave 'The _____ is _____'. Reach into the bag and take out another object and use the same structure sentence to describe it, e.g. 'The bird is small'.
Now pass the bag round the group and let children take objects out and describe them using the same sentence structure. Write their sentences up on the board or onto strips of paper.
Variation, differentiation and extension – this activity can be done with lots of different simple sentence constructions, e.g. 'I don't like the _____ because_____.'
Assessment focus – I can say a simple sentence with a given structure.

15. Colourful sentences (1)

CLL E Extend their vocabulary, exploring the meanings and sounds of new words. **CLL F** Speak clearly and audibly with confidence and control and show awareness of the listener. **CLL R** Write their own names and other things such as labels and captions and begin to form simple sentences, sometimes using punctuation.

Reception Literacy Objectives
T12 through guided and independent writing;
• write labels or captions for pictures and drawings;
• write sentences to match pictures or sequences of pictures.
T13 to think about and discuss what they intend to write, before writing it;

Strand 5

Specific Learning Outcomes – to write simple sentences with a given structure.
Group – guided.
Resources – Copymaster 60. Coloured paper.
What to do – photocopy the word classes onto the appropriate colour of paper. Enlarge and make a class set. Make a set of coloured large dots on a board in front of the children. The order should be blue, green, red, yellow, black. (Blue=determiners, green=nouns, red=verbs, yellow=adjectives, black=punctuation.) Give out the cards to the children and ask them to 'Get up and go!'. They need to make themselves into groups of five in the order shown and they should make some simple sentences, some of which will make more sense than others!
Variation, differentiation and extension – use the same colour coding and ask the children to brainstorm lists of nouns to write onto green cards and adjectives to write onto yellow cards. Try some other determiners such as 'a/an', 'that/this' etc. Play again with this new set of cards.
Assessment focus – I can make a simple sentence using a given structure.

---

16. Colourful sentences (2)

CLL E Extend their vocabulary, exploring the meanings and sounds of new words. **CLL F** Speak clearly and audibly with confidence and control and show awareness of the listener. **CLL R** Write their own names and other things such as labels and captions and begin to form simple sentences, sometimes using punctuation.
Reception Literacy Objectives:
T12 through guided and independent writing;
• write labels or captions for pictures and drawings;
• write sentences to match pictures or sequences of pictures.
T13 to think about and discuss what they intend to write, before writing it;
Specific Learning Outcomes – to write simple sentences with a given structure.
Group – guided.
Resources – Copymasters 60 and 61. Coloured paper and coloured pens. Blu-tack. Paper and pencils.
What to do – follow on from the previous activity. Photocopy the word classes onto the appropriate colour of paper. Prepare Copymaster 61 by colouring in the dots in the appropriate colour and order of blue, green, red, yellow. These dots are for the children to match the coloured paper strips on and to stick on with Blu-tak. Explain to the children that they have to order the words and match them in the order that you will show them.
Demonstrate what to do by spreading all the words out in front of you and picking up a blue word to match to the first blue dot. Read the word and stick it down. Pick up a green word, read it and stick it down after the blue word. Continue with the red, then yellow word and end with the punctuation mark on the white paper. Re-read the sentence aloud and explain that you are ready to copy the sentence. Write the sentence underneath. Support the children as they undertake the activity. Encourage them to read the sentence aloud both whilst they are making the sentence and when they have made it.
Variation, differentiation and extension – use the same colour coding but let children make up their own sets of nouns and adjectives to add into the collection. Once set up, this can become an independent activity. If all the pieces are laminated the game will last.
Assessment focus – I can compose and write a simple sentence using a given structure.

---

17. Ketchup on your cornflakes

CLL E Extend their vocabulary, exploring the meanings and sounds of new words. **CLL F** Speak clearly and audibly with confidence and control and show awareness of the listener. **CLL R** Write their own names and other things such as labels and captions and begin to form simple sentences, sometimes using punctuation.
Reception Literacy Objectives
T12 through guided and independent writing;
• write labels or captions for pictures and drawings;
• write sentences to match pictures or sequences of pictures.
T13 to think about and discuss what they intend to write, before writing it.
Specific Learning Outcomes – to write and explore simple sentences with a given structure.
Group – guided.
Resources – the book *Ketchup on your Cornflakes?* by Nick Sharrat. Copymaster 62.
What to do – look at the book *Ketchup on your Cornflakes?* and explore some of the funny combinations possible, e.g. *Baked beans in your bath tub?*
Explain to the children that you are going to make a book like this.
Use the writing frame on Copymaster 62 and show them what will happen when several are collected together and cut in half to make a book.
Variation, differentiation and extension.
1 Make similar books by splitting interesting sentences like this.
2 Try some extended sentences or different word orders on strips of paper. For example, make a set of cards using the following sentence structure: *The grey elephant was swimming slowly.*
Shuffle the cards up. Let children pick a set of cards in a certain order and draw a picture to go with the sentence that they copy.
Assessment focus – I understand when a sentence does not make sense.

Theme 16 Challenging early writing

18. Drama Day (Using drama as a starting point for writing)

CLL E Extend their vocabulary, exploring the meanings and sounds of new words. **CLL F** Speak clearly and audibly with confidence and control and show awareness of the listener. **CLL R** Write their own names and other things such as labels and captions and begin to form simple sentences, sometimes using punctuation. **CLL K** Use their phonic knowledge to write simple regular words and make phonetically plausible attempts at more complex words.

Reception Literacy Objective
T7 to use knowledge of familiar texts to re-enact or to re-tell to others, recounting the main points in correct sequence
T12 through guided and independent writing
- experiment with writing in a variety of play, exploratory and role-play situations;
- write their own names; to write labels or captions for pictures and drawings;
- write sentences to match pictures or sequences of pictures;
- experiment with writing and recognise how their version matches and differs from convention version, e.g. through teacher response and transcription.

W14 to write letters using the correct sequence of movements.

Specific Learning Outcome – begin to write simple narratives and recounts, dictate and invent own compositions. To think about what to write before writing it.

Group – shared/guided and collaborative.
Resources – Copymaster 63.
What to do – discuss what the routine of a typical day is, e.g. getting up and having breakfast, going to school, doing some work, lunchtime, afternoon session, playing after school, going to bed.

Act out using drama the events and routines for this pattern. Prompt the children to think of a character other than themselves that they are going to pretend to be.

Explore different scenarios e.g. *My happy day – the character is really happy and good things happen all day.*

My lucky day – lucky things happen at each point through the day.
My bad day – problems and unlucky things happen all day.
Using shared writing write the following frame up on the board:
_____'s bad day by _____
At breakfast_____
On the way to school _____
In _____
At lunchtime_____
In the afternoon_____
After school_____
At bedtime_____

This should be used to model a bad day based upon one of the children's retellings. They could act out each part of the day, before the telling you the sentence that goes with the drama freeze frame. Orally rehearse the sentence before demonstrating to the children how to write the sentence. Each freeze frame might have one or two captioning sentences. The first sentence can be constructed by using the supporting connective phrases, e.g. *Sarah's bad day by Tamara. At breakfast Sarah spilled her milk over the table. She lost her book bag and said 'This is going to be a bad day!' On the way to school Sarah got lost and was very late. In maths Sarah got all the sums wrong. The teacher said 'You are having a bad day!'.*

Children should develop their own versions based on their drama. For each page they can draw a picture and caption using one or two sentences as modelled by you. Remind them to rehearse the sentence before they write it. These books can be read and shared during review or plenary sessions.

Variation, differentiation and extension – use this kind of format to develop other simple recount and narrative sequence frames. They can be added to the class library of books for reading. The text could be word processed to develop class big books or take-home books.

Assessment focus – I can write a sentence to go with a picture.
I can write a story and talk about my ideas.
I can draw a picture to help me with my writing.
I can tell my teacher what I want him/her to write for me.

19. Story faces ('I am feeling … because')

CLL E Extend their vocabulary, exploring the meanings and sounds of new words. **CLL F** Speak clearly and audibly with confidence and control and show awareness of the listener. **CLL R** Write their own names and other things such as labels and captions and begin to form simple sentences, sometimes using punctuation. **CLL K** Use their phonic knowledge to write simple regular words and make phonetically plausible attempts at more complex words.

Reception Literacy Objective
T12 through guided and independent writing
- write their own names; to write labels or captions for pictures and drawings;
- write sentences to match pictures or sequences of pictures;
- experiment with writing and recognise how their version matches and differs from convention version, e.g. through teacher response and transcription.

W14 to write letters using the correct sequence of movements

Specific Learning Outcome – dictate and invent own compositions.
Think about what to write ahead of writing it.
Use experience and drawing as a basis for writing and understand the difference between drawing and writing.
Group – guided.
Resources – Copymaster 64. Mirrors; a tape-recorder or Dictaphone.
What to do – *Physical feelings:* Sit the children in a

Strand 5

space. Model some physical effects of being in different settings and situations *e.g. pretend you are shivering and that you are really cold*. Prompt the children to guess where you are and why you might be so cold. Let them pretend they are really cold, walking round talking in a shivery voice and rubbing themselves. When you say 'freeze frame' the children should stand stationary. Walk in amongst them and ask them why they are so cold, where they are, how they got there, what they think they will do next etc. If you have a Dictaphone, tape some of these sentences. Explore some other feelings, *e.g. really hot, really wet, etc*.

Emotional feelings: Sit the children in a circle with a mirror between pairs of children. Tell them to look carefully at your face. Model an expression such as a really angry face, a happy face, a sad face, a shocked face etc. Prompt the children to suggest how you are feeling and what might have made you feel like that. Let them ask you questions (this works well when another adult is prompting the children to question you). Let the children copy some of your expressions and look at themselves in the mirrors.

Suggest an emotion, e.g *You are feeling....really angry*!, and pass a pebble around the circle to start a circle chant. The children have to show that emotion with their face. They can practise in the mirror. When the child gets the pebble they say: '*I am feeling really angry because*'. Explore a range of emotions in this way. Use an enlarged copy of Copymaster 9 to model drawing an expression on a face. Model looking in the mirror at your own expression *e.g. show a really scared face, wide eyes, wide mouth and emphasise this in your drawing, e.g. draw your eyebrows raised and wrinkles on the forehead, caricature the expression by talking about how scared you are, and draw your hair standing on end etc*. Ask the children for suggestions as to why you were so scared. And then tell them, alternatively do the same but with an extremely happy and laughing face – why were you so happy? Explain that you are drawing the picture but that you are writing the words, forming letters and spelling words, using the strategies children have been taught elsewhere.

Let the children experiment with facial expressions and fill in Copymaster 9 by drawing a detailed picture of their expression and then explaining why they felt like this. Constrain the choices available to the children the first few times they undertake this activity, *e.g. ask them all to do a happy face rather than letting them choose their face*. Guide the children by prompting them to put more detail into their picture, using line texture, exaggeration and to talk about the picture as they draw it. Once the face is drawn let them discuss what has prompted this strong feeling and they can draw this inside the folded Copymaster 64. Remind the children of the strategies to support independence in their writing.

Let children share their booklets and writing with the group. Talk about the differences between drawing and writing.

Variation, differentiation and extension – once children are familiar with this activity, it can form an independent activity in the writing area. It can also be used to explore character feelings at significant points in stories.

Assessment focus – I know that I draw pictures and spell words to write.
I can draw a picture to help me with my writing.
I can tell my teacher what I want her to write for me.
I can write a sentence to go with a picture.
I can write a story and talk about my ideas.

---

20. Consequences (verb pictures) Day 1 and 2

CLL E Extend their vocabulary, exploring the meanings and sounds of new words. **CLL F** Speak clearly and audibly with confidence and control and show awareness of the listener. **CLL R** Write their own names and other things such as labels and captions and begin to form simple sentences, sometimes using punctuation. **CLL K** Use their phonic knowledge to write simple regular words and make phonetically plausible attempts at more complex words.

Reception Literacy Objective
T12 through guided and independent writing
* write their own names; to write labels or captions for pictures and drawings;
* write sentences to match pictures or sequences of pictures;
* experiment with writing and recognise how their version matches and differs from convention version, *e.g. through teacher response and transcription*.

W14 to write letters using the correct sequence of movements.

Specific Learning Outcome – to use experience and drawing as a basis for writing To think about what to write ahead of writing it. Dictate and invent own compositions Group – guided.
Resources – Copymasters 65 and 66.

What to do – prepare a number of action words (verbs), *e.g. running, throwing, chasing, falling, catching, giving*, by writing them on cards. Prompt the children by miming the action, *e.g. throwing or running*. Explore different intensities of each verb, *e.g. running, walking*, and directions and prepositions, *e.g. from, to, on, off, below*. Enlarge Copymaster 65 and fold in half so only the left hand side is visible to the children. Model drawing a picture of a target action on the left hand side of Copymaster 65, *e.g. running*.

In this example the person running should be headed left (away from the fold in the centre of the paper). Model the dialogue you have with yourself as you draw the picture, explaining how you draw the figure and how you put in the detail and add texture to the drawing. Let the children draw a similar picture. Ensure that the figure they draw is headed away from the fold.

Theme 16 Challenging early writing

Revisit the action words but encourage the children to think about what is causing the action or what will happen as a result of the action. *E.g. Throwing – who are you throwing to? What is being thrown? Where is this all happening? Running – what are you running away from? What is chasing you?*
Return to Copymaster 65, unfold it and draw a picture of what is chasing the person. Add details into the background. Explain that you are drawing lines to make the picture.
Model rehearsing aloud the sentence that will caption the picture. Show the children how you write this sentence using the shared writing strategies. Explain that you are spelling the words in order to write.
Ask the children to talk to their friend to share what they were running away from, then share the ideas with the class. Ask the children to rehearse the sentence that they will use to caption the picture with a friend and let some children share their sentences.
Let the children draw their pictures and caption the pictures with their own sentences.

21. Consequences Day 3 and 4

Objectives and resources outlined above.
Revisit the action words and let children act out their scenarios. Children should work in pairs. Let them think about what happened after this and act this out.
Return to Copymaster 65, fold it in half again, so that the picture is in the middle. On what is now the back of a small booklet draw a picture to illustrate what happened next. Model the writing of a sentence to caption this picture. Let children work on the resolution of their action in the booklets that they have been making.

Look at the booklets that have been made. Discuss what might have happened just before the scene in the centre of the booklet. What made this happen? How did you come to be there? Where are you? Prompt children to work in pairs to act out their scenarios from beginning to end. Let pairs of children show the class the stories they have made up. Children could use the story telling mask to retell their story.
Return to Copymaster 65. Model drawing the picture that precedes the action in the centre spread. Rehearse the sentence that sets the scene for the action that will follow. Let children work on their booklets.

Children should have an opportunity to share their storybooks with friends and other children in the class. They could form part of the class library.

Variation, differentiation and extension – once children are familiar with this format they can be introduced to Copymaster 66. They should be introduced to the idea that this book tells what happened in the past, as opposed to what is happening now, in the present tense (the difference between 'I was' and 'I am'). Once children have worked through this structure and are familiar with it, they can use the four-page booklet as a way of structuring simple narrative events. They should work through them from beginning, to action in the middle, and resolution at the end. This booklet can be used as a resource for independent activity in a writing area. Copymaster 66 can be given to the children to take and use at home.

Assessment focus –
I know that I draw pictures and spell words to write.
I can draw a picture to help me with my writing.
I can tell my teacher what I want him or her to write for me.
I can write a sentence to go with a picture.
I can write a story and talk about my ideas.

22. Information and communication technology

CLL L Explore and experiment with sounds, words and texts. **CLL K** Use their phonic knowledge to write simple regular words and make phonetically plausible attempts at more complex words. **CLL Q** Attempt writing for different purposes, using features of different forms such as lists, stories and instructions
Reception Literacy Objectives
T12 through guided and independent writing;
• experiment with writing in a variety of play, exploratory and role-play situations;
• experiment with writing and recognise how their own version matches and differs from conventional version, e.g. through practitioner response and transcription;
T15 to use writing to communicate in a variety of ways, incorporating it into play and everyday classroom life, e.g. recounting their own experiences, lists, signs, directions, menus, labels, greeting cards, letters
Specific Learning Outcomes – to be able to use a keyboard and a mouse to enter and manipulate text and writing.
Group – guided.
Resources – a range of appropriate software; computer.
Suggestions:

Strand 5

Talking word processor Pre-configured texts to be read to children	Dictation practice – child dictates from a simple story to another child who has to type up the story without seeing the book. Let the talking word processor read the story back. Compare pronunciation and spellings.	Use talking storybook software to interact with a multimedia story
Find information out from an interactive CD-ROM	Type up text written and drafted elsewhere	Create environmental print to contribute to room labelling or Word Wall work.
Teacher has created simple sentences on tiles but they are jumbled up, children have to unjumble (Clicker screens, especially Clicker Literacy screens)	Starspell computer programme to practise spellings of letter combinations	My World story screens to provide interactive story environments to aid retellings
Picture sequencing	Instruction and barrier games One child has already made a picture and printed it out. Instructs another child by giving oral instructions. Compare to original.	Teacher has created text but sentences are jumbled up, e.g. a nursery rhyme. Children have to unjumble, sequence and print out to compare to original.
Touch typing software	Language games and vocabulary games.	Use drop down menus in art programme etc....

Assessment focus

I know where the letter keys on the keyboard are and I can enter text.

Theme 17) Early motor skills and handwriting

Early Learning Goals for Handwriting
Reception Literacy Objectives for Handwriting

CLL S Use a pencil and hold it effectively to form recognisable letters, most of which are correctly formed.
W12 to use a comfortable and efficient pencil grip;
W13 to produce a controlled line which supports letter formation;
W14 to write letters using the correct sequence of movements

1. Motor Skill Moments

CLL S Engage in activities requiring hand-eye co-ordination, Use one-handed tools and equipment (yellow), Draw lines and circles using gross motor movement, Manipulate objects with increasing control (blue).
Specific Learning Outcome – To develop Motor skills and co-ordination of whole-body Gross Motor skills and hand/ finger Fine Motor Skills.
Group – shared, guided, collaborative and independent.
Resources – As specified
Suggestions:

Cutting out activities. Draw wavy lines and cut out using scissors.	Jigsaws, puzzles, picture matching.	Sequencing and matching games and activities, snap, alphabetical order games etc.
Modelling materials- Clay, plasticine, play dough, edible dough	Kinaesthetic – drawing on backs, drawing on boards,	Feely bags with tactile and unusual shaped objects inside.
Letter shapes and tactile letters	Sewing cards	Threading beads onto laces to make patters.
Painting/printing Shape/ mark making with water etc. Finger painting	Unusual textures e.g. 'gloop' – cornflour, water and paint in trays.	Decorative patterns in paint and water – spirals and waves etc.
Drawing – pictures to match texts; Details in pictures include textures	Sticks with ribbons on the end for skywriting	Nursery rhymes and finger rhymes
Finger Puppets	Computer with appropriate software – keyboard skills, mouse co-ordination.	Treasure hunt for letters and objects to match initial letter in sand.
Sandwriting with fingers and tools for mark making and textures in sand.	Small construction toys and equipment. Small world figures and trains and vehicles.	Could include activities from the visual/auditory/tactile activities and games and games from the Progression in Phonics:
Chopsticks and tweezers – picking up small objects and moving them with chopsticks develops the tripod grip.	Glue and sand pictures. Put the glue onto the picture and sprinkle sand, glitter etc. to make pictures. Practises finger thumb grip.	Washing liquid bottles full of water to squirt large shapes and patterns onto floors and walls on a hot day.
Draw very large shapes onto the playground with chalk for children to run around.	Turn all the lights out and use torches to make shapes on the walls and ceiling.	Marbles and marble runs, pick up sticks, domino runs etc.
Collage pictures	Paper folding and Sellotape	Cooking activities

Variation, differentiation and extension –
As appropriate to match the needs of individuals. Children may use both hands through the Foundation Stage, but most children will have a preferred hand by the end of Foundation 2. Where possible, gently introduce children to the tripod grip for holding tools as appropriate and certainly as they begin to use mark-making tools.

Assessment focus –
I have good control of my gross and fine motor movements.

Strand 6

2. Brain Workout

CLL S Engage in activities requiring hand-eye co-ordination (yellow). Draw lines and circles using gross motor movements (blue). Begin to use anticlockwise movement and retrace vertical lines (green).
Specific Learning Outcomes – To build gross motor skills and hand-eye co-ordination through multi-sensory co-ordinated movements.
Group – shared, guided.
Resources – Copymaster 67 – Brain Workout prompt poster.

What to do –
Use the directions on the Brain Workout poster to encourage children to exercise and develop hand-eye and body co-ordination. These exercises also give the brain a refreshing break and work out and are good to re-energise children when concentration starts to lapse.
Variation, differentiation and extension – n/a.
Assessment focus –
I can co-ordinate my body with Brain Workout exercises.

3. The Three Letter Roots

CLL S Begin to use anticlockwise movement and retrace vertical lines.
Reception Literacy Objectives
W12 to use a comfortable and efficient pencil grip;
W13 to produce a controlled line which supports letter formation;
W14 to write letters using the correct sequence of movements.
Specific Learning Outcome – To learn to form the three basic movements for letter formation.
Group – Guided.
Resources – Suggestions from motor skill moments (previous activity). Copymaster 68.
What to do – it is useful to establish these three shapes (l, c, r) with children using some of the gross and fine motor movements from the previous activity. They are referred to in the National Literacy strategy as 'l = the long ladder', 'c = the curly caterpillar', 'r = the one arm robot'.

These rhymes or variations of them are helpful to introduce to the children to help them begin to have the language to talk about letter formation. The rhymes are on Copymaster 68.
Variation, differentiation and extension –
There is no need to introduce formal handwriting worksheets to young children. Use opportunities in paint, sand and with mark making tools to reinforce basic shapes without referring to them as letters. E.g. 'Draw the wheels on this very long lorry.'
Try and gently encourage children to adopt the tripod grip, holding the pencil between the thumb and forefinger with the pencil resting on the third finger, but don't force this on children, as they need to be gradually introduced to it. Pencil grips and triangular pencils can help if their use is checked to see if they are being used properly. Also check children are not gripping the pencil; too tightly.
Assessment focus –
I can form the Three Basic Shapes.

Theme 18 — Developing motor skills and handwriting

4. Snake letters/snake letter snacks

CLL J Hear and say the initial sound in words and know which letters represent some of the sounds.
CLL S Begin to form recognisable letters.
Reception Literacy Objective:
W2 Read letter(s) that represent(s) the sounds: a-z, ch, sh, th;
W2 Write each letter in response to each sound: a-z, ch, sh, th;
W14 to 'write' letters using the correct sequence of movements.
Specific Learning Outcome – to learn the correct formation of lower case letters.
Group – guided.
Resources – plasticine, playdough, edible dough. Copymaster 69.
What to do – let the children experiment with the dough or plasticine. Let them explore rolling out long thin sausages and exploring what shapes they can make with these 'snaking sausages'. Can they make a circle and some other shapes?
Enlarge Copymaster 69 and cut out to select the letters for the focus of the session. Talk about the name of the letter and the sound (phoneme) that corresponds to the letter. Tell the children to put their finger onto the eye of the snake and to track down and round the snake's body to form the letter.
Let the children roll out the plasticine or dough to make long thin sausage snakes. Form the snake into the shape of the letter. These could be laid onto the letter templates if they are laminated. Put a head and an eye onto the snake. Track your finger down the snake's body. Choose and make another letter.
Variation, differentiation and extension –
if snakes are made from dough they can be baked and eaten! Make the sound of the letter as you eat it. Eat the letters in your name !
Assessment focus – I can correctly form the letters of the alphabet.

5. Feely letters

CLL J Hear and say the initial sound in words and know which letters represent some of the sounds.
CLL S Begin to form recognisable letters
Reception Literacy Objective:
W2 Read letter(s) that represent(s) the sounds: a-z, ch, sh, th;
W2 Write each letter in response to each sound: a-z, ch, sh, th;
W14 to 'write' letters using the correct sequence of movements.
Specific Learning Outcome – to learn the correct formation of lower case letters.
Group – guided.
Resources – Water, washing up liquid bottles (empty), gloop (cornflour, water and paint), paint, collage materials and glue. Copymaster 69.
What to do – enlarge Copymaster 69 and cut out to select the letters for the focus of the session. Talk about the name of the letter and the sound (phoneme) that corresponds to the letter. Tell the children to put their finger onto the eye of the snake and to track down and round the snake's body to form the letter.
Outside, on a warm dry day, fill the empty washing up liquid bottles with water and let children squirt letter shapes onto the playground. Reinforce the phoneme that goes with each letter as they make the mark.
Make up some 'gloop' using corn flour, water and a bit of paint for colour. Let the children make letter like shapes in the gloop. Laminate the snake letters and put them in the bottom of the gloop tray. Let the children to trace the letter.
Enlarge the snake letters on Copymaster 69 and cut them out. Ask children to paint glue onto the letter and sprinkle sand onto the glue to make tactile letters. Alternatively, other collage materials could be used to make the letters tactile when dry. Put the feely letters into a bag or box. Children have to identify the phoneme/letter by feeling the letter.
Variation, differentiation and extension – mix up some paint. Use a surface such as a tray/ table or large piece of plastic. Provide some small pots with which to pour the paint. One child has a letter snake and instructs another child by telling them, for example, to 'start at the top, pour down, back up a little and round'. The child pouring the paint compares the paint trail with the letter snake. Try another letter and swap over.
The above could also be done with the washing up water bottles.
Assessment focus – I can form the letters of the alphabet correctly.
I know which phoneme goes with which letter.

Copymaster 1

Share and tell circle prompts

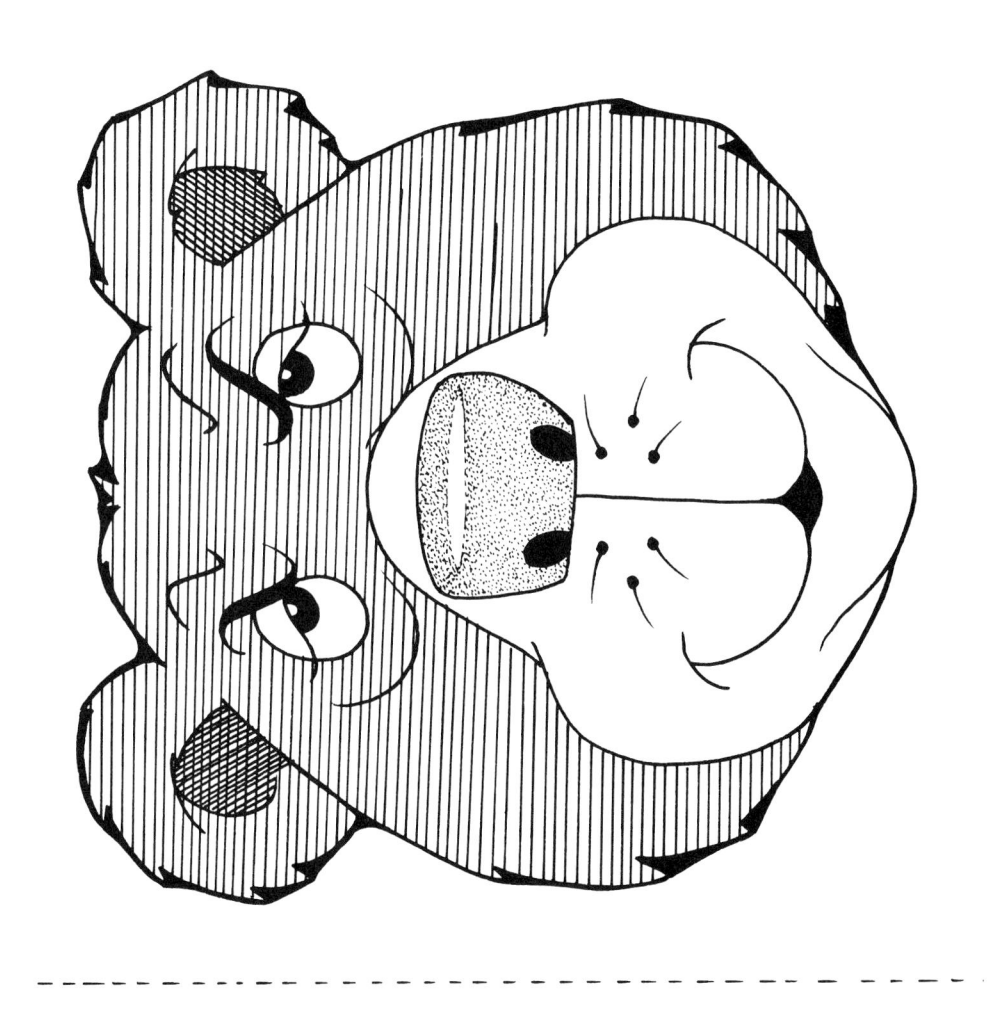

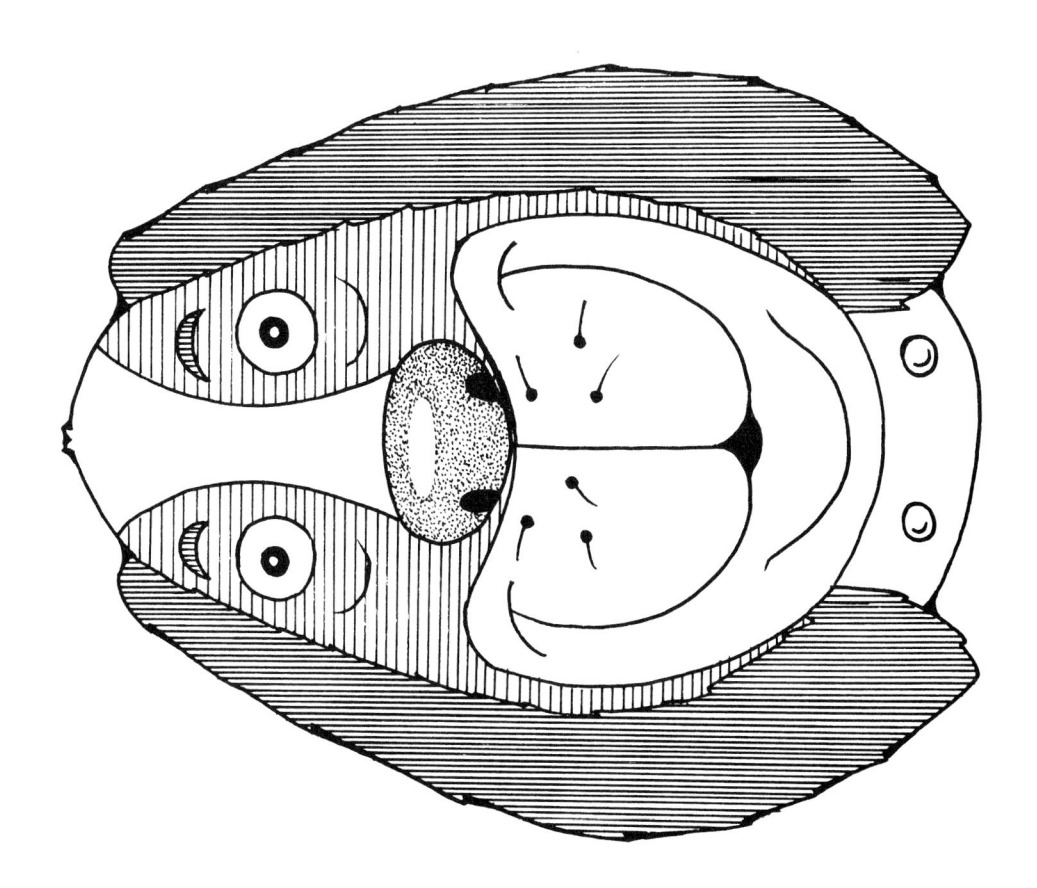

75

Copymaster 2

Group observation sheet

Date: Activity:

> Key:
> ✓ hand up ⊘ hand up and asked a question
> ▽ prompted to ask a question ▼ prompted to ask a question and asked a question
> | question was relevant — question not relevant

Name	Contribution code	Questions	Descriptive language offered	Notes

Copymaster 3

The story-telling mask

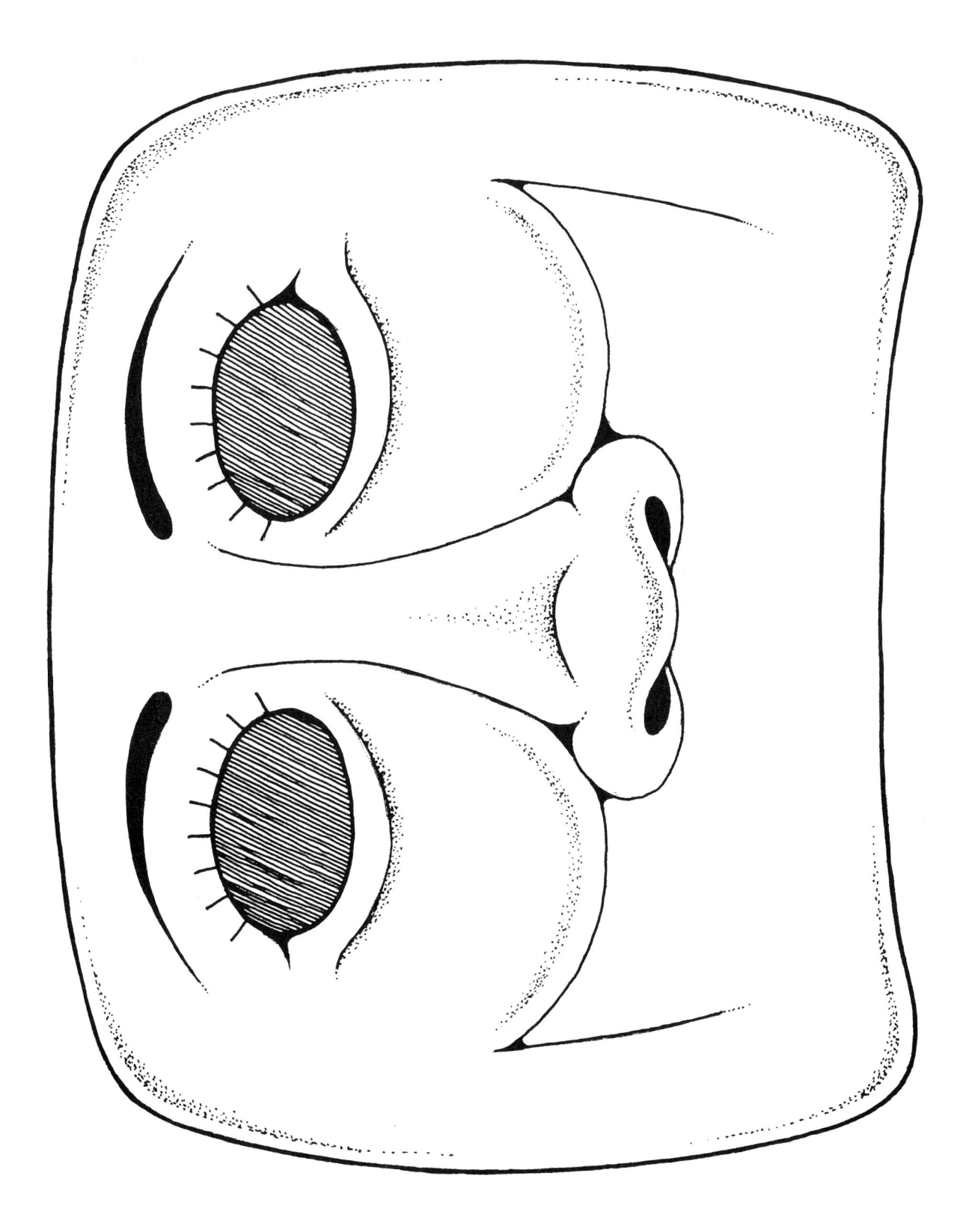

77

Copymaster 4

Star Child Reward Vouchers

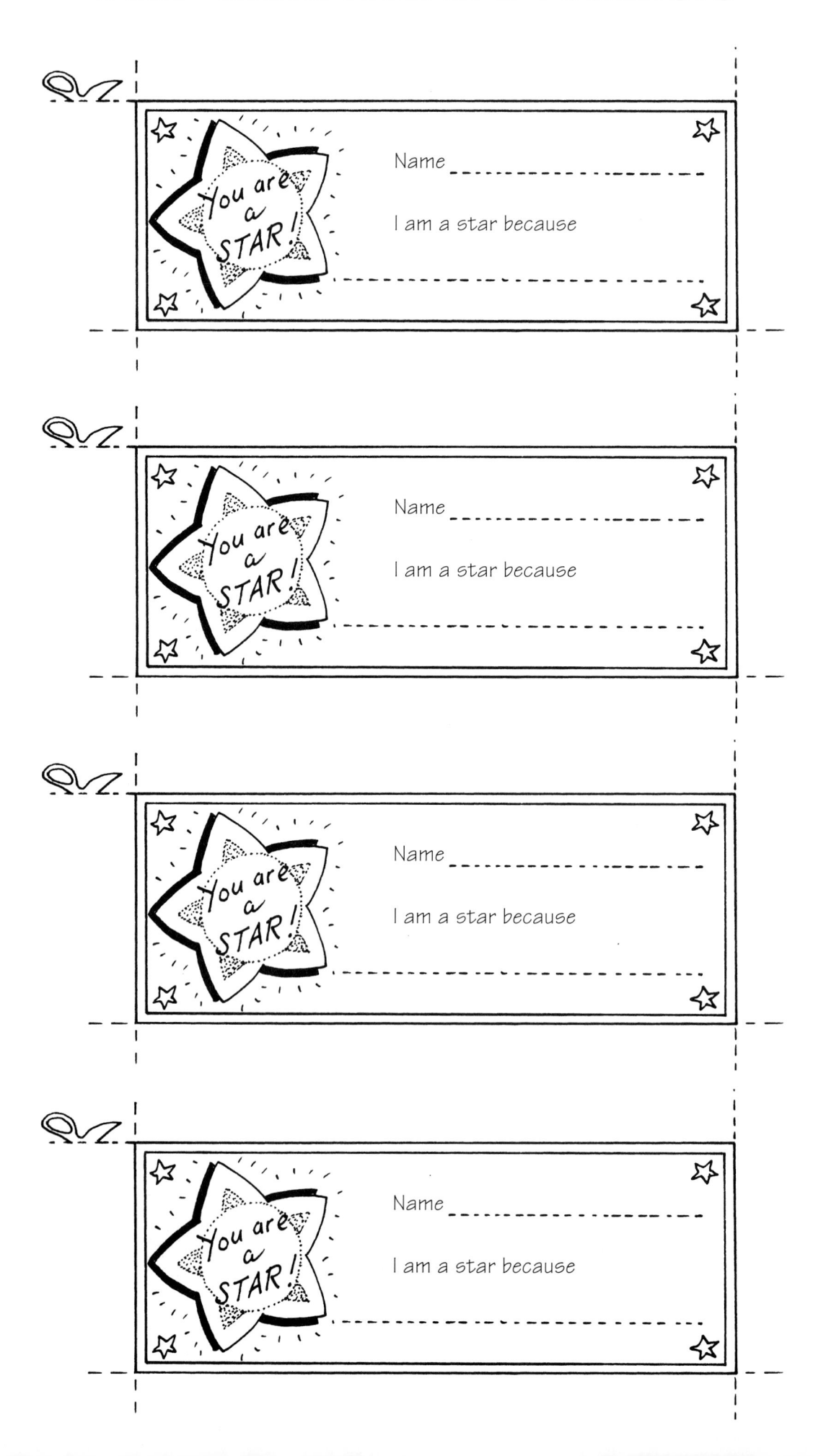

You are a STAR!

Name _____

I am a star because _____

You are a STAR!

Name _____

I am a star because _____

You are a STAR!

Name _____

I am a star because _____

You are a STAR!

Name _____

I am a star because _____

Copymaster 5

What has Mr Sock been up to?

What did Mr Sock do wrong?

How can he do it right?

Copymaster 6

Share and tell circle prompts

What would you like to know about it?

I could improve it by ....

This is a ....

It looks like ....

It can ....

I made it by ....

The best thing about it is ....

First I ....
Then I ....
Finally I ....

It was difficult to .... but I ....

Tell us your news

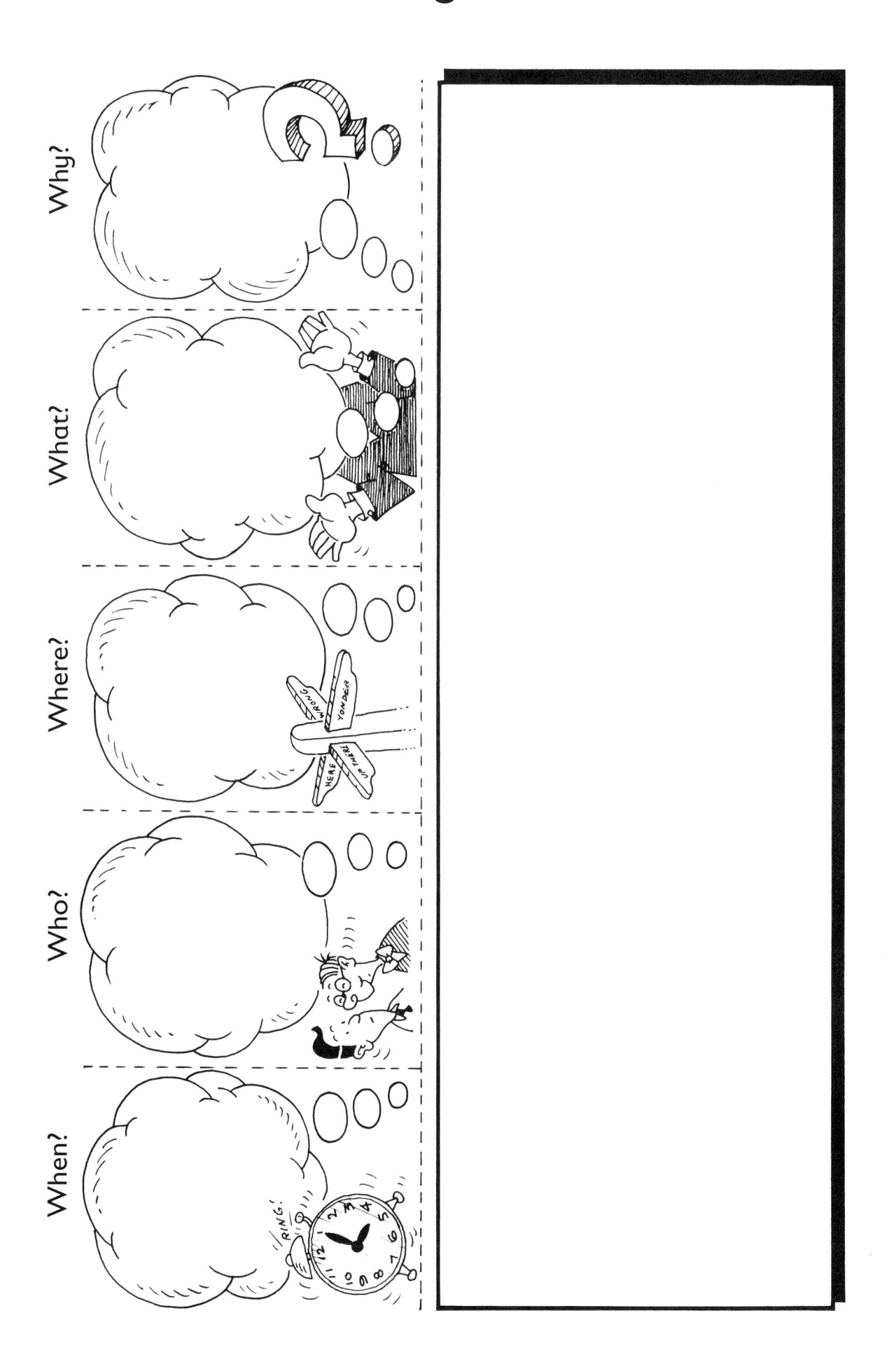

Why?

What?

Where?

Who?

When?

Copymaster 7

Copymaster 8

What comes next?

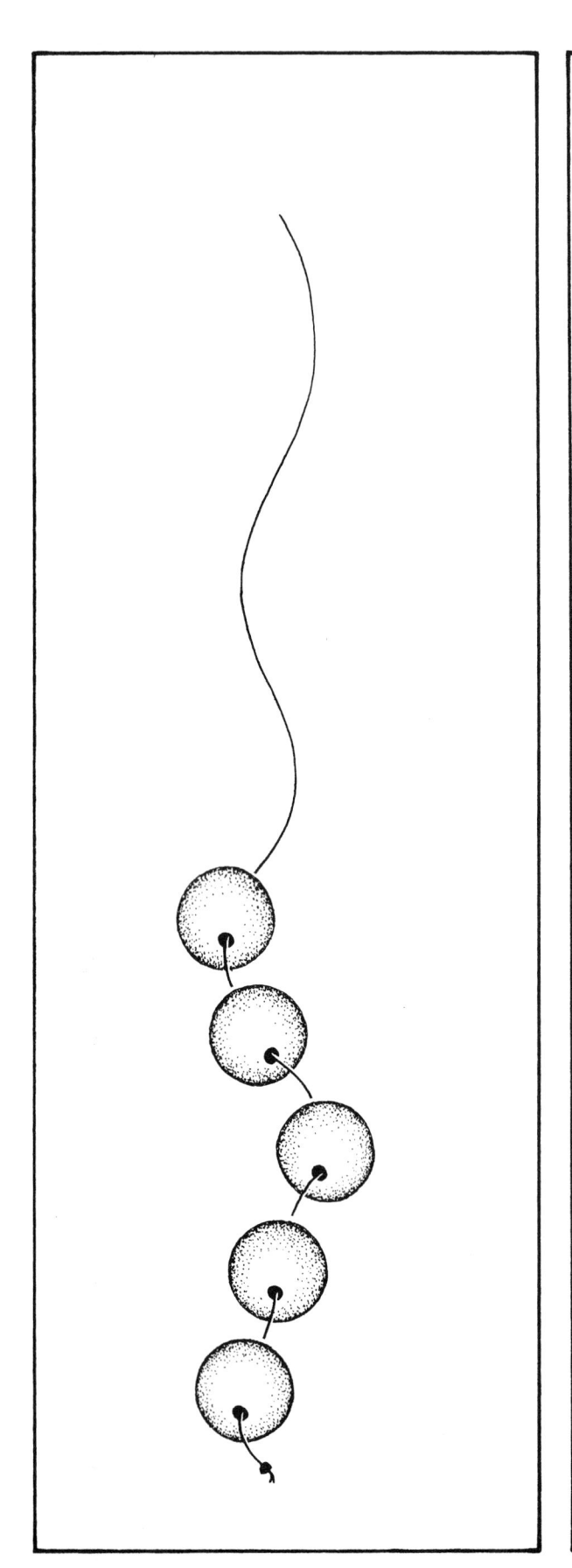

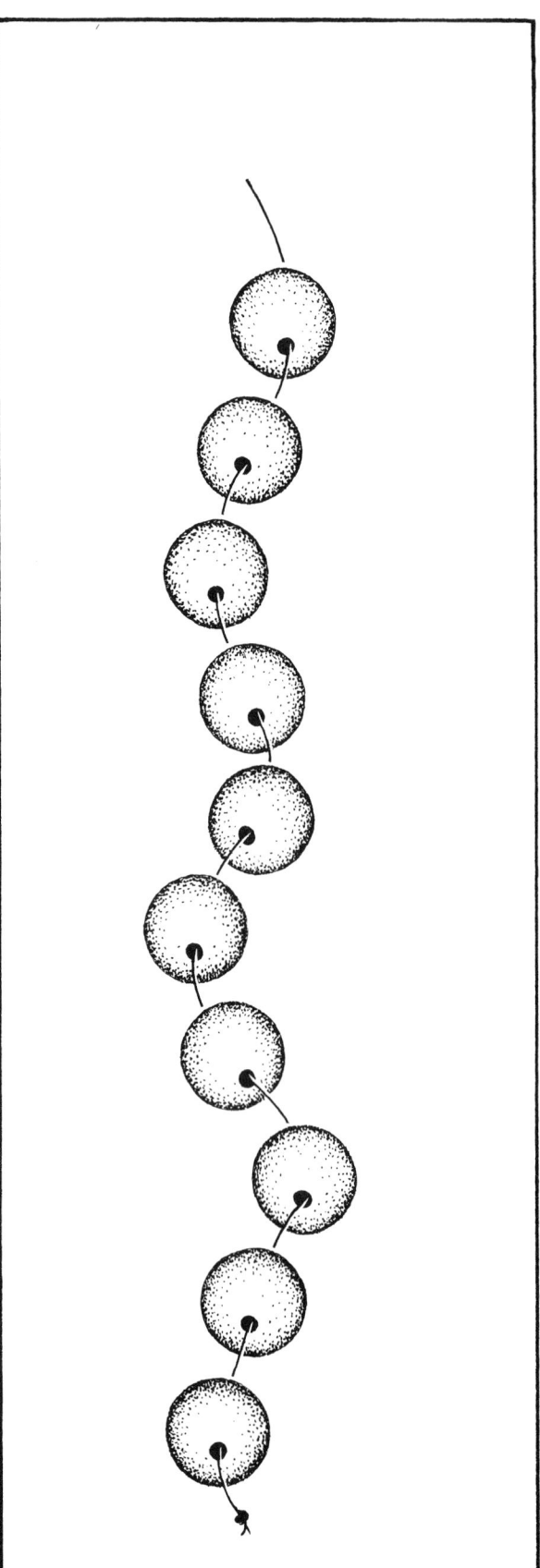

82

Copymaster 9

Funny face

Copymaster 10

Face parts

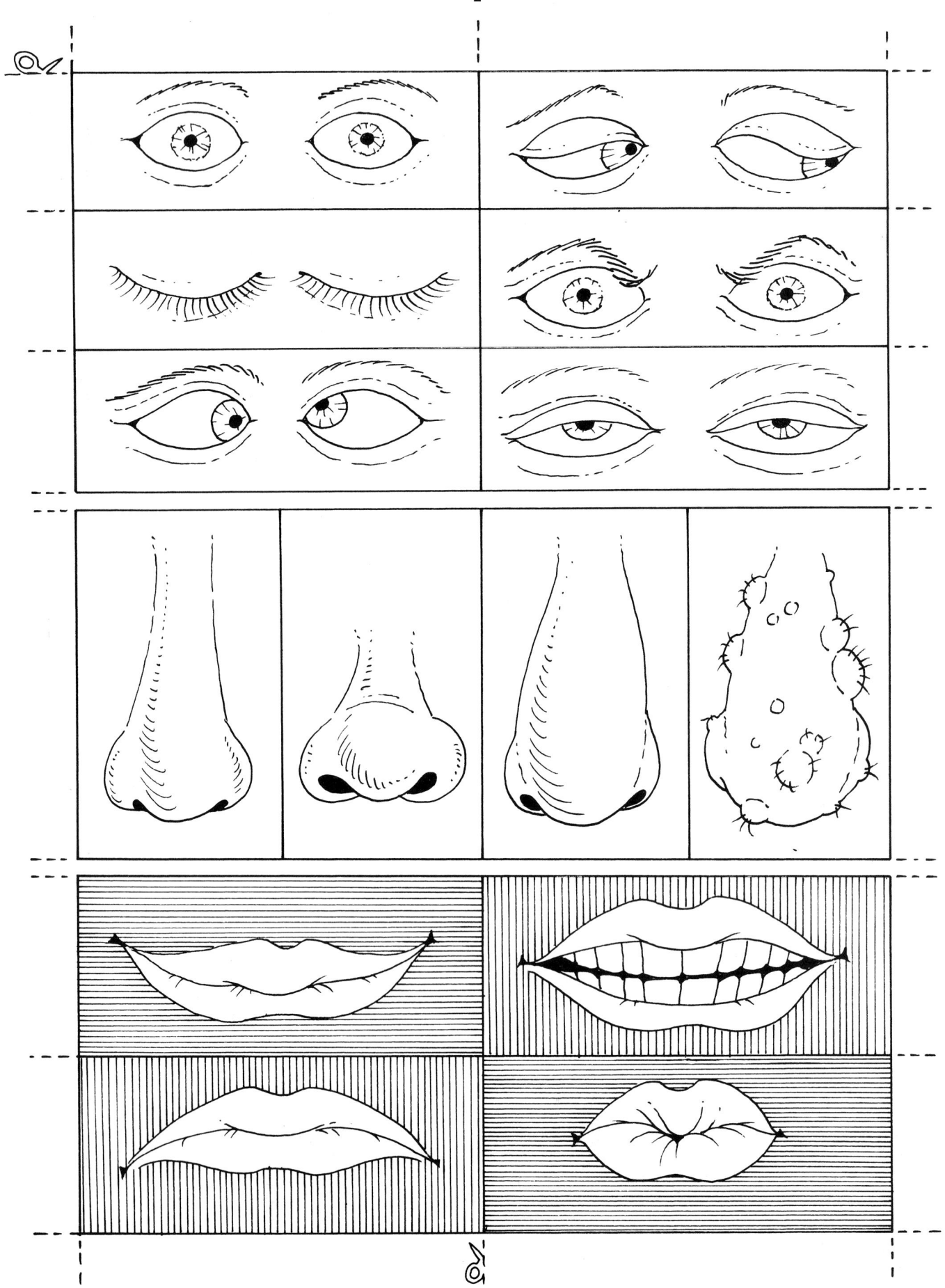

84

Copymaster 11

Crazy creature background

Copymaster 12

Crazy creature parts

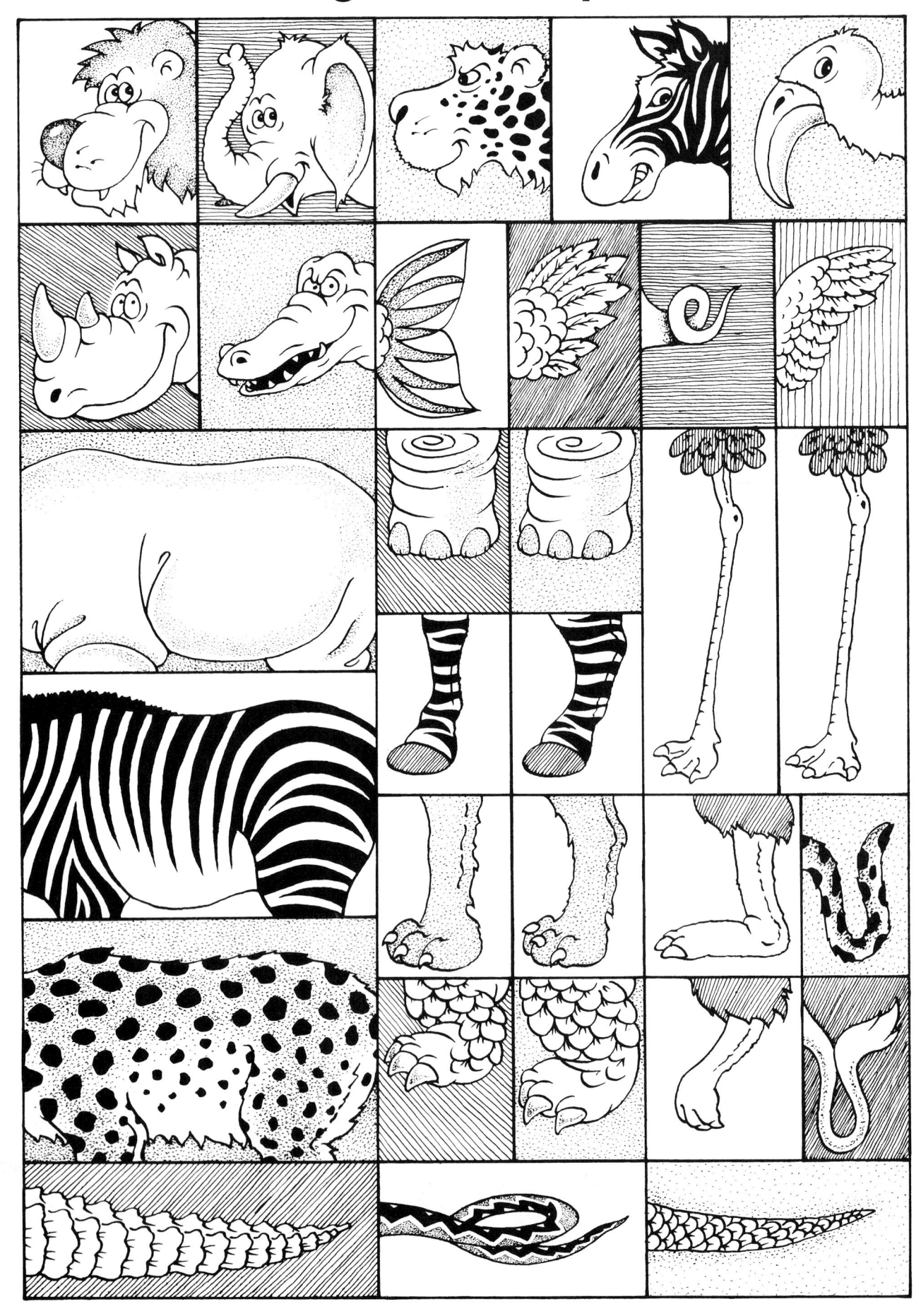

Copymaster 13

Where in the house?

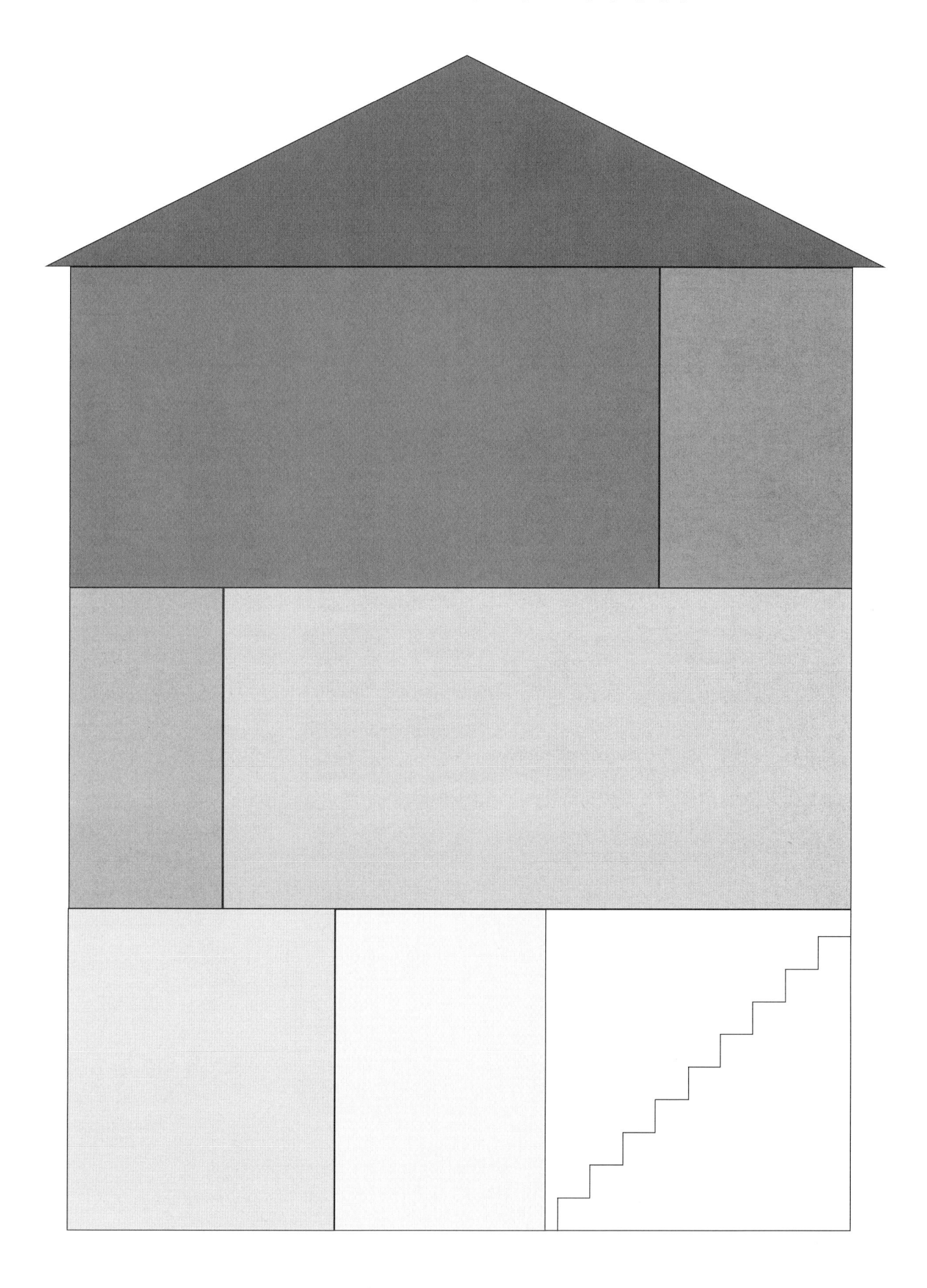

87

Copymaster 14

House furniture

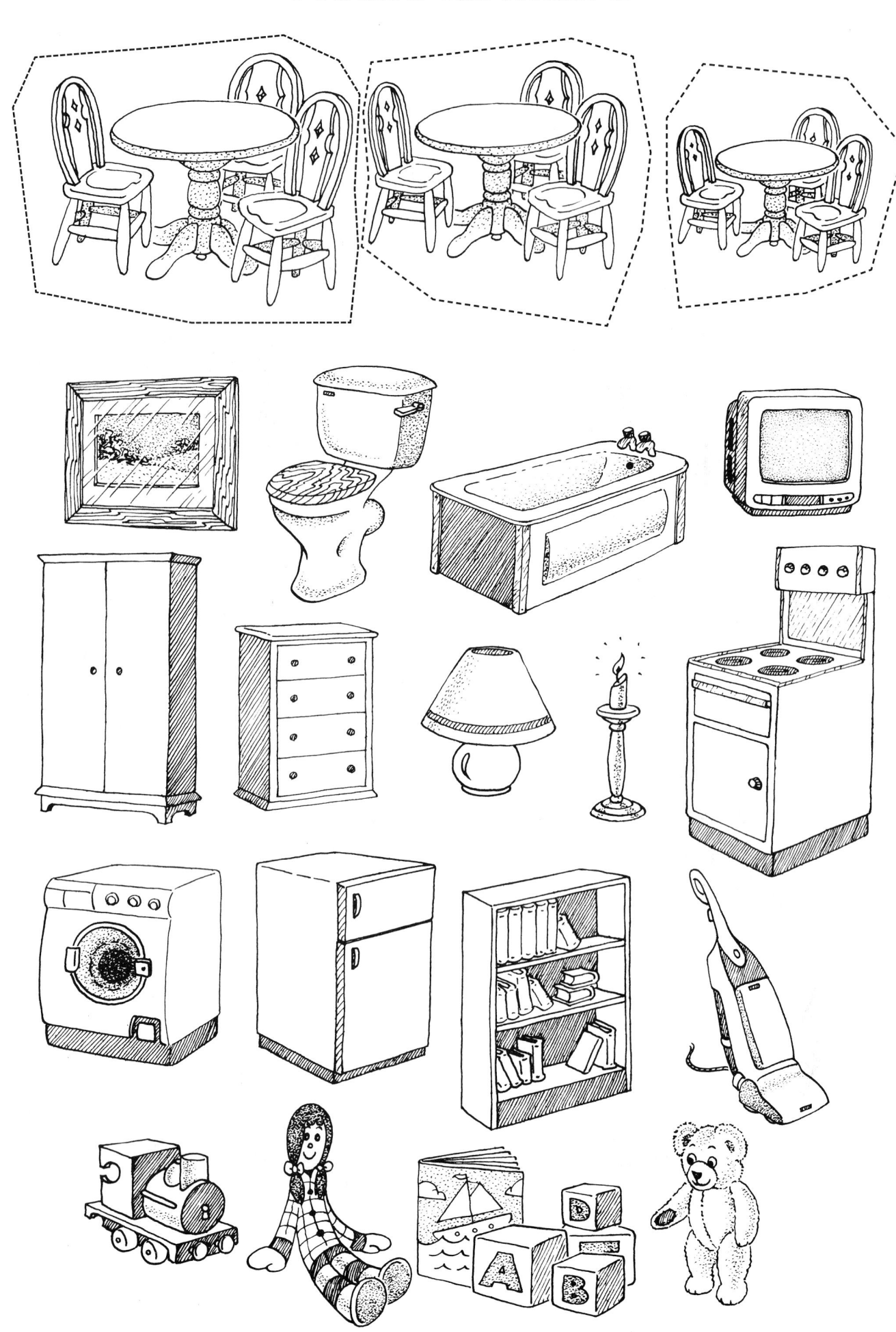

Robo-Kid mask

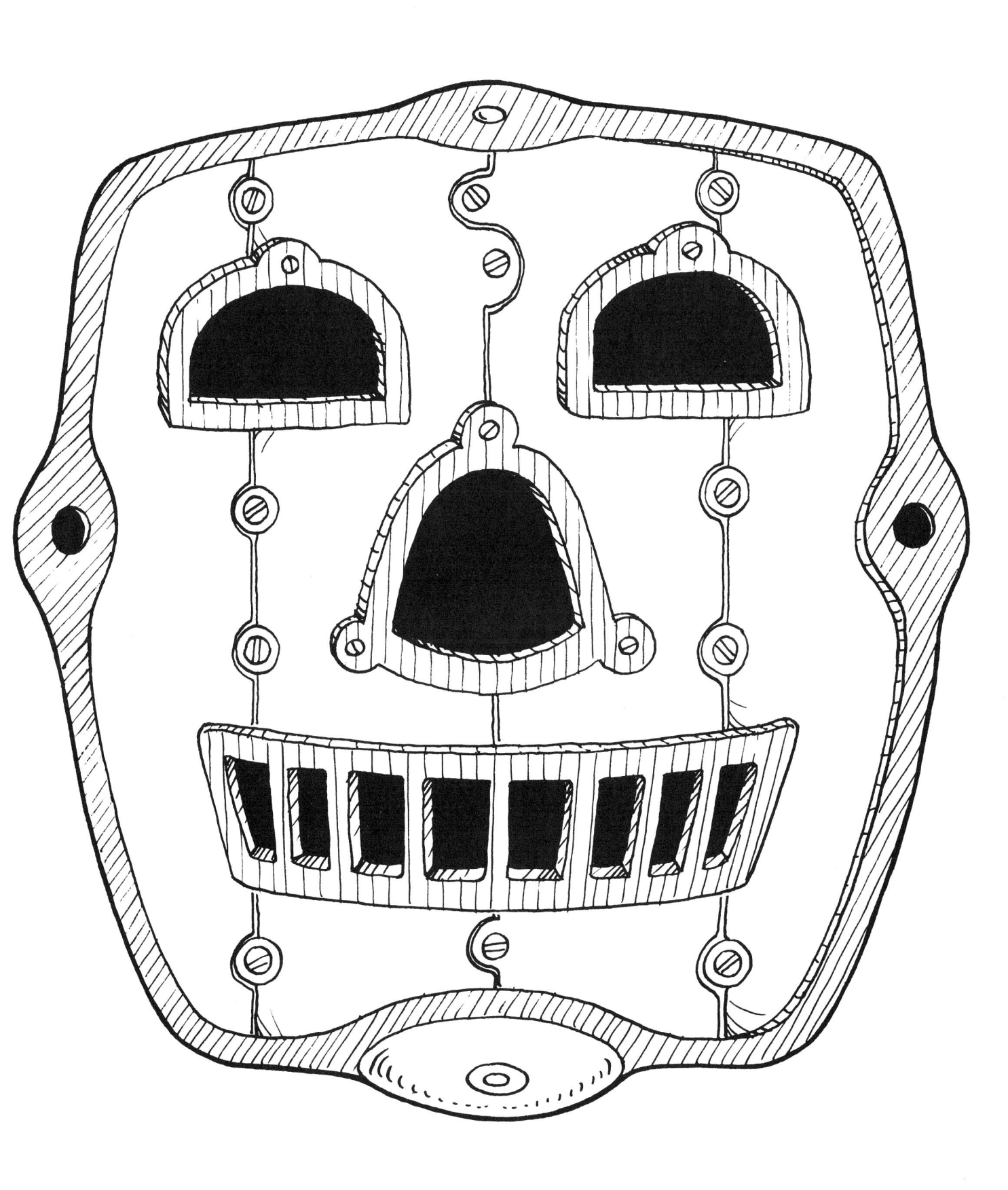

Copymaster 16

An ear signal

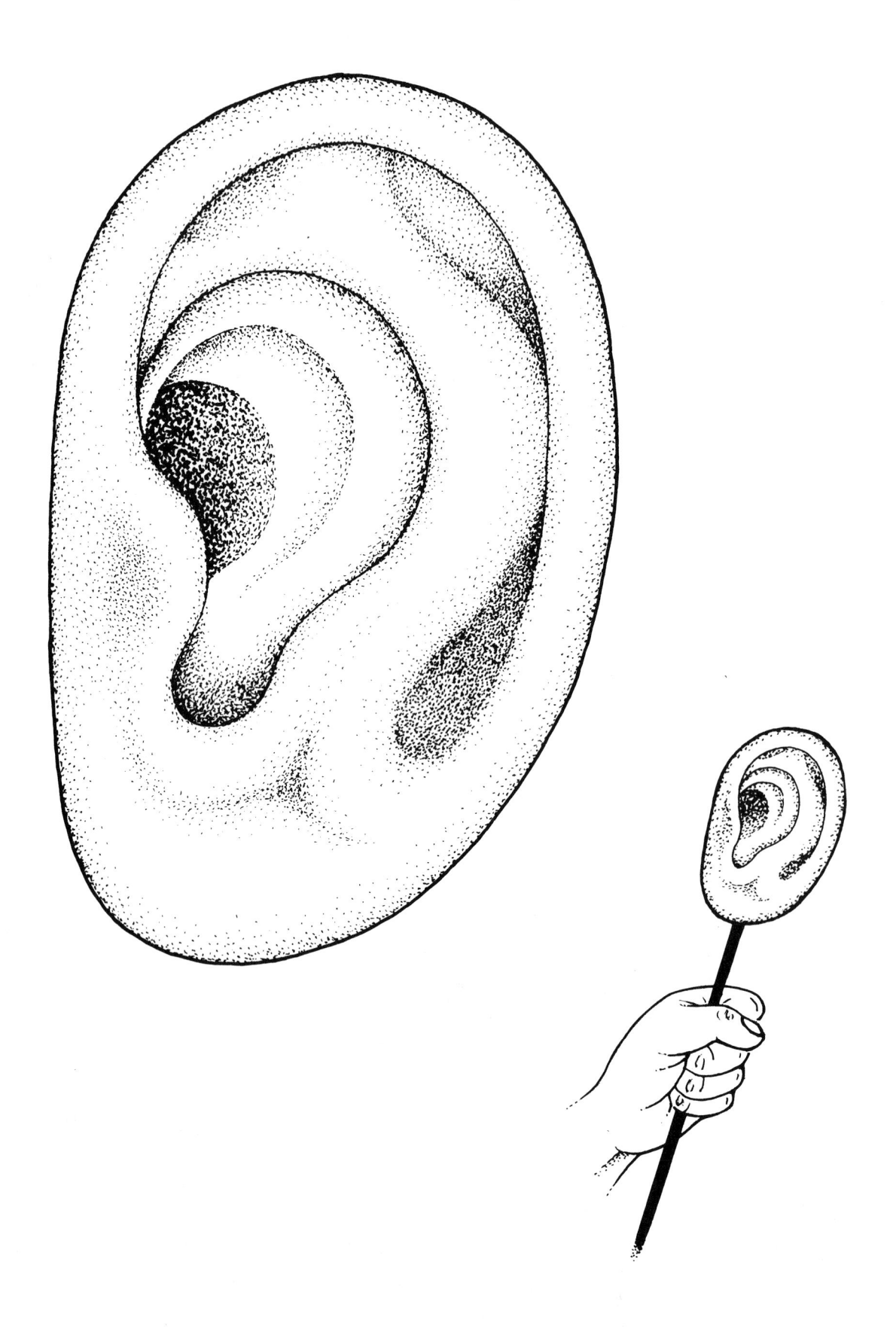

Tap-symbols

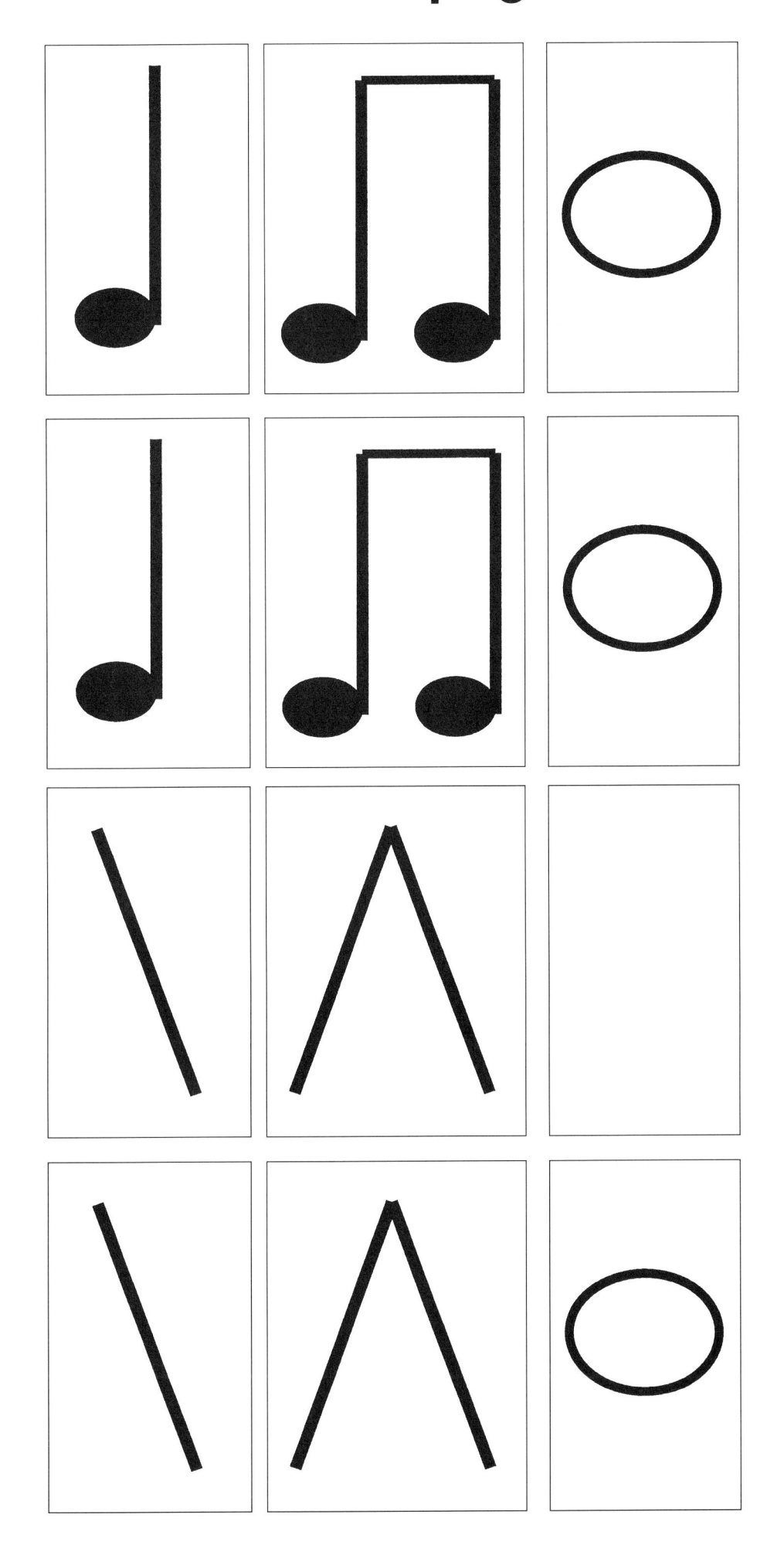

Instrument pictures

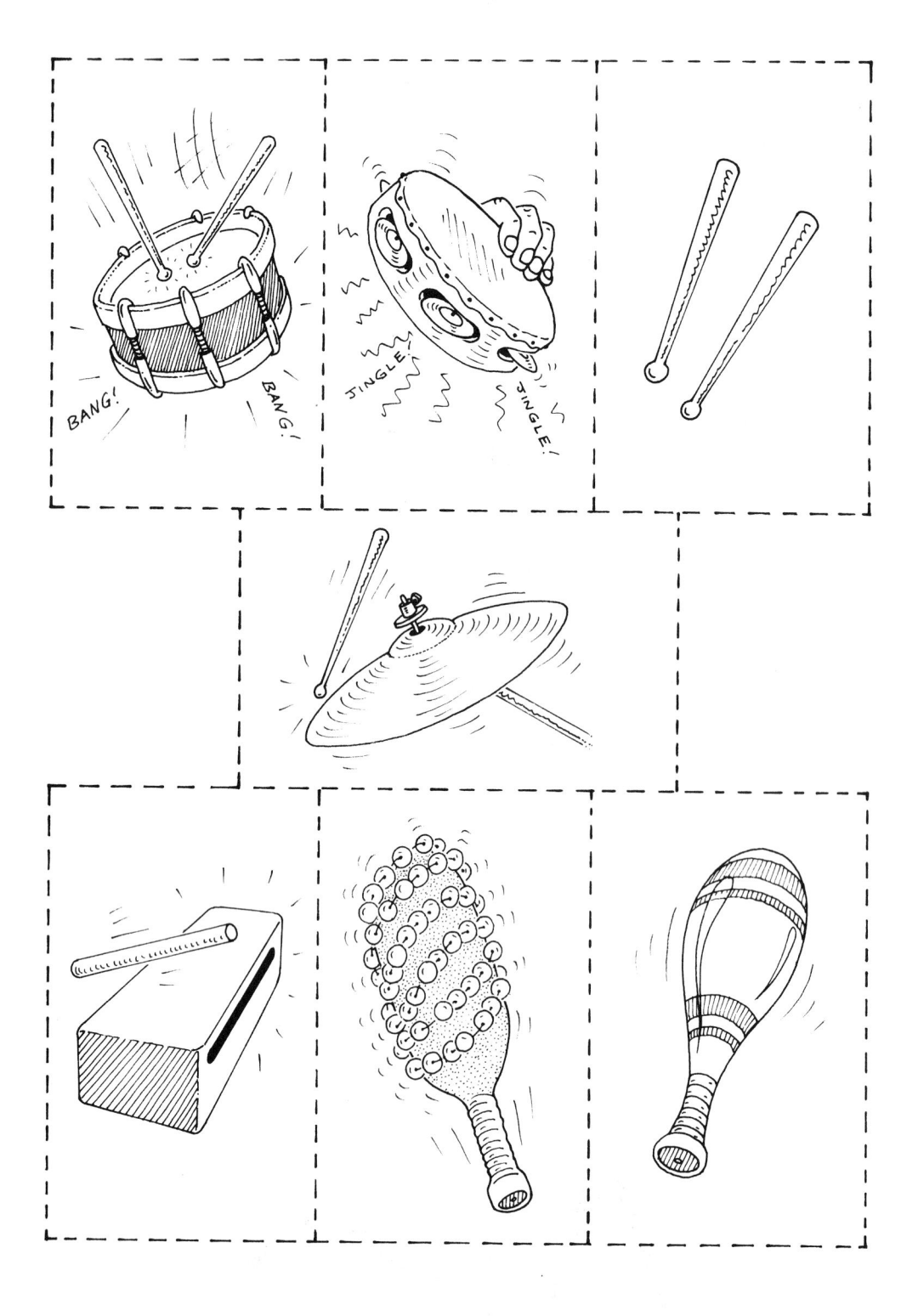

Copymaster 19

Composing grid for music

Copymaster 20

Composing grid for segmentation and blending practice

94

Copymaster 21

Sound Buttons

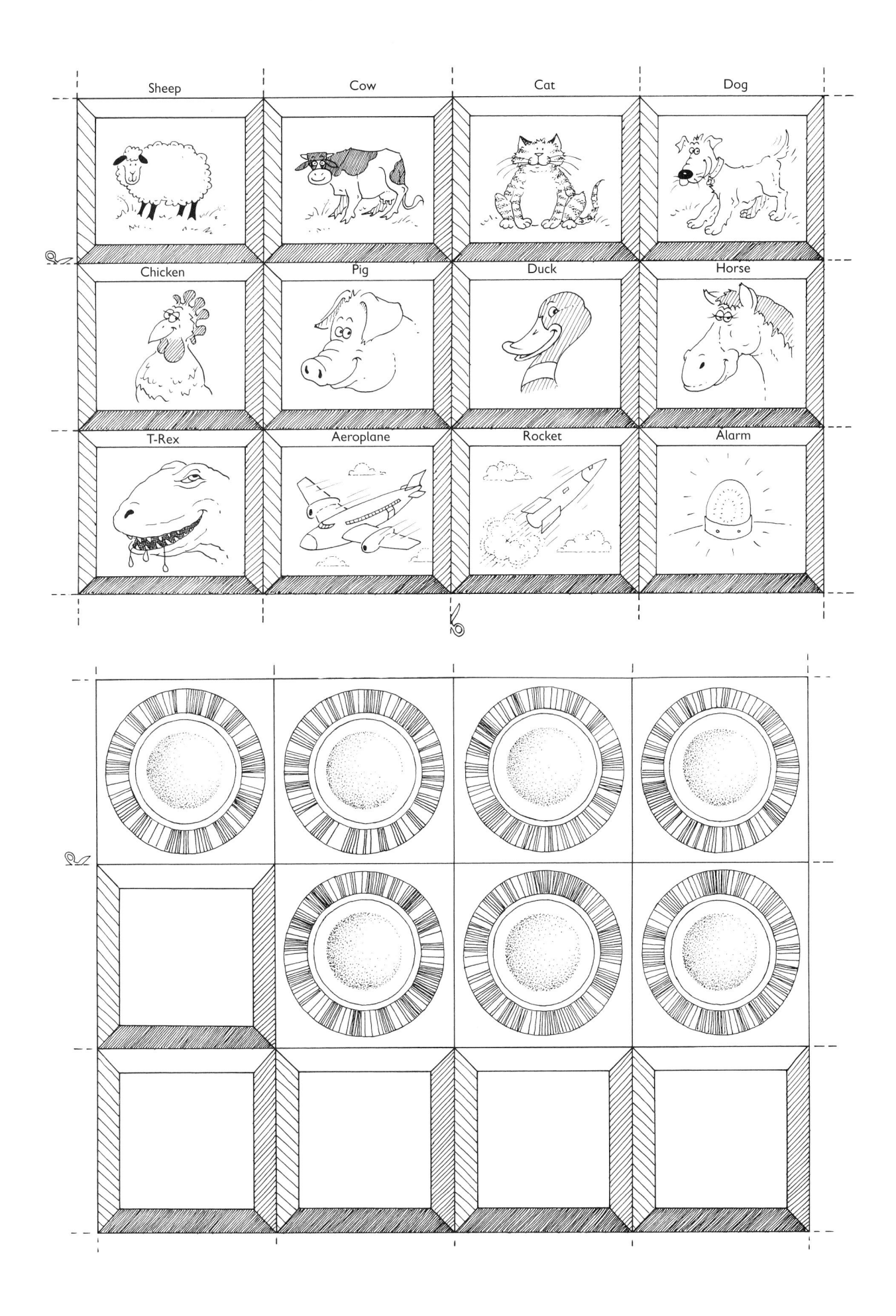

Sheep Cow Cat Dog

Chicken Pig Duck Horse

T-Rex Aeroplane Rocket Alarm

95

Finger rhyme examples

The wheels on the bus

The wheels on the bus go round and round,
Round and round, round and round.
The wheels on the bus go round and round
All day long.
The bell on the bus goes ding-ding-ding-
Ding-ding-ding, ding-ding-ding.
The bell on the bus goes ding-ding-ding.
All day long.
The wheels on the bus go round and round, round and round, round and round.
The wheels on the bus go round and round, all day long.

The door on the bus shuts chsh-chsh, chsh-chsh, chsh-chsh!
The wipers on the bus go swishy-swashy, swishy-swashy, swishy-swashy!
The horn on the bus goes beep-beep-beep, beep-beep-beep, beep-beep-beep!
The babies on the bus go wah-wah-wah, wah-wah-wah, wah-wah-wah!
The people on the bus go chitter-chatter, chitter-chatter, chitter-chatter!

Row, row, row your boat

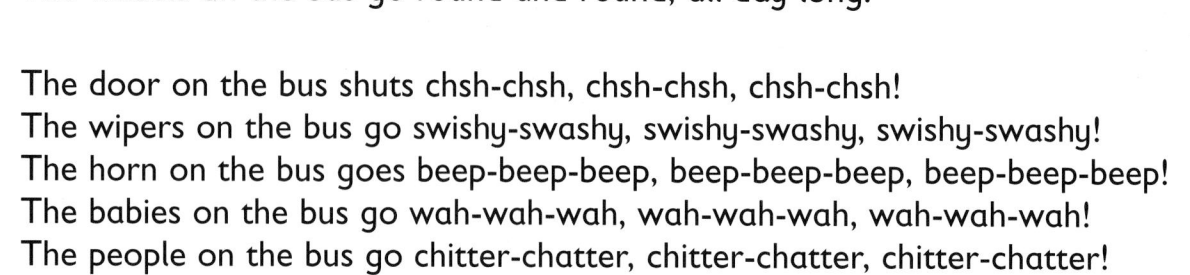

Row, row, row your boat
Gently down the stream
Merrily, merrily, merrily, merrily, life is but a dream.
Row, row, row your boat
Gently down the stream
Merrily, merrily, merrily, merrily, life is but a dream.
If you see a crocodile, don't forget to scream.

Miss Polly had a dolly

Miss Polly had a dolly who was sick, sick, sick,
So she phoned for the doctor to be quick, quick, quick.
The doctor came with his bag and hat
And knocked at the door with a rat tat tat.
He looked at the dolly and shook his head
And said "Miss Polly, put her straight to bed."
He wrote a pad for a pill, pill, pill.
"I'll be back in the morning with my bill, bill, bill."

Finger rhyme examples

The brave old Duke of York

Oh, the brave old Duke of York,
He had ten thousand men;
He marched them up to the top of the hill,
And he marched them down again.
And when they were up, they were up,
And when they were down, they were down,
And when they were only halfway up,
They were neither up nor down.

Heads, toes, knees and nose

Heads, toes, knees and nose,
Touch your head and touch your toes,
Touch your knees and touch your nose.
Stand up and count to ten then touch your toes,
Head, toes, knees, and nose.
Touch your head and touch your toes.
Touch your head and touch your nose,
Touch your knees and touch your toes.
Stand up and count to ten then touch your toes,
Head, nose, knees, toes.
Touch your head and touch your nose.
Touch your head and touch your nose,
Touch your knees and touch your nose.
Stand up and count to ten then touch your toes.
Head, nose, knees, nose,
Touch your head and touch your nose.

One finger, one thumb

One finger, one thumb keep moving.
One finger, one thumb keep moving.
We all stay merry and bright.
One finger, one thumb, one arm, keep moving.
One finger, one thumb, one arm, keep moving.
We all stay merry and bright.
One finger, one thumb, one arm, one leg, keep moving.
One finger, one thumb, one arm, one leg, keep moving.
We all stay merry and bright.
One finger, one thumb, one arm, one leg, stand up, sit down, keep moving.
One finger, one thumb, one arm, one leg, stand up, sit down, keep moving.
We all stay merry and bright.

Finger rhyme examples

How is the finger family?

Tommy Thumb, Tommy Thumb,
Where are you?
Here I am, here I am,
How are you?
Peter Pointer, Peter Pointer,
Where are you?
Here I am, here I am,
How are you?
Toby Tall, Toby Tall,
Where are you?
Here I am, here I am,
How are you?
Ruby Ring, Ruby Ring,
Where are you?
Here I am, here I am,
How are you?
Baby Small, Baby Small,
Where are you?
Here I am, here I am,
How are you?
Fingers All, Fingers All,
Where are you?
Here we are, here we are,
How are you?

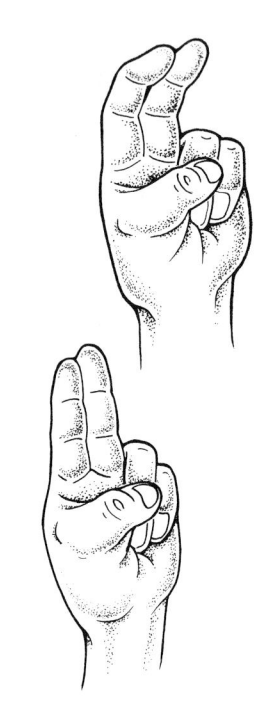

Cuento hasta diez.

Uno, dos y tres, (one, two, and three,)
Cuatro, sinco, seis, (four, five, six.)
Siete, ocho, nueve, (seven, eight, nine,)
Cuento hasta diez. (I count to ten.)
La la la la la; la la la la la,
La la la la la; la la la la la.
La la la la la; la la la la la.

Funny bunny

Here is a bunny
With ears so funny
And here is a hole in the ground.
At the first sound she hears
She pricks up her ears
And pops right into the ground.

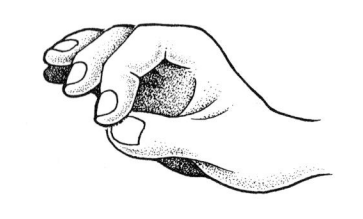

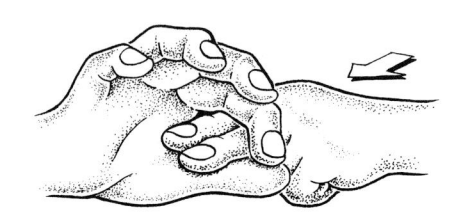

Humpty Dumpty

Humpty Dumpty, sat on a wall.
Humpty Dumpty, had a great fall.
All the King's horses
And all the King's men
Couldn't put Humpty together again.

Humpty Dumpty sat on a cat

Humpty Dumpty sat on a bat

All the King's horses
   And all the King's men
Told Humpty never
   To sit down again.

Humpty Dumpty went to Lumpty
To get his cheese and meat.
But when he got there
The shops were all bare
So he had nothing to eat.

Hampty Dampty

Heeping Deeping

Higgledy Piggledy

Bixing Fixing

Hippity Dippity

Copymaster 26

Word count

The little mouse came up the stairs.	*The elephants ran fast.*	*You are kind.*	**Sam jumps.**	Humpty Dumpty sat on the wall.	I am a good boy and I like to look at lots of books.	Once upon a time there were three bears: a baby bear, a mummy bear and a gruff and hairy: daddy bear.	Is this the longest sentence ever written?	**'This sentence does not have any words in it at all, does it?'**	*This sentence has five words.*	*This is a very long sentence with ten words in.*	**Sam jumps.**

Etc...

Sentence trains

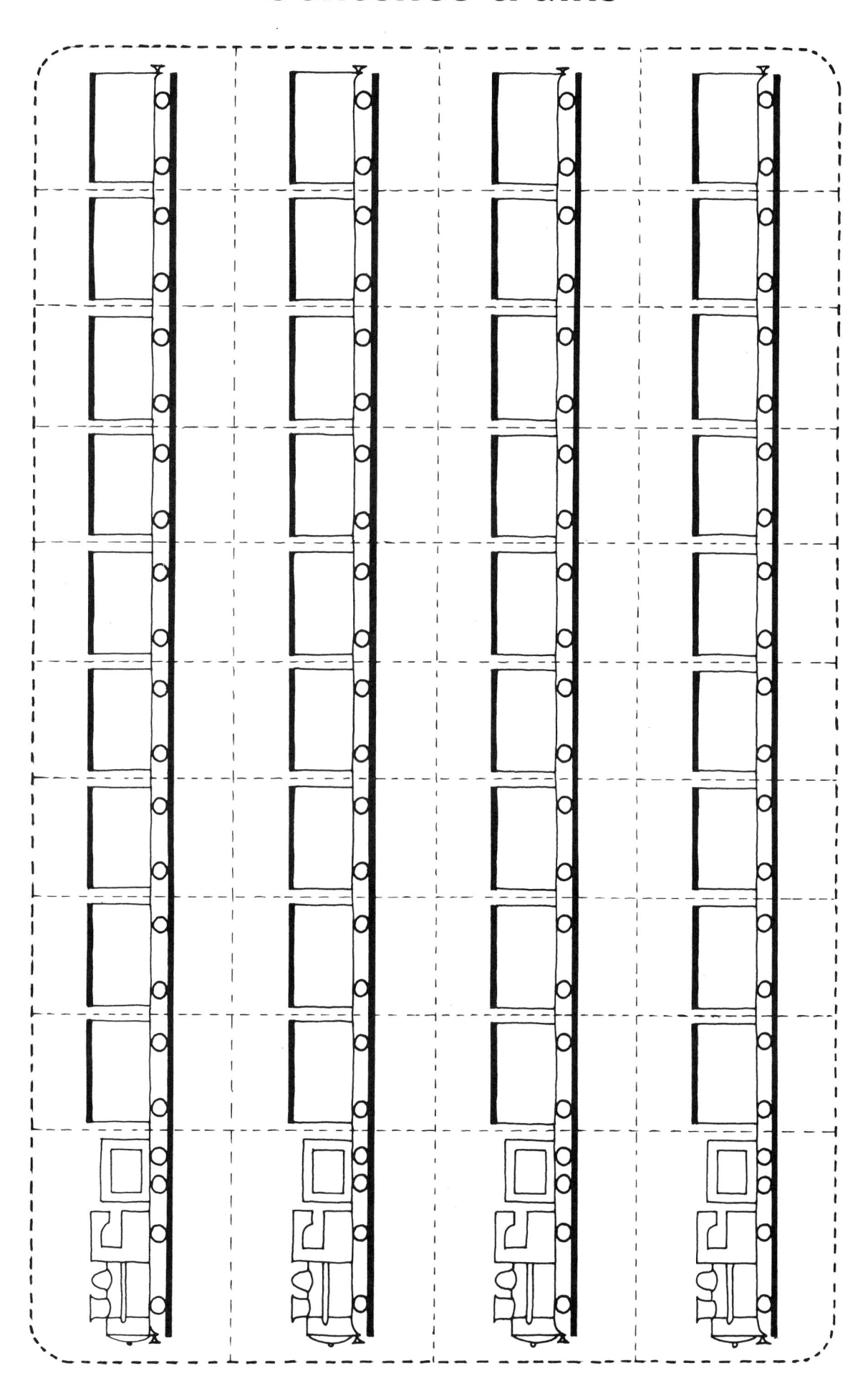

Copymaster 27

Copymaster 28

Syllable Sally

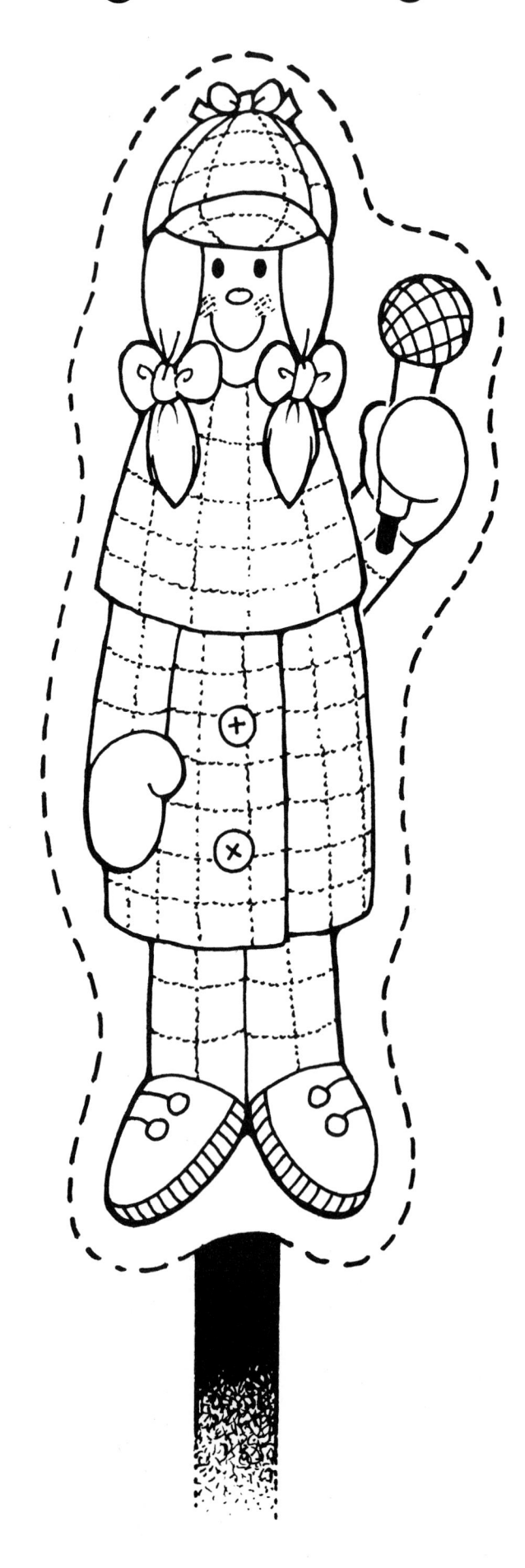

M.A.P.s

/b/ action – beating a drum.

/c/ action – fingers as scissors cutting.

/d/ action – shovelling sand over the shoulder

/f/ action – hand makes a fish and weaves from side to side

/g/ action – hands under arm pits to /g/g/g/g/.

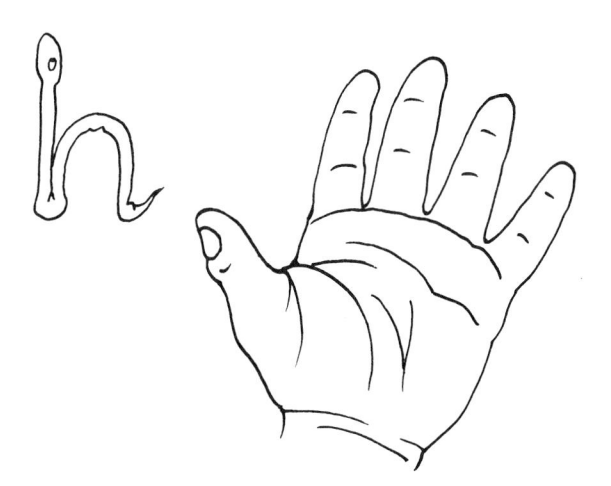

/h/ action – open hand as you make /h/ sound.

Copymaster 30

M.A.P.s

/j/ pouring from a jug with a /j/j/j/

/l/ action – 2 hands, one makes a fist to make the lamp base, the other on top a lamp shade. Tap top hand up and down to /l/l/l/.

/m/ action – hands under chin as if in thought, eyes up – make /m/ sound.

/n/ action – shake head and point finger as you say /n/n/n/.

/p/ action – pretend to be pumping with a bicycle pump /p/p/p/

/qu/ action – use hand to make duck's head, open and close thumb as you /qu/qu/qu/

Copymaster 31

M.A.P.s

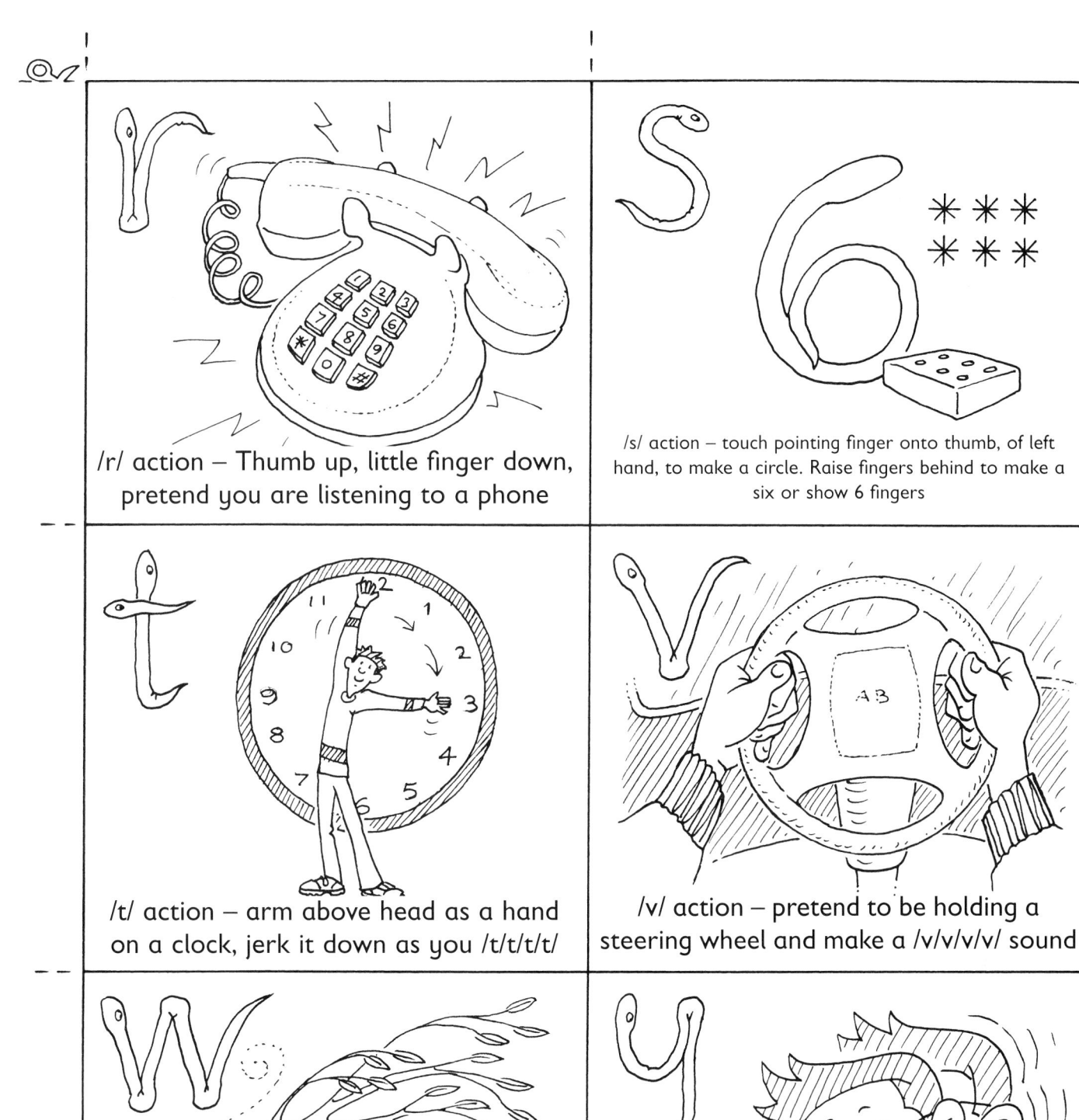

/r/ action – Thumb up, little finger down, pretend you are listening to a phone

/s/ action – touch pointing finger onto thumb, of left hand, to make a circle. Raise fingers behind to make a six or show 6 fingers

/t/ action – arm above head as a hand on a clock, jerk it down as you /t/t/t/t/

/v/ action – pretend to be holding a steering wheel and make a /v/v/v/v/ sound

/w/ – action – blow /w/ onto the palm of your hand. Move your hand away.

/y/ action – nod head – /y/y/y/y/

Copymaster 32

M.A.P.s

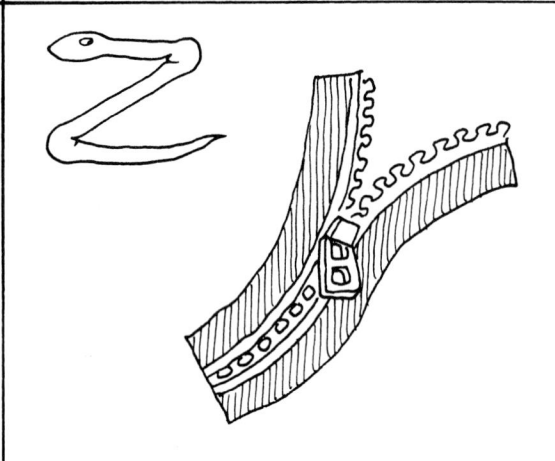

/z/ action. Hand out – palm up – pointer finger from other hand runs up palm to /z/z/z/.

/x/ action – arm up and hand like a goose neck and head. Flick hand back and forth to /kss/kss/kss/ sound.

/a/ action – arms apart – bring them together with a clap and a /a/a/a.

/e/ action – hand into fist, egg-shaped-tap with finger like a spoon whilst saying /e/e/e/e/.

/i/ action – finger beckoning to /i/i/in.

/o/ action – put your hat /o/o/o/n your head.

M.A.P.s

/u/ action – point up whilst saying /u/u/u/p.

/ch/ action – arms by side to make train movements /ch/ch/ch/.

/sh/ action – finger in front of mouth – /sh/sh/sh/

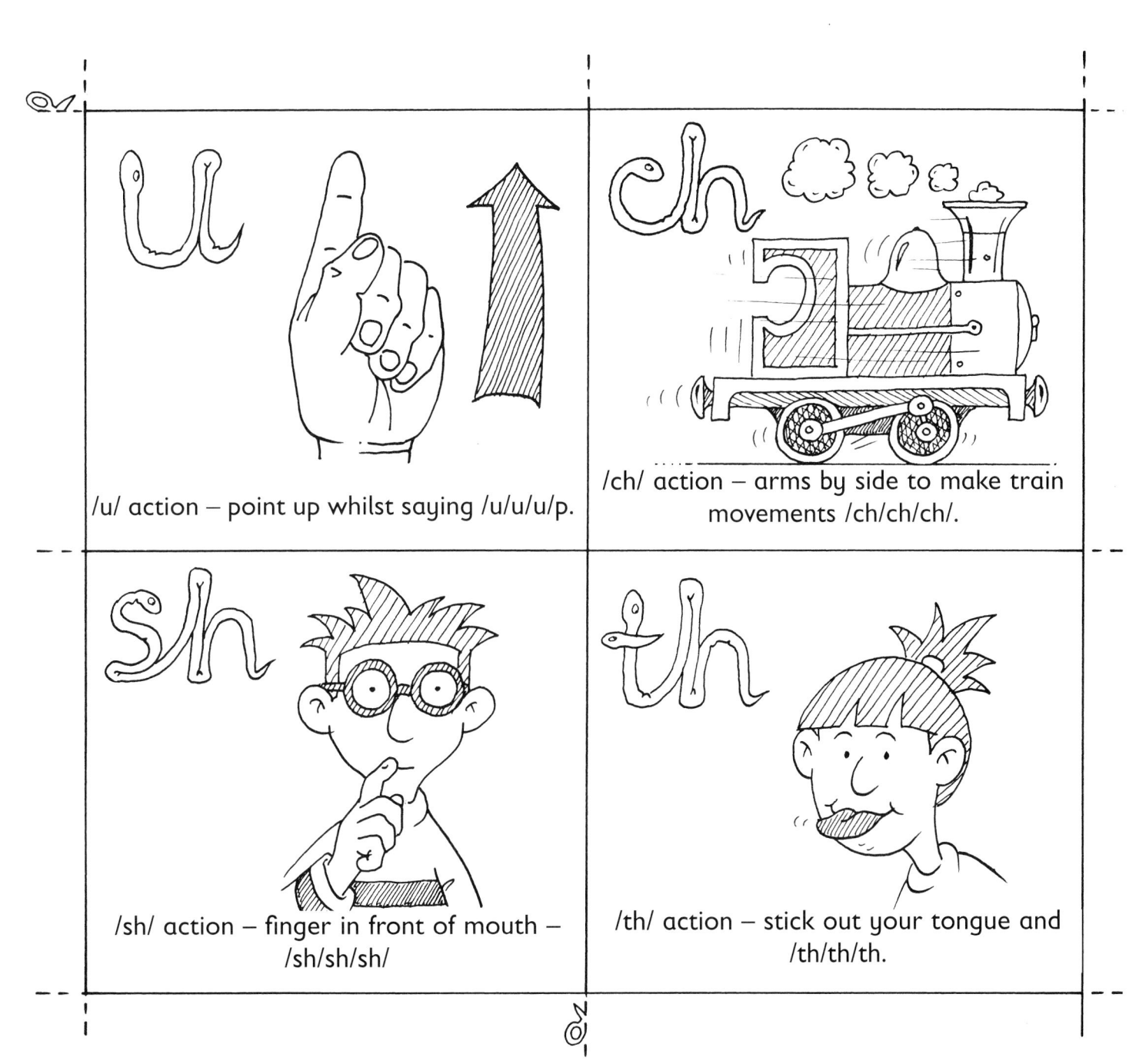

/th/ action – stick out your tongue and /th/th/th.

Copymaster 34

Master set of letters (1)

ch	sh	th
d	j	p
k	h	n
c	g	m
b	f	l

Copymaster 35

Master set of letters (2)

v	a	
t	z	u
s	y	o
r	x	i
qu	w	e

Copymaster 36

Pop the phoneme

The naughty microphone

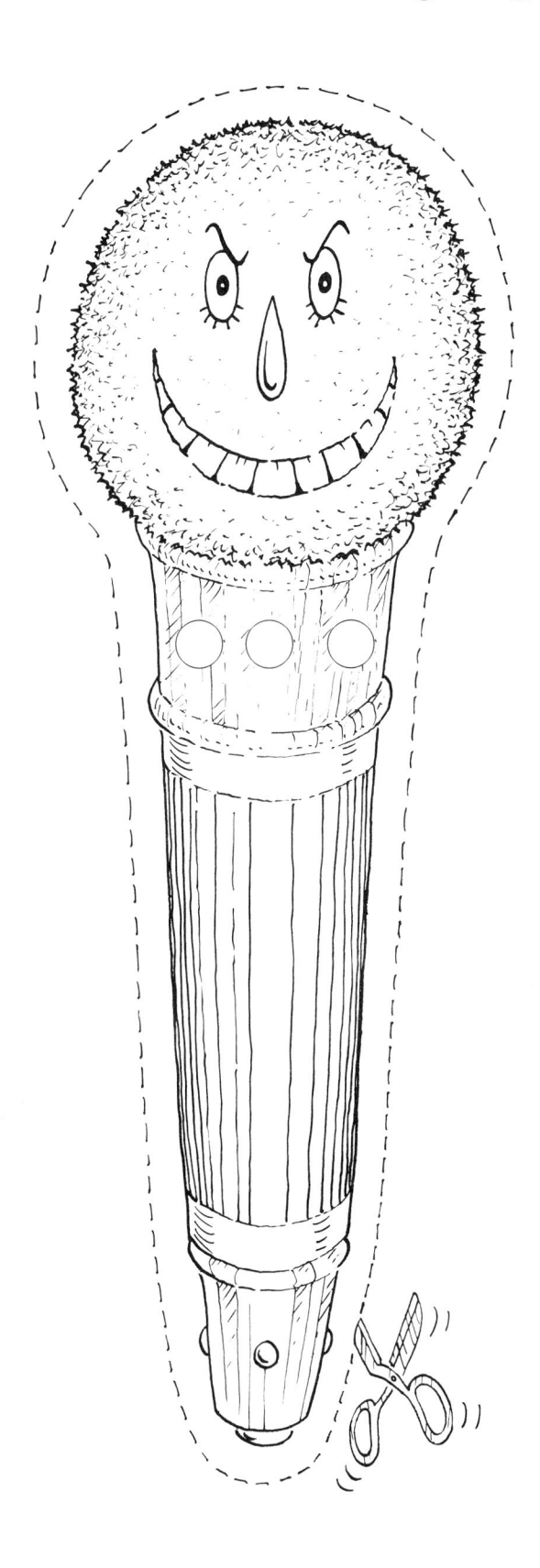

Photocopy onto card and laminate. Put a X in the first circle if you are dropping initial phonemes, middle circle for medial phonemes and last circle for final phonemes.

Use a + signal if you are adding a phoneme, indicate where you will add it in the word by putting the + into the appropriate circle.

Use a <-> Sign to indicate that you will be changing a phoneme; again select the circle to show if it will be in the initial, medial or final position

Copymaster 38

Phoneme substitution fans

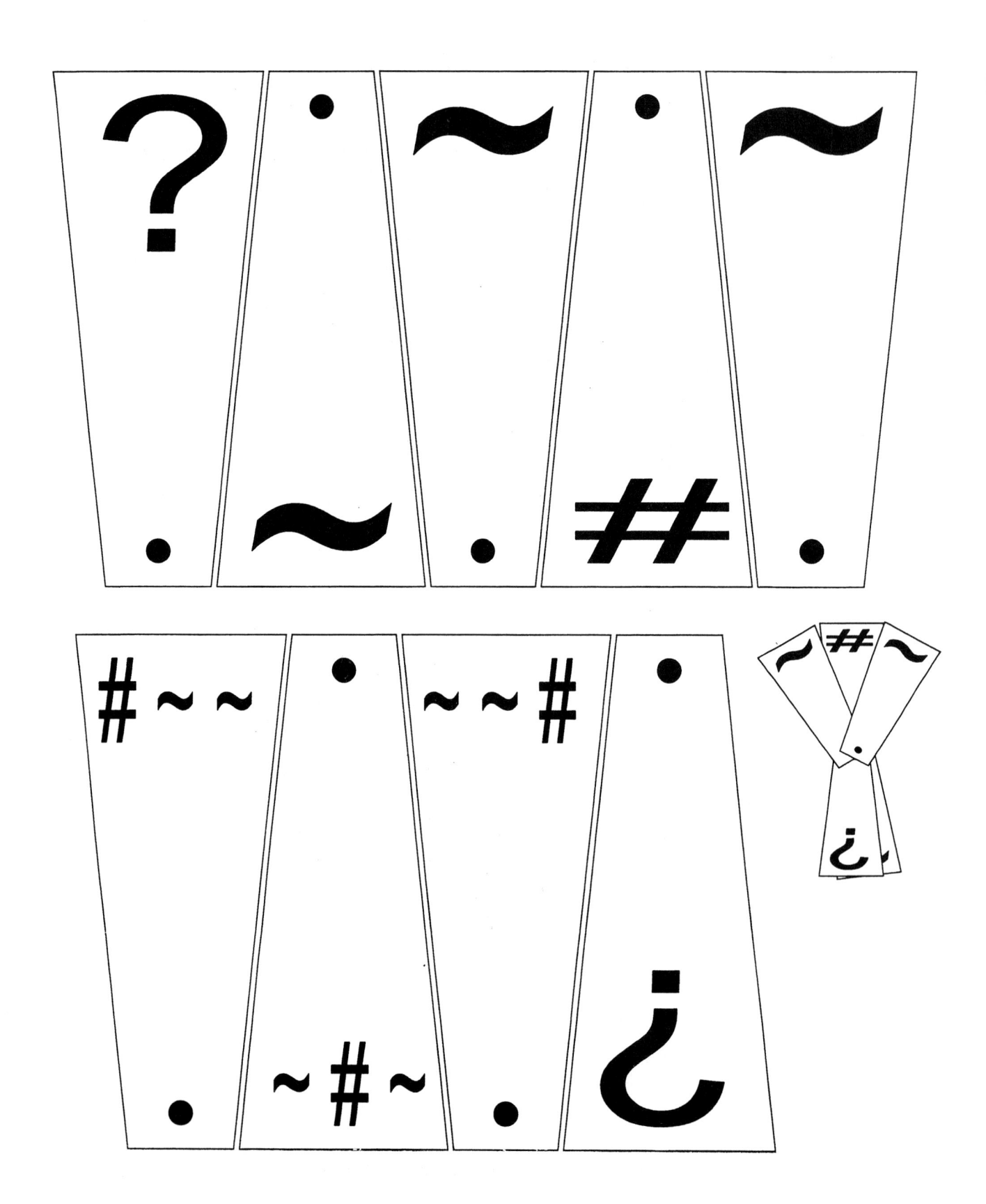

112

MAPs long vowel phonemes

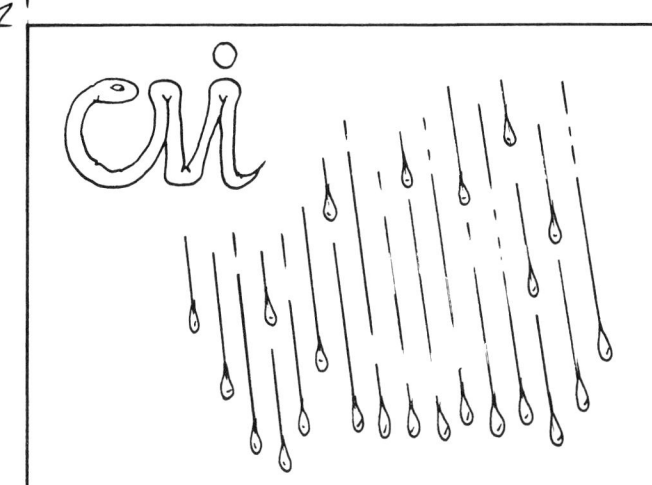

/ai/ action – pitter, patter fingers going /ai/ai/ai/

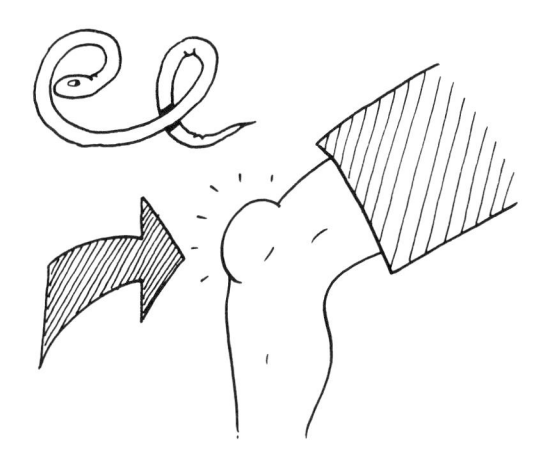

/ee/ action – point to your knee and bend your knee with /ee/ee/ee/.

/oo/ action – run fingers down from neck to chest as if straightening a tie /ie/ie/

/os/ – to fingers on head to make horns and /oa/oa/oa/

/oo/ action – hands in front swaying as a ghostly /oo/oo/oo/ is made.

Copymaster 40

MAPs long vowel phonemes

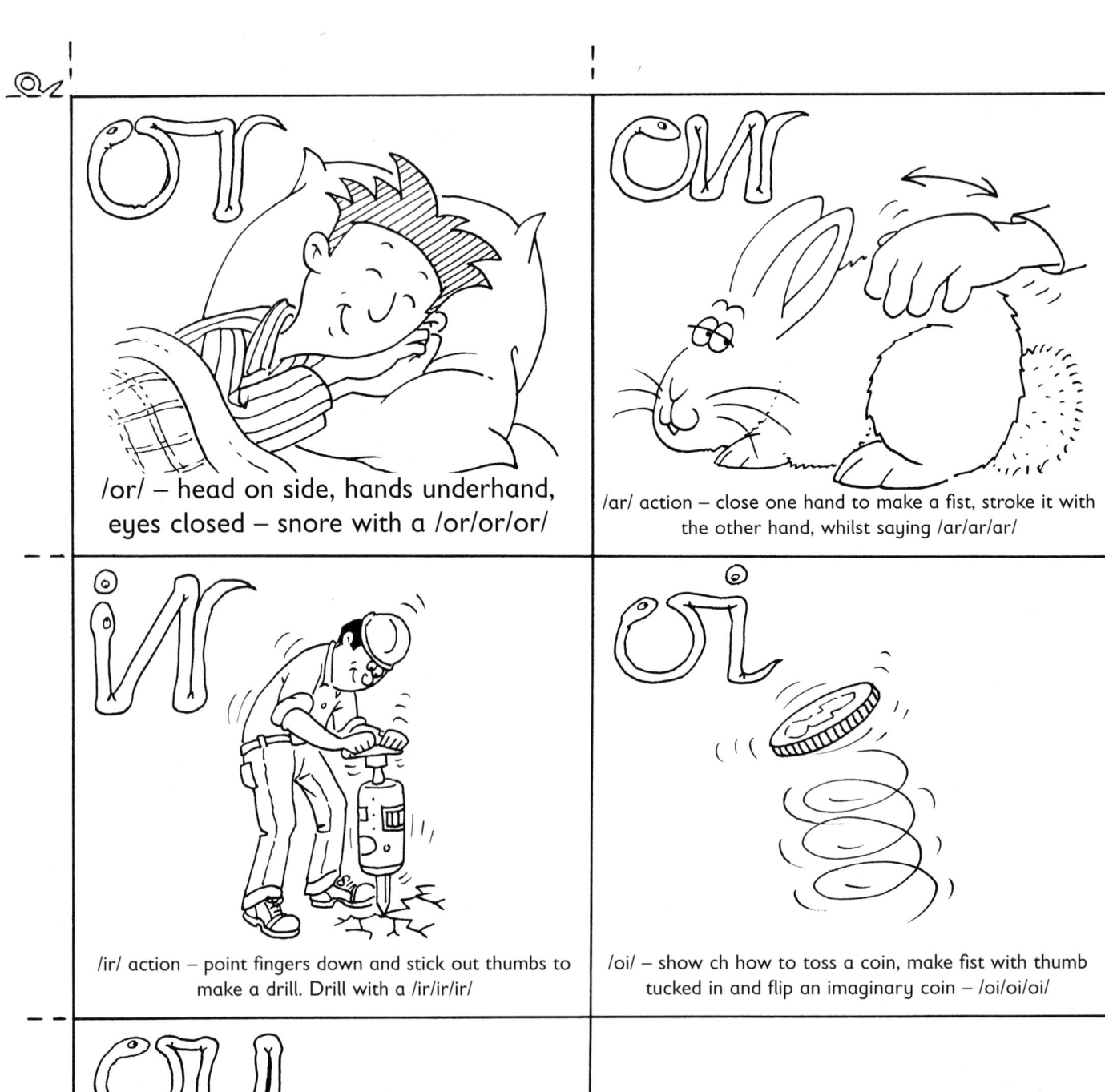

/or/ – head on side, hands underhand, eyes closed – snore with a /or/or/or/

/ar/ action – close one hand to make a fist, stroke it with the other hand, whilst saying /ar/ar/ar/

/ir/ action – point fingers down and stick out thumbs to make a drill. Drill with a /ir/ir/ir/

/oi/ – show ch how to toss a coin, make fist with thumb tucked in and flip an imaginary coin – /oi/oi/oi/

/ou/ – put two hands and arms together to make a triangle – grow the mountain with each /ou/ou/ou/

114

Long vowel snap (1)

a	ai	ay	a-e
e	ee	ea	ie
e-e	ie	igh	y
i-e	i	o	oa
o-e	oe	oo	ew
ue	u-e	or	aw
ir	er	ur	oi
oy	ou	ow	air
ear	are	ear	eer

Copymaster 42

Long vowel snap (2)

ere	oo	u	ou
o			

---

a ai, ay, a-e	e, ee ea ie e-e	ie igh, y, i-e, i	o, oa ow, o-e, oe	oo ew, ue, u-e
or aw	ir er, ur	oi oy	ou ow	air ear are
ear eer ere	oo u ou o			

Use this table to check if you are not sure.

High frequency words

I	go	come
went	up	you
day	was	look

are	the	of
we	this	dog
me	like	going

big	she	and
they	my	see
on	away	mum

Copymaster 44

High frequency words

it	at	play
no	yes	for
a	dad	can

he	am	all
is	cat	get
said	to	in

Word Wall chants

Each day while 'doing the Word Wall' the class chants the selected words. This will support struggling readers and provide multi-sensory ways of over-learning the spelling and structure of the words. The chants included here are designed to be fun and engaging and therefore to aid memory. These chants provide templates for practitioners to invent their own following the interests of their pupils. Many more examples of chants like these can be found at www.k111.k12.il.us/lafayette/fourblocks/word_wall_chants.htm
Start by encouraging children to apply their phonic skills and give you the phonemes and sounds of letters, quickly move towards a flexibility and ability to give the phonemes or letter names. Many of these chants can be used with syllabic and phonic segmentation and blending activities as well as with learning high frequency irregular vocabulary.

Any time chants

M.A.Ps-
Use the mnemonic multi-sensory cues from the M.A.P.s activities to spell out the word as quickly as possible. Practitioner has the word- mimes it out using the actions, children have to guess the word, spell the word using plastic letters, write the word on a whiteboard/ piece of paper.
Practitioner picks word on Wall- mimes it out, children have to point to the word they think after every letter.

Sit down chants

Movie star kisses Put your hands to your mouth. Throw each letter a kiss, like a film star at the Oscars.	**Opera** Sing the letters in opera fashion.	**Nose** Hold your nose and spell it.
Beat it Beat it out on your lap.	**Cheer it** Like a cheerleader (Give me an 'h', etc.).	**Snap and clap** Snap the vowels and clap the consonants.
Volcano Start at a whisper, get louder with each letter, explode when you say the word at the end.	**Marshmallow clap** Almost like a clap but you stop just before the hands touch each for each letter.	**Slow-motion** Hold the sound of each letter for a second or two.

Copymaster 46

Word Wall chants

Sit down or stand up chants

Hand jive Pair children up/ clap hands for consonants and lap clap for vowels, hands in the air as you say the word.	**Steps (at the Disco)** Hand starts at the stomach for each letter, hand up for consonants, hand down for vowels (e.g. John Travolta in *Saturday Night Fever!*).	**Mexican Hat Dance** Alternate feet in front.
Stomper Stomp out each letter with your foot.	**Yo-yo** Pretend to have a yo-yo in each hand. Decide which will be consonants and which vowels. Say a letter with each yo-yo move and a double loop the loop when you say the word at the end.	**Robot** Segment the word in a r-o-b-o-t voice. Really good for syllable and phoneme segmentation.

Stand up chants

Blast off Start crouch at floor, as you say each letter get a little higher, jump into the air as you say the word.	**Back tracer** Trace the letter on the back of the person in front of you. This is best done in a circle so everyone is tracing on the back of someone else. Close your eyes and feel the letters.	**Heads-tummies-tails** Pat your head for tall letters, pat your tummy for short letters, and pat your bottom for letters with tails.
Be the letter Like the YMCA song.	**Chopper** Pretend to swing the axe for each letter, pretend the tree is falling over at the end and say the word in the style of 'TIMber!'.	**Weight lifter** Pretend to lift each letter, in the style of a weight lifter, grunting the letter as you lift. Say the word in an exhausted way at the end.
Alphabet arms Set up word or sequence of letters, *e.g. the alphabet.* Under each letter draw an arrow < left hand, > right hand, ^ both hands up, # clap, ~ wave etc. Children mime the actions as they say the letters.	**Double doodle** Put both arms out in front and trace a figure of eight (on side) for each letter.	**Motorcycles** Pretend you are on a bike and do a wheelie for each letter.

Copymaster 47

Whole class observation

Pupil name	Hand up	Asks question	Incorrect answer/ contribution	Answers question	Offers contribution	Does not participate/ behaviour ☹	Notes

Wordo!

Beginner's Wordo

Wordo Challenge

Cross the river and beat the troll

Copymaster 50

Blank origami book

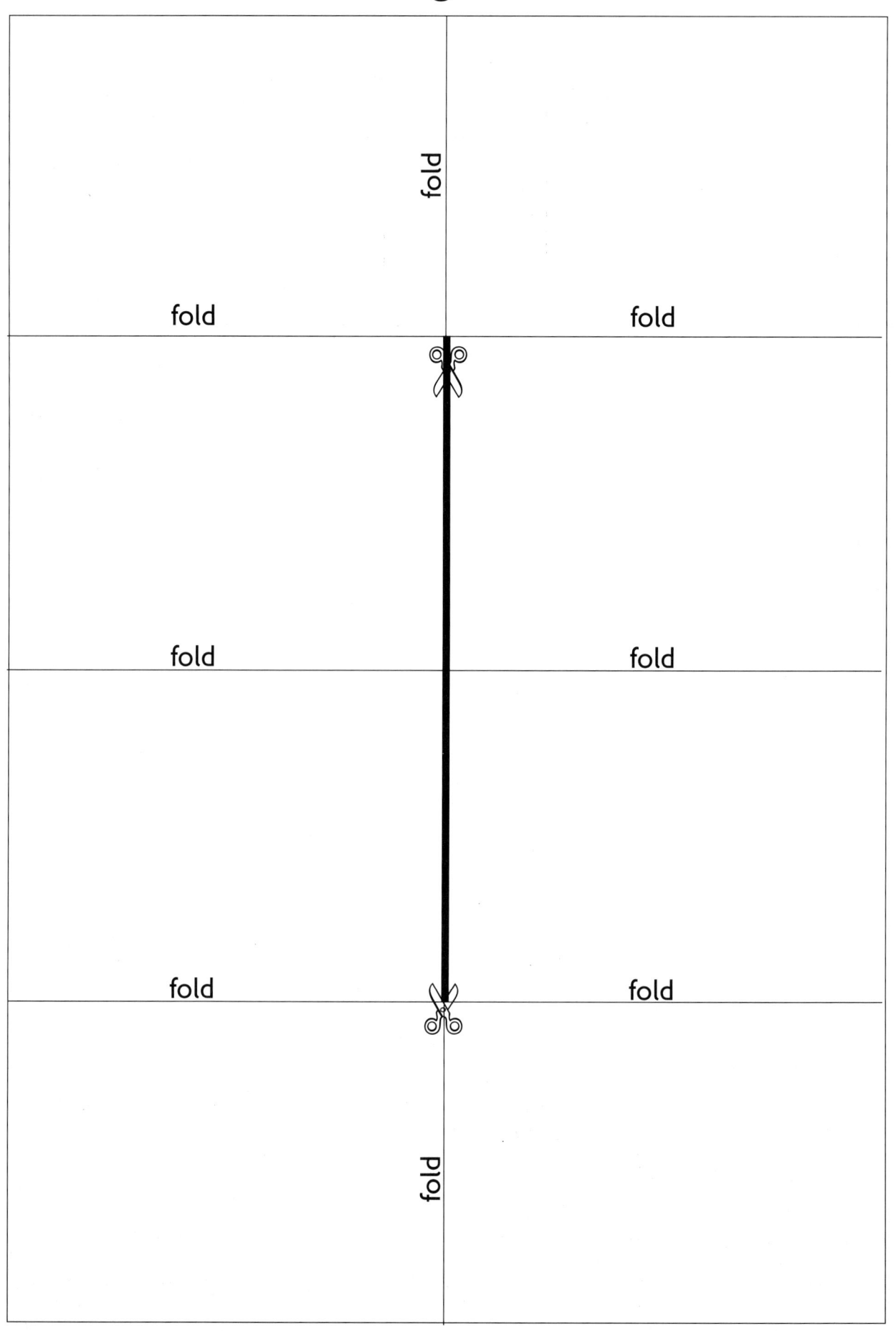

fold

fold   fold

fold   fold

fold   fold

fold

124

Copymaster 51

Blanks for shop

Date _____

Royal Bank of Swindon

□□□□□□□□□

Signed _____

credit card

0794 3215 8621

00-03   9742   2004

My list:

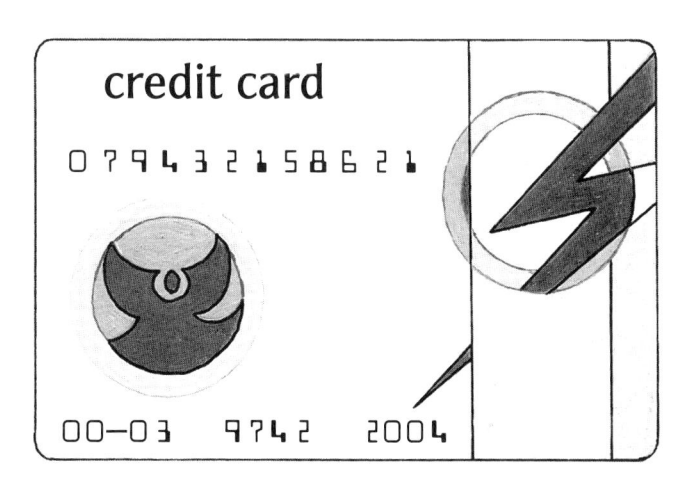

-
-
-
-
-
-
-
-
-
-

Receipt:

-
-
-
-
-
-
-

125

Copymaster 52

Blanks for shop

For Sale

costs

costs

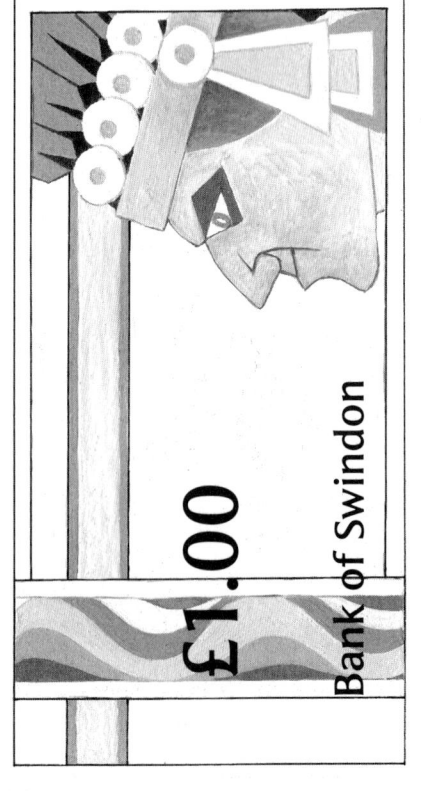

£1.00 Bank of Swindon

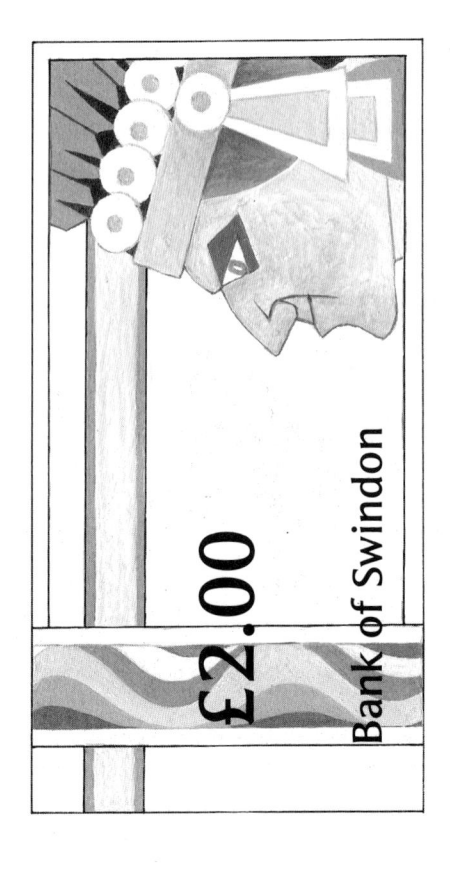

£2.00 Bank of Swindon

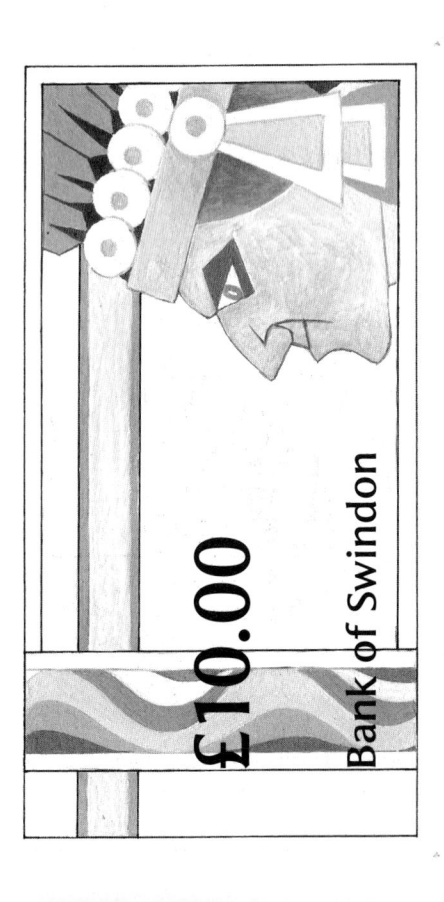

£10.00 Bank of Swindon

Copymaster 53

Blanks for hospital

✚ First Aid card

-
-
-
-
-
-
-

Nurse

Doctor

Patient

Medical records   Date:

Name _____

DOB _____

What is wrong?

_____

_____

_____

Copymaster 54

Blanks for hospital

Name _____

Date _____

No Smoking

Waiting Room

Surgery

X-ray

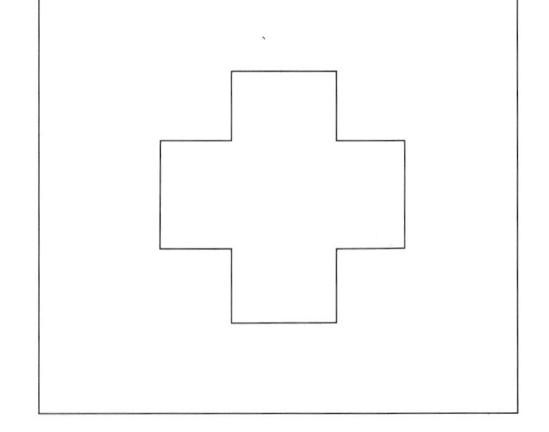

Exit

Blanks for house

Dear _____

List to do!
-
-
-
-
-
-
-

Message
For _____

Copymaster 56

Blanks for travel agents

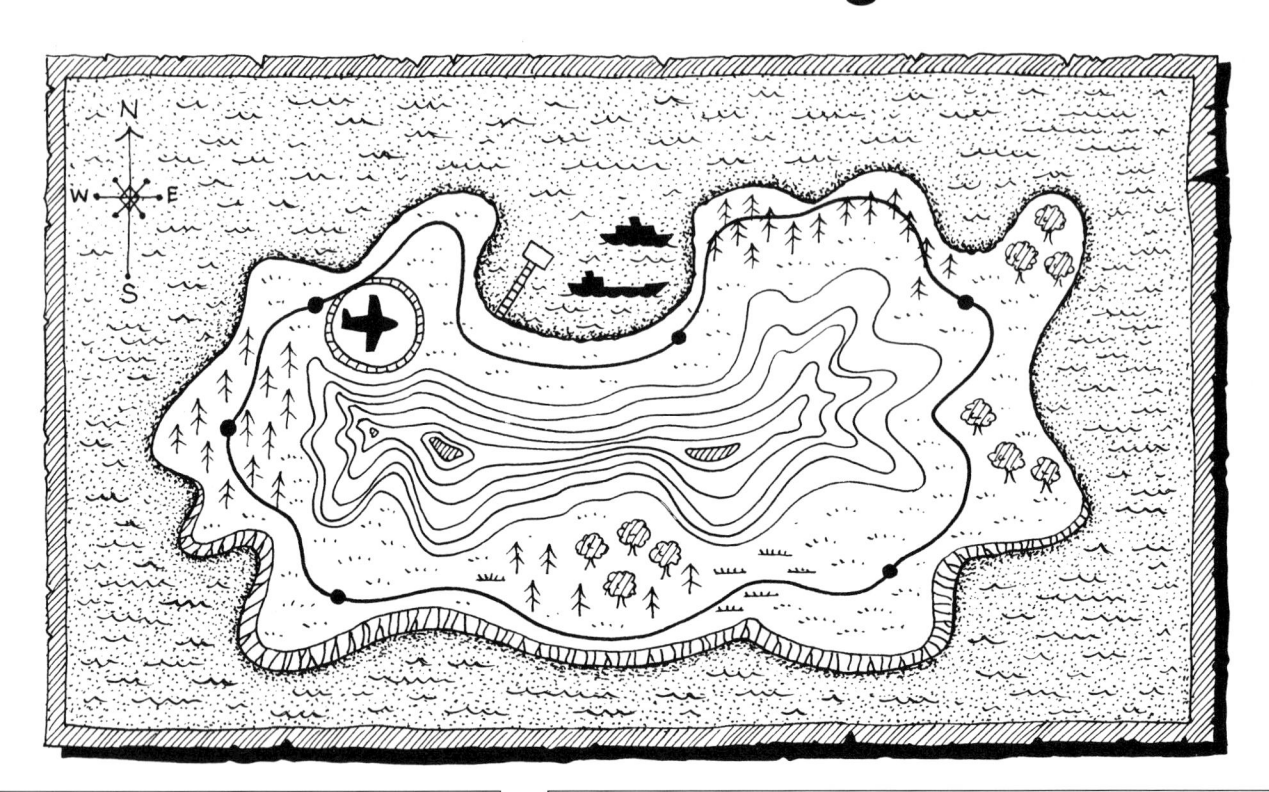

Holiday snaps

Holiday snaps

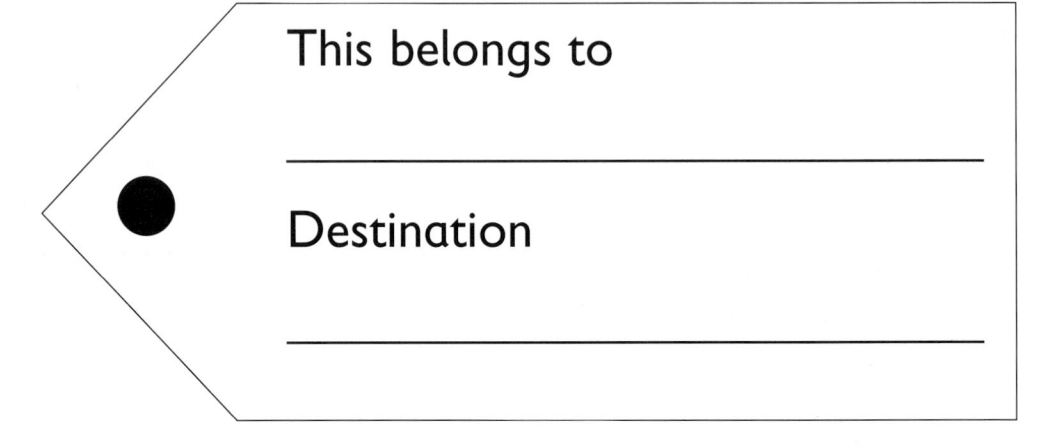

This belongs to
_____

Destination
_____

Copymaster 57

Blanks for travel agents

Travel:

Details:

Sign here
_____

Passport

Name: _____
0545 456546 32

Ticket

to: _____

by:

on: _____

Booking Form

_____
_____
☐ ☐ ☐ ☐ ☐ _____

Copymaster 58

Blanks for restaurant/café

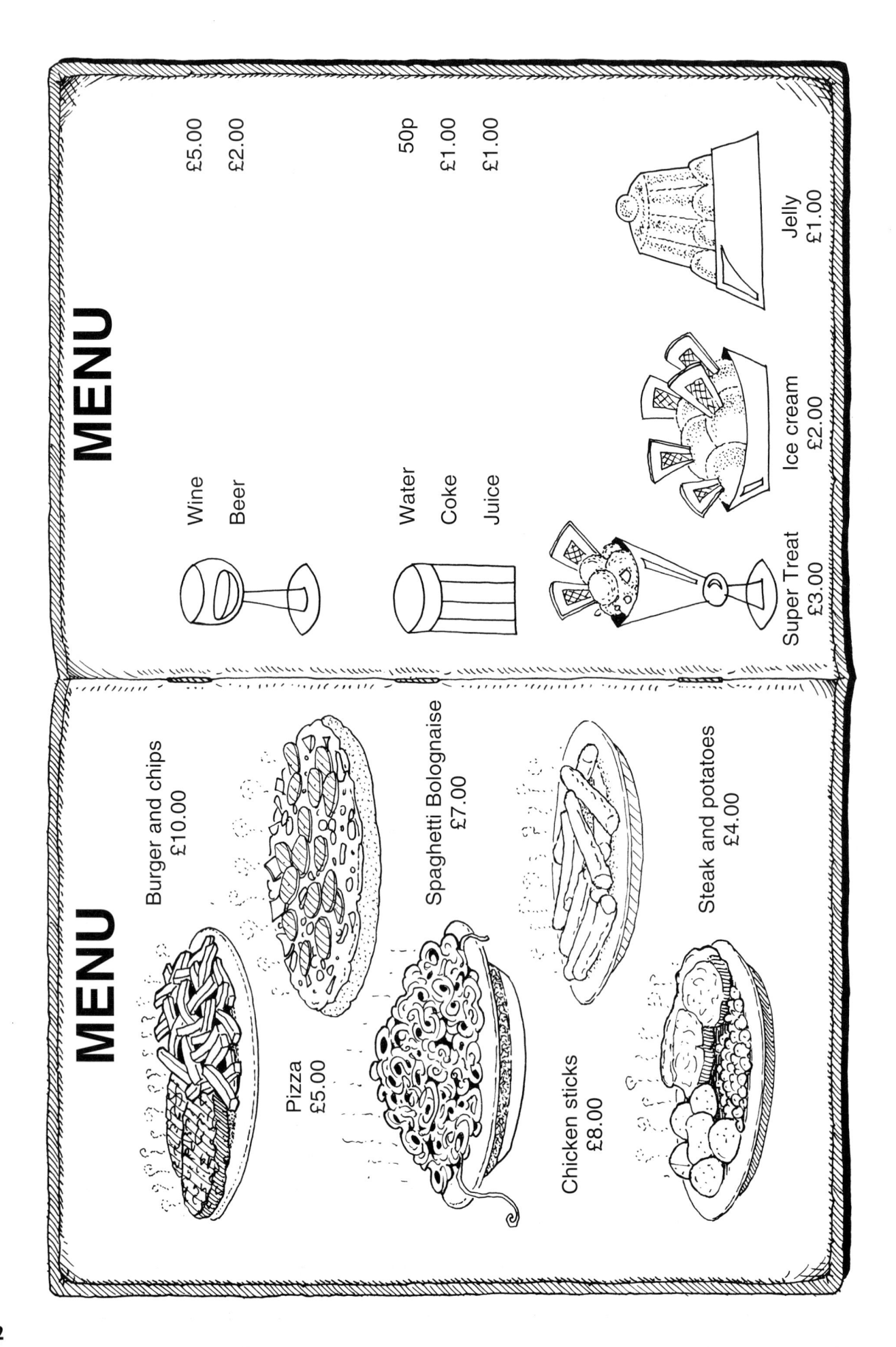

MENU

Wine £5.00
Beer £2.00

Water 50p
Coke £1.00
Juice £1.00

Super Treat £3.00
Ice cream £2.00
Jelly £1.00

MENU

Burger and chips £10.00
Pizza £5.00
Spaghetti Bolognaise £7.00
Chicken sticks £8.00
Steak and potatoes £4.00

Copymaster 59

Blanks for restaurant/café

Bookings

2.00 _____

3.00 _____

4.00 _____

5.00 _____

6.00 _____

7.00 _____

8.00 _____

9.00 _____

10.00 _____

Shopping list

-
-
-
-
-
-
-

Bill

-
-
-
-
-
-

Total _____

Copymaster 60

Colourful sentences

Blue words

The	The	A	A
The	The	A	A

Green words

puppy	cat	sheep	fish
girl	boy	dog	car
pizza	lolly	ant	worm

Red words

is	is	was	was
is	is	was	was

Yellow words

brown	blue	white	good
wet	hungry	hot	cold
bad	fast	slow	gone

White cards for punctuation

.	.	.	.

Copymaster 61

Colourful sentences

w	w	w
y	y	y
r	r	r
g	g	g
b	b	b

Colour in the dots, blue, green, red, yellow, white.

Copymaster 62

Ketchup on your Cornflakes?

Do you like

_____

✂------------------------------------

on your

_____

Copymaster 63

The bad day origami book

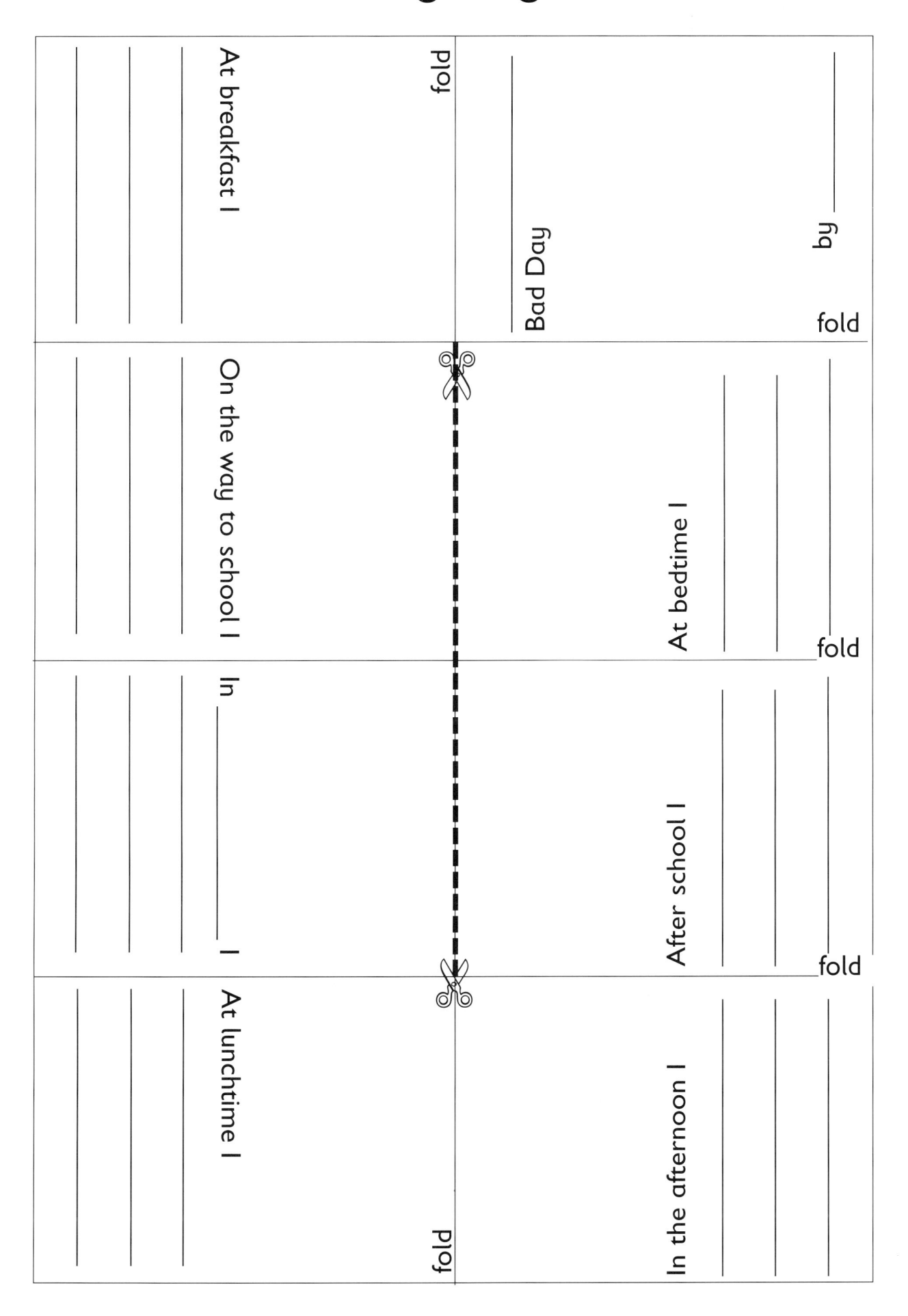

At breakfast I

On the way to school I

At lunchtime I

Bad Day

by

At bedtime I

After school I

In the afternoon I

In _____ I

fold

Copymaster 64

Story faces

Fold to make a booklet. Draw an expressive face on the cover and explain what made you feel this way inside.

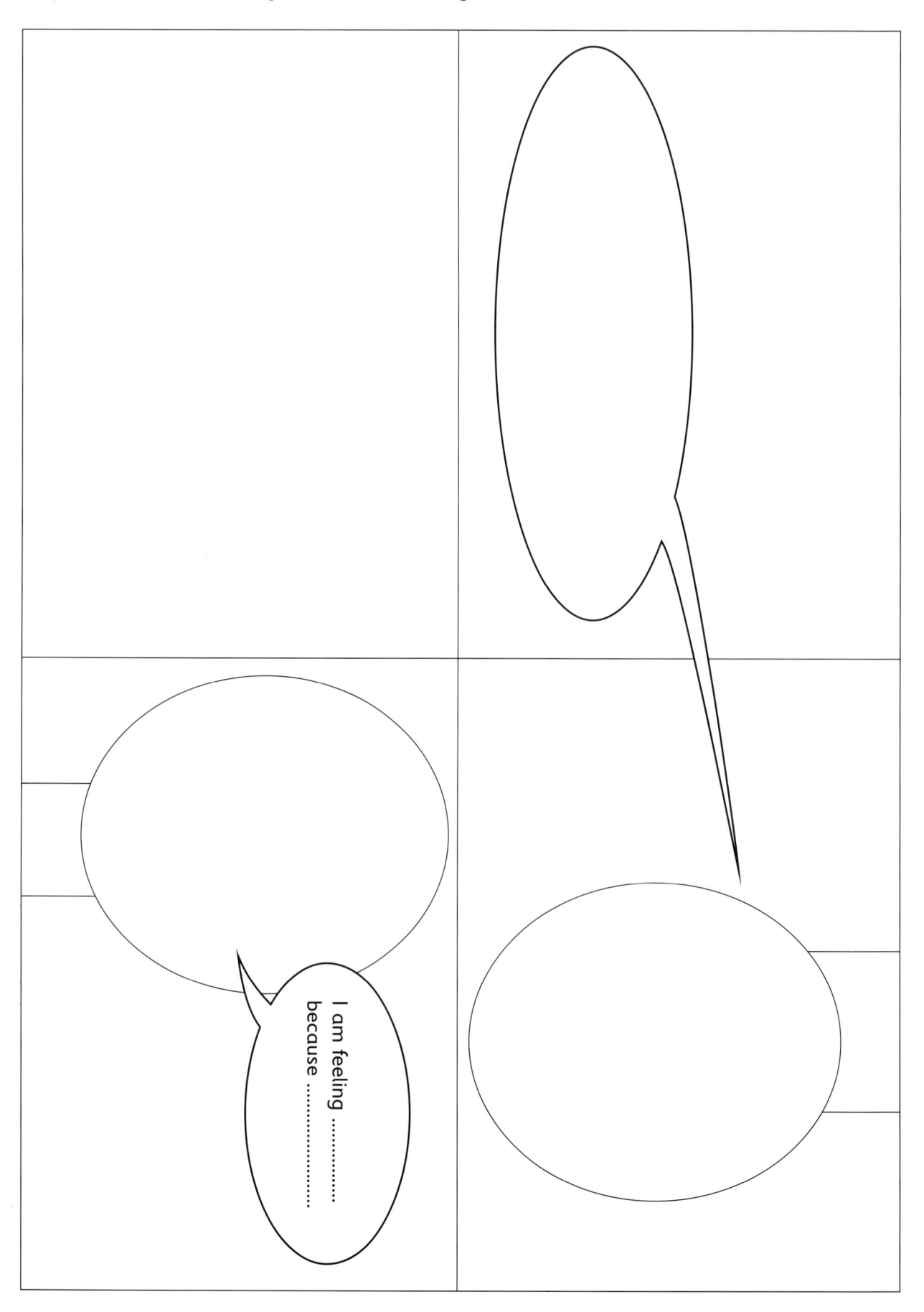

I am feeling .... because ....

138

Consequences template

I am

Copymaster 66

Consequences booklet

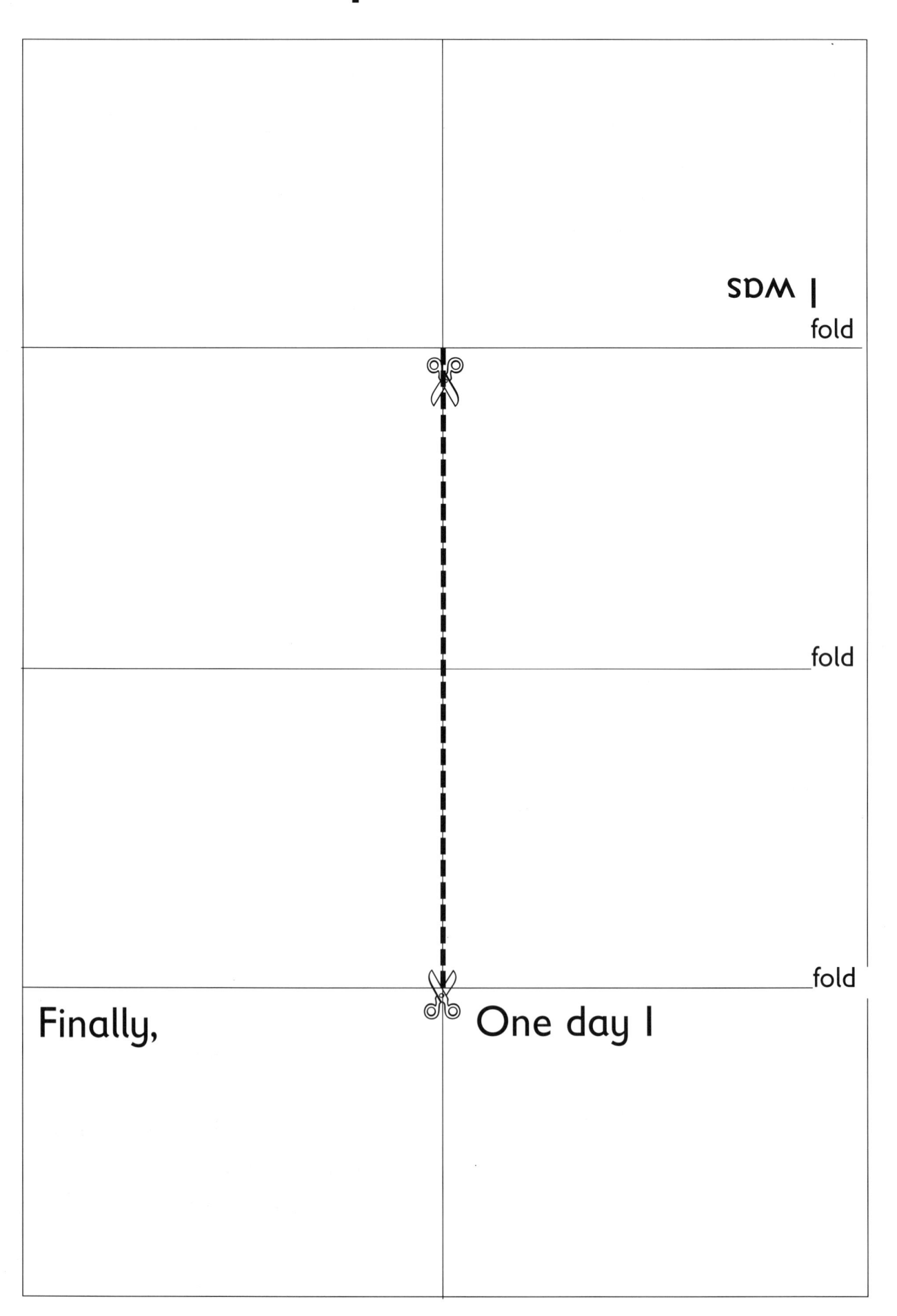

SDM 1

fold

fold

fold

Finally,　　　　　One day I

140

Brain Workout prompts

Cross crawl

- Move opposite arms and legs as if walking on the spot.
- Reach in opposite directions.
- Reach behind the body to touch the raised foot.
- Move arms as if front crawling when swimming.
- Do all of the above to music!

Lazy 8s ∞

- Activates both sides of the brain and body.
- First left hand and lazy ∞s in front, the right and then both hands.
- Close your eyes, open your eyes.
- Use sticks with streamers.
- Do them in fingerpaint, sand or with paint brushes.

Double Doodle

- Set up a vertical board, chalk, white, paint easel, paper etc – draw a line down the, middle. Let the child have two appropriate mark making tools.
- Using both hands and tools at once draw/paint cut both sides at the same time.
- Double Dooddle in the air mirroring both hands.
- Double Doodle with sticks with streamers.

Butterfly 8s

- Draw imaginary lazy 8s on the ceiling, in front of you.
- Use alternate hands.
- Make the 8 shape look like a butterfly.
- Double Doodle the butterfly onto the ceiling.

Rub a dubs

Rub you tummy – pat your head. Swap hands. Swap head and tummy over.

Keywords

- Write letters in the air in front of you.
- Write your name.
- Write a keyword.
- Close your eyes – draw a shape, draw a circle, draw a triangle.
- Use both hands.
- Make them do the opposite to each other.

The three letter roots

The Long Ladder
Is the longest in town.
You start at the top
And slide all the way down.

The Curly Caterpillar's
Crunching sound
Starts at the top
And crunches back round.

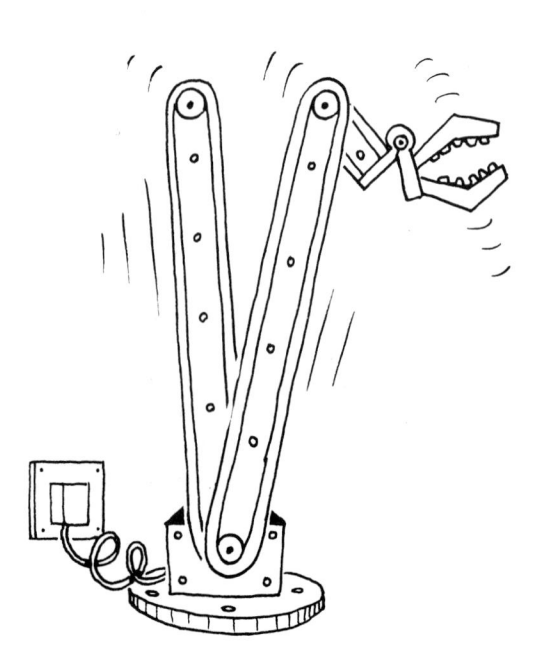

The One-arm Robot
Is helpful to know.
You start at it's head
And go down to its toe.
Stop right there!
It will do you no harm
So you can bounce back up
And shake its arm.

Copymaster 69

Letter snakes

z r g y e
a i u o t
x c f b k
m d h i p
l s n q w
v ch sh j
th

Copymaster 70

Environmental print

fridge	switch	door	bath
chair	window	bed	cupboard
draws	television	sink	tap
floor	letterbox	picture	cooker
table	door handle	toys	mess

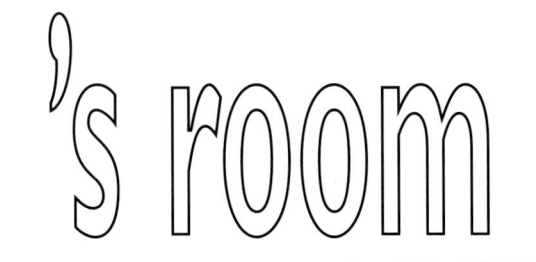

'S room

Glossary

These definitions are taken from the NLS glossary of terms on the Standards website www.standards.dfee.gov.uk. There is a fuller definition of terms at this Internet address.

alliteration
a phrase where adjacent or closely connected words begin with the same phoneme: *one wet wellington; free phone; several silent, slithering snakes.*

analogy
perception of similarity between two things; relating something known to something new; in spelling, using known spellings to spell unknown words: *night-knight-right-sight-light-fright*; in reading, using knowledge of words to attempt previously unseen words.
Emphasis on analogy encourages learners to generalise existing knowledge to new situations.

blend
the process of combining phonemes into larger elements such as clusters, syllables and words. Also refers to a combination of two or more phonemes, particularly at the beginning and end of words, *st, str, nt, pl, nd.*

blurb
information about a book, designed to attract readers, usually printed on the back or inside flap of book jacket. Informs the prospective reader about genre, setting, etc

consonant
A consonant is a speech sound which obstructs the flow of air through the vocal tract; for example, the flow of air is obstructed by the lips in *p* and by the tongue in *l*. The term also refers to those letters of the alphabet whose typical value is to represent such sounds, namely all except *a,e,i,o,u*. The letter *y* can represent a consonant sound (*yes*) or a vowel sound (*happy*).

cue
a source of information. In reading, children may use contextual, grammatical, graphic and phonological cues to work out unfamiliar words. Fluent readers orchestrate different cues and cross-check.

decode
literally, this means to convert a message written/spoken in code into language which is easily understood. In reading, this refers to children's ability to read words – to translate the visual code of the letters into a word.

digraph
two letters representing one phoneme: *b<u>a</u>th; tr<u>ai</u>n; <u>ch</u> / <u>ur</u>/ <u>ch</u>.*

frameworks – writing frame/oral (thinking) frame
a structured prompt to support writing or the retelling of a story or series of events. A writing frame often takes the form of opening phrases of paragraphs, and may include suggested vocabulary. It often provides a template for a particular text type. In the same way questions and prompts can support thinking and talking when recounting an experience or a line of thought.

genre
this term refers to different types of writing, each with its own specific characteristics which relate to origin (legend/folk tale) or reader interest area – the types of books individuals particularly choose to read: adventure, romance, science fiction.
Texts with these specific features – often related to story elements, patterns of language, structure, vocabulary – may be described as belonging to a particular genre. These attributes are useful in discussing text and in supporting development of writing skills.
Texts may operate at different levels, and so represent more than one genre; some will be combinations, for example historical romance.

grapheme
written representation of a sound; may consist of one or more letters; for example the phoneme s can be represented by the graphemes *s, se, c, sc* and *ce* as in *<u>s</u>un, mou<u>se</u>, <u>c</u>ity, <u>sc</u>ien<u>ce</u>.*

guided reading
a classroom activity in which pupils are taught in groups according to reading ability. The teacher works with

Glossary

each group on a text carefully selected to offer an appropriate level of challenge to the group. Usefully thought of as a 'mini lesson'. Challenge may be in terms of reading cues and strategies, language and vocabulary, or sophisticated aspects of grammar, inference, skimming and scanning.

guided reading sessions have a similar format:
a. the teacher introduces the text, and sets the purpose for reading, for example reminding pupils of strategies and cues which will be useful, or asking them to gather particular information;
b. pupils read independently, solving problems as they read through the text. More fluent readers will read silently. The teacher is available to offer help when it is needed. S/he then guides pupils to appropriate cues, for example use of syntax, picture cues, initial letter;
c. the teacher discusses the text with the pupils, drawing attention to successful strategies and focusing on comprehension, referring back to the initial focus.

guided talk
a classroom activity in which pupils are grouped by oral ability. The teacher works with each group on a task carefully selected to offer an appropriate level of challenge to the group. Usefully thought of as a 'mini-lesson'. Challenge may be in terms of questioning, particularly open-questioning, and support can come from prompts and phrases to scaffold the learner as they reconstruct their learning and thinking with support from the practitioner.

guided writing
a classroom activity in which pupils are grouped by writing ability. The teacher works with each group on a task carefully selected to offer an appropriate level of challenge to the group. Usefully thought of as a 'mini lesson'. Challenge may be in terms of spelling, letter formation, simple punctuation, language and vocabulary, or sophisticated aspects of generic structure, planning and editing, use of imagery and so on.

innovation on text
a classroom strategy in which the practitioner uses a familiar text as the model for a piece of new writing: *Georgina and the Dragon; The Very Hungry Kittens; Burglar Barry*.

letter string
a group of letters which together represent a **phoneme** or **morpheme**.

metalanguage
the language we use when talking about language itself. It includes words like *sentence, noun, paragraph, preposition*. Those who understand these concepts are able to talk about language quite precisely; thus, acquisition of metalanguage is seen as a crucial step in developing awareness of and proficiency in communication, particularly written language.

mnemonic
a device to aid memory, for instance to learn particular spelling patterns or spellings: *I Go Home Tonight; There is a rat in separate*.

modelling
in literacy, this refers to demonstration of an aspect of reading or writing by an expert for learners. This would support direct instruction.

onset
the onset of a word or syllable is the initial consonant or consonant cluster: *clang; trike; sun*. Some words or syllables have no onset: *or; out; end; at; on; earth*.
see **rime**

phoneme
a phoneme is the smallest contrastive unit of sound in a word. There are approximately 44 phonemes in English (the number varies depending on the accent). A phoneme may have variant pronunciations in different positions; for example, the first and last sounds in the word 'little' are variants of the phoneme /l/. A phoneme may be represented by one, two, three or four letters. The following words end in the same phoneme (with the corresponding letters underlined):
to
shoe
through

phonological awareness
awareness of sounds within words – demonstrated for example in the ability to generate rhyme and alliteration, and in segmenting and blending component sounds.

reading searchlights
the model used by the National Literacy strategy to represent the automatic cueing systems used by fluent readers as they problem-solve their way through extracting meaning from text.

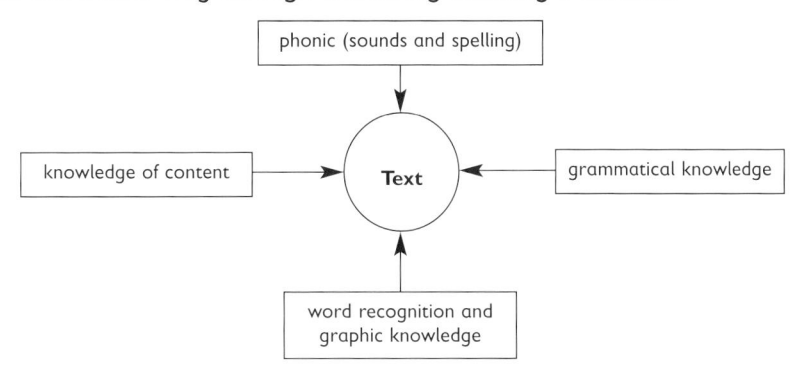

```
                    phonic (sounds and spelling)
                                |
                                v
  knowledge of content  ---->  Text  <----  grammatical knowledge
                                ^
                                |
                    word recognition and
                     graphic knowledge
```

Successful teaching equips children with as many of these searchlights as possible. Each sheds a partial light, but together they make a mutually supporting system. The fewer the searchlights the reader can switch on, the more dependent he/ she is on a single one and if that should fail, the reader will be stuck. The more searchlights we can teach children to switch on simultaneously, the less they will need to rely on a single one and the less it will matter if one fades or goes out. This model can equally well be applied to successful writing, in that a successful writer has to manage all these strategies at once in order to organise the thinking, language and motor skills to produce written text.

rhyme
a rhyme occurs when words share the same stressed vowel phoneme, e.g. *she/tea, way/delay* and subsequent consonant(s) e.g. *sheet/treat, made/lemonade* and final unstressed vowel e.g. *laughter/ after*.

rime
that part of a syllable which contains the vowel and final consonant or consonant cluster if there is one: *at* in *cat*; *orn* in *horn*; *ow* in *cow*. Some words consist of rime only: *or, ate, eel*.
see **onset**

scaffolding
describes the support given by a teacher to allow a child to work at their 'cutting edge'. It is the interim stage between the dependence of an adult demonstrating and modelling a strategy or skill and the independent application of this skill by the learner. Scaffolding can take the form of adult support, usually through carefully chosen language or it take the form of the support offered by a task, for example, a framework such as a writing frame can scaffold a child's writing and enable them to work at an ability beyond that which they would be able to do independently.
See **frameworks**; **guided reading**, **guided talk**, and **guided writing**

segment
to break a word or part of a word down into its component phonemes, for example: *c-a-t; ch-a-t; ch-ar-t; g-r-ou-n-d; s-k-i-n*.

sentence
a sentence can be simple, compound or complex.
A simple sentence consists of one **clause**:
It was late.
A compound sentence has two or more clauses joined by *and, or, but* or *so*. The clauses are of equal weight (they are both main clauses):
It was late but *I wasn't tired*.

Glossary

In writing, we mark sentences by using a capital letter at the beginning, and a full stop (or question mark or exclamation mark) at the end.

shared reading
in shared reading the teacher, as an expert reader, models the reading process by reading the text to the learners. The text chosen may be at a level which would be too difficult for the readers to read independently. The teacher demonstrates use of cues and strategies such as syntax, initial letter, re-reading. Learners have opportunities to join in with the reading, singly or chorally, and are later encouraged to re-read part or all of the text.

shared writing
a classroom process where the teacher models the writing process for children: free from the physical difficulties of writing, children can observe, and subsequently be involved in, planning, composition, redrafting, editing and publishing through the medium of the teacher. Shared writing is interactive in nature and is appropriate for teaching all forms and genres.

syllable
each beat in a word is a syllable. Words with only one beat (*cat, fright, jail*) are called monosyllabic; words with more than one beat (*super, coward, superficiality*) are polysyllabic.

text
language organised to communicate. Includes written, spoken and electronic forms.

vowel
a phoneme produced without audible friction or closure. Every syllable contains a vowel. A vowel phoneme may be represented by one or more letters. These may be vowels (*maid*, or a combination of vowels and consonants (*start; could*).

Notes

Notes

Notes

Notes